## Let the Diva turn you into a disciple of do-ahead!

Diane Phillips, the Diva of Do-Ahead, has taught her sold-out cooking classes for 15 years to more than 40,000 students around the country. Now she shares her secrets for fabulous, foolproof festive meals that can be prepared in advance, freeing you to enjoy holidays with family and friends.

**A ROSH HASHANAH DINNER:**
Roasted Sweet Potatoes,
Parsnips, Beets, and
Carrots, page 211

**A MEDITERRANEAN EASTER DINNER:** Mint Pesto-Crusted Lamb Racks with Cucumber-Mint Salsa, page 125

NEW YEAR'S EVE COCKTAILS AND SMALL BITES:
Crostini Bar, page 43, with Gorgonzola-
Walnut Topping, page 45; Sweet Pepper
and Parmigiano Topping, page 45; Roasted
Eggplant Topping, page 44

**A PASSOVER SEDER:**
Chocolate Meringues Filled with
Fresh Raspberries, page 96

**A CHRISTMAS DINNER:**
Roasted Tomato and Pesto
Cheesecake with Polenta Crust,
page 283

**A VALENTINE'S DAY SWEETHEART DINNER:**
Salmon Wellingtons Stuffed
with Crab and Asparagus,
with Lemon-Dill Velouté
Sauce, page 78

**A MEMORIAL DAY PICNIC:**
Tuna Niçoise Sandwich,
page 148

**A CHRISTMAS BREAKFAST:**
Denver Omelet Casserole,
page 274

**AN ALL-AMERICAN FOURTH OF JULY BARBECUE:**
Red, White, and Blue
Ice Cream Cake, page 195

AN ALL-AMERICAN FOURTH OF JULY BARBECUE:
Grilled Stuffed Burgers, page 180

THE DIVA'S FAMOUS DO-AHEAD THANKSGIVING DINNER:
Recipes begin on page 241

**A HALLOWEEN PARTY FOR ALL AGES:**
Build-Your-Own-Pizza Bar, page 224

**A FATHER'S DAY PARTY:**
Margaritaville Grilled
Chicken, page 166, with
Confetti Peppers and
Onions, page 167

**A MOTHER'S DAY BREAKFAST:**
Fresh Fruit Parfaits with
Orange Mascarpone Crème,
page 138

# Happy Holidays

FROM THE

*Diva of Do-Ahead*

ALSO BY DIANE PHILLIPS

Perfect Party Food

The Perfect Basket

The Ultimate Rotisserie Cookbook

The Soup Mix Gourmet

Pot Pies

It's a Wrap!

The Perfect Mix

# Happy Holidays

FROM THE
## *Diva of Do-Ahead*

## A Year of Feasts to Celebrate
## with Family and Friends

Diane Phillips

THE HARVARD COMMON PRESS • *Boston, Massachusetts*

**The Harvard Common Press**

535 Albany Street

Boston, Massachusetts 02118

www.harvardcommonpress.com

Printed in the United States of America

Printed on acid-free paper

*Library of Congress Cataloging-in-Publication Data*

Phillips, Diane.

 Happy holidays from the diva of do-ahead : a year of feasts to celebrate with family and friends /
Diane Phillips.

   p. cm.

 Includes index.

 ISBN 1-55832-320-1 (hardcover : alk. paper ) — ISBN 1-55832-321-X (pbk. : alk. paper)

 1. Holiday cookery. 2. Menus. I. Title

 TX739.P53 2006

 641.5'68—dc22                                                                                  2006002869

ISBN-13: 978-1-55832-320-9 (hardcover); 978-1-55832-321-6 (paperback)

ISBN-10: 1-55832-320-1 (hardcover); 1-55832-321-X (paperback)

Special bulk-order discounts are available on this and other Harvard Common Press books.
Companies and organizations may purchase books for premiums or resale, or may arrange
a custom edition, by contacting the Marketing Director at the address above.

Book design by Night & Day Design

Front cover and insert page 1 photographs by Brian Smale;

food and prop styling by Steven DeJoy; makeup by Mary Erickson

Photograph on pages 84 and 86 provided by iStockphoto

All other photographs by Becky Luigart-Stayner;

food styling by Ana Price Kelly; prop styling by Jan Gautro and Fonda Shaia

2 4 6 8 10 9 7 5 3 1

For my family—Chuck, Carrie, and Ryan—
for making every day a happy holiday.
Thanks, guys, this one's for you.

## ACKNOWLEDGMENTS

Celebrations are more than the food and decor; it is the guests who make the magic happen and turn celebrations into cherished memories. The same can be said of writing a book about celebrations; I would be remiss if I didn't thank my fellow revelers.

A toast to my family: my husband, Chuck, who helps make any celebration fun; our daughter, Carrie, whose zest for life makes parties more interesting and colorful; and our son, Ryan, who can be counted on to serve as bartender and all-around host-in-training.

My agent, Susan Ginsburg, has been a constant source of support and encouragement. I'm not sure what I've done to deserve the best cookbook agent on the planet, but I must be living right. Thanks also to her calm, patient assistant, Emily Saladino.

Thanks to all my road families, the staffs, volunteers, and students at the cooking schools where I teach across the country for allowing me to celebrate in their kitchens.

I would be remiss if I didn't toast the remarkable team at Great News! Cooking School here in San Diego for giving me a kitchen to call home. Their graciousness in allowing us to shoot the cover photo there was more than I could have hoped for, and I could not have imagined doing it anywhere else, because they have become my family. A standing ovation to Ron and Devora Eisenberg, Allison Sherwood, Sara Rose, Erika D'Eugenio, and the other dedicated staff members and volunteers who make my time in the kitchen here in San Diego so much fun—and to the students here in San Diego, you rock!

On the production side of things I would like to thank the entire gang at The Harvard Common Press for taking this book from conception to reality. A toast to publisher Bruce Shaw and the rest of the crew: Valerie Cimino, Jane Dornbusch, Virginia Downes, Pat Jalbert-Levine, Abby Collier, Betsy Young, Megan Weireter, Howard Stelzer, Ellie Levine, Janice Geary, Amy Etcheson, and copyeditor Jayne Yaffe Kemp.

I was blessed to work with photographer Becky Luigart-Stayner and stylists Jan Gautro, Fonda Shaia, and Ana Price Kelly for the interior photos. The cover photo is the result of photographer Brian Smale's creativity and style, and I am so grateful that he was willing to leave Seattle to work here in San Diego. Thanks also to art director Ralph Fowler and stylists Steven DeJoy and Mary Erickson for a day filled with fun—that's a lot to celebrate!

# Contents

# Preparing for
# the Happiest of Holidays

Holidays conjure up memories of the past and visions of the future. Most of us have delicious memories of cookouts on the Fourth of July, a beautifully prepared Thanksgiving dinner, breakfast in bed we made for Mom on Mother's Day, or the annual neighborhood Halloween parties of our childhoods. We also may have grown-up nightmares about these same holidays, given the anxiety associated with preparing and serving a holiday meal. Not only is there food anxiety, but there is also the family anxiety created by so many relatives under one roof, critiquing everything from the table setting to your children's manners to your new hairstyle. Putting a meal on the table is a feat even when you don't have all those people in your house! If you don't have a game plan, you'll be in for the legendary Excedrin headache.

This is where I come in: I'm the coach to help you get the dinner prepared ahead of time so you can enjoy your family and friends. Holidays aren't only about the past and the future—they are also about making the most of the present! Think of me as the Diva of Do-Ahead. I help you get over the food anxiety so that you can deal on your own with your family anxiety. (Medication and therapy may be the only true way to deal with that!) I'll give you the plan, the recipes, and the confidence to pull off memorable holiday parties: everything from a romantic dinner for two on Valentine's Day to a lavish Thanksgiving feast for as many people as you'd like to invite, all without the hassle of last-minute prep and party angst.

Holiday parties should be filled with the joy of hosting and sharing your home and food with your family and friends. Whether it's a backyard bash for Dad on Father's Day or an elegant Passover Seder, each holiday has its own great make-ahead menu as well as countdowns and helpful hints for decorating and serving. I love to entertain, and I teach thousands of students all over the country my approach to entertaining by breaking down recipes into simple, do-ahead steps that allow you to put together a menu easily, even for a large group. Preparing your dishes in advance, then reheating them just before serving or serving them at room temperature gives you an edge so that you can relax and enjoy your party. Trust me, this isn't the time to challenge your culinary abilities, so the recipes are straightforward but still delicious, with easy-to-find ingredients and simplified methods of preparation. If you want to farm out recipes to your family and friends, choose from the menu, then copy recipes for them to prepare. Make sure that when the party is over, you give them copies of the other recipes, or a copy of this book—share your do-ahead savvy with others.

## Getting Started

Okay, so you've decided that you are going to have a holiday party. (Or maybe you've been pushed into it by relatives who tell you it's your turn.) Now what do you do? First, figure out how many people will be there. I know this advice may sound simplistic, but you should invite only people you want to be around. I once read that a famous hostess accepted dinner invitations only from people she wanted to ask to her house. Then she didn't have to feel guilty for not having recipro-cated other invitations. Nothing is worse than having to endure the know-it-all who will domi-nate the table with opinions on everything from politics to the price of watercress. That being said, for family holidays you may have little choice but to hope that the know-it-all is going elsewhere! If not, take a deep breath and remember that such gatherings occur only a few times a year, and you will get through this one. Remember, I'll take care of the stress over the food, you just keep deep breathing and smiling when the know-it-all wants to know why you aren't in the kitchen fussing!

Invitations can be extended by phone or via e-mail (check out www.evite.com) for informal holidays such as the Fourth of July or Halloween. For casual entertaining, two weeks is sufficient time for sending invitations. RSVPs should be received five days before the event. More formal holiday invitations should be sent four to six weeks ahead, and RSVPs are expected 10 days before. Written invitations are still preferable for more formal holidays such as Thanksgiving or Passover—no, this is not old-fashioned. Your invitation should include the time of the party, appropriate dress, and what will be served, be it dinner, hors d'oeuvres, or lunch, for example. Make sure to plan a starting and ending time for your parties; if people come for dinner at 6:30 P.M., chances are they will be gone by 10:00 or 11:00 at the latest. The later the festivities begin, the later guests will stay. The bottom line: How late do you want to be up washing dishes?

Be a good host and give your guests an idea about the dress for the party—casual, formal, or informal—so that they don't show up in flip-flops when everyone else is in stilettos. Polite guests will tell you ahead of time about food allergies or other dietary restrictions, but to be safe I usually ask when they RSVP. A simple "Is there anything you can't eat?" will save you from a lot of headaches at party time. Asking ahead also helps you to know if there are vegetarians in the crowd so that you can plan for them as well. One night we had a large dinner party, and I'd made a particularly luxurious main dish that was filled with cream and cheese only to have one of our guests state (for all to hear), "I can't eat dairy products." Frankly, this is the person you don't invite back; it's your guests' responsibility as well as yours to make sure that they are comfortable and will have something to eat. Fortunately for this guest, I had rice and salad on the menu, but she also missed out on the whipped-cream cake for dessert.

Next up is figuring out how much food you will need for the number of guests you will have. For main courses, pick-up type appetizers (single serving on a skewer or a puff pastry bite, for example), and desserts, multiply by 1. In other words, you're counting on a full serving per person: If a recipe says that it serves 8 and you are having 16 for dinner, double the recipe. For all other food items, such as salads, dips, spreads, sauces, veggies, and casseroles, you don't need quite so much food. Multiply upward in half increments to determine the right amount of food. So if a recipe serves 8 and you are having 16 guests, increase the recipe by half rather than doubling it. How do I know this, you might ask? After more than 20 years of catering and party giving, as well as teaching cooking classes throughout the country, I've figured out that these are good proportions that won't leave you with lots of extra food that goes to waste. In one particular Thanksgiving class that I taught, the prep staff quadrupled the recipe for do-ahead mashed potatoes to serve 50 students, and they had to be eating those mashed potatoes way into the New Year. Sometimes a little goes a long way!

After you've settled on your food quantities, write out a detailed shopping list (check out my Web site, www.dianephillips.com, for a great entertaining shopping list that you can download and print). Then write out a detailed do-ahead calendar (also on the Web site) with each task clearly marked for the appropriate day. In addition to the recipe prep, make sure to include chores that are not kitchen-related: shopping; cleaning the house; polishing the silver; setting the table; rolling flatware into napkins; renting tables, chairs, silver, glassware, or china, if necessary; and buying and arranging flowers.

For planning purposes, if you are having a large dinner, allow 45 minutes to 1 hour for cocktails and mingling. If it's a smaller family gathering, you can be looser. But if people are late, begin dinner without them; it's their responsibility to be on time. Dinner should take about 90 minutes, but can go longer if the conversation is flowing. Often you may want a break from the table between dinner and dessert to stretch your legs and allow your meal to settle, so you can allow a half hour if you wish. Dessert will take about 45 minutes. Grazing parties such as the New Year's Eve party (see page 16), at which you're serving cocktails and tidbits, should be between 3 to 6 hours long, depending upon how formal the occasion is. I generally figure about 4 hours and then some (remember that people may be going to other parties before or after yours) for the type of party I have included for New Year's Eve.

## In the Kitchen

Before you begin, if you haven't had your oven calibrated in a while, you might want to invest in a Taylor oven thermometer (about $20), which you can buy at a gourmet retailer and even some

hardware stores. This tool will give you an accurate reading if, for example, you have your oven set to 350°F but it's actually heating to 300°F. Polder makes a remote thermometer probe that can be used for testing doneness for meats, but it also monitors your oven temperature and will beep if it isn't correct. Nothing will bake as it is supposed to if your oven is off by 25 degrees, especially cookies, cakes, and other sweets. You can also call your oven manufacturer's service person to come out and calibrate it for you, which will cost about $150 but may make the difference between items correctly baked and those that burn or are underdone.

For any party, you will need lots of ice. Don't think your automatic ice maker will be able to supply what you need, no matter how far in advance you start storing the ice. Buy the ice—it's inexpensive—then put it in coolers. That way you can lavishly ice down the wine, beer, champagne, and sodas. For large parties, you can fill your washing machine with ice and stand your white wine and liters of soda in it. The ice will drain out and you won't need to lug around coolers or borrow extras. You will need 3/4 to 1 pound of ice per person for icing and filling drinks. When I got married, we received four ice buckets as gifts, which at the time I thought was at least three too many. Little did I know then how invaluable they would be. You can make your own ice buckets using galvanized metal tubs or deep glass bowls, or put traditional ice buckets out on your counter, but you will need at least one. Make sure to have a good set of tongs for lifting the ice out of the bucket.

Serving utensils are important, and I recommend that you make sure ahead of time that each utensil that you will use for serving is efficient and in working order. If you are serving salad, buy a nice set of tongs rather than relying on spoon-and-fork-type salad servers. Tongs help to gather up the salad, and when guests are balancing a plate and everything else, the separate spoon and fork salad servers are awkward and unwieldy.

Have your prep knives professionally sharpened every two to four months, depending upon how much you use them. Never put your knives in the dishwasher, because the high heat will damage the blades and make them dull.

Use wooden or plastic cutting boards, which will not dull your knives like glass and other hard materials. Make sure you have the right knives for the job; if you don't own a good carving knife, it's a good idea to buy one before the big Thanksgiving feast. Ask your retailer if you can hold the knife to see if it fits your hand—some knives can feel awkward or too heavy, and it's better to test-drive before you spend money. Most reputable retailers are more than happy to allow you to try their knives. If you are lucky enough to have a cooking school in the area, chances are it gives knife-skills classes, and that is a great way to test-drive lots of knives.

Start your prep times and your party with a clean trash can and a clean dishwasher or sink. That way you won't have to empty trash or wash dishes during the party or while you are prepping; you can neatly dispose of trash and hide dishes in the dishwasher. And do your cleanup when the party ends instead of waiting till the next morning. Believe me, it's much easier to get it started the night before with a load in the dishwasher and the other items stacked to be done the next day rather than having to face it all the next morning.

Coffee is essential after a large dinner, and if you don't own a coffee urn, it's a good idea to invest in several thermal carafes that will store coffee. That way you can make several pots and store them in the carafes an hour before the party starts rather than trying to get your 4-cup Mr. Coffee to keep up with demand. Zojirushi makes a large pump pot that holds about 20 cups of coffee, and I use that for all my parties. If you think you need more storage, or wish to make both decaffeinated and regular, then buy two pump pots. Coffee bars will also sell you insulated boxes of brewed coffee, and some will even provide the cups, stirrers, and extras such as sugar and cinnamon. Check with your favorite coffee bar to see if it can supply your coffee, especially if you are giving a large party.

## Kitchen Tools

Everyone needs a few gadgets and utensils to make party prep easier. I'm not suggesting that you buy out your local gourmet cookware store, but you might want to add a few things to your already existing supply. When you have the right tools, everything seems to go more smoothly.

*Swivel peeler*: I recommend that you buy a new swivel peeler. It's amazing how many people still have an old aluminum model that's rusted and very dull. Oxo Good Grips is a great company, and it manufactures an inexpensive peeler that makes life easier, whether you are peeling vegetables or making chocolate curls. The company offers both a serrated version (for peeling peaches and tomatoes) and a regular style. Buy both, and you won't be sorry!

*Microplane zester*: This gadget is terrific for grating citrus zest, whole nutmeg, cinnamon sticks, fresh ginger, chocolate, and small amounts of cheese for garnish. It's a tool I wouldn't be without in my kitchen. I must use it at least once a day, and it goes right into the dishwasher.

*Whisks*: Whisks are great for making sauces and stirring liquids together. I recommend that you buy a sauce whisk (narrow) and a balloon whisk (fatter). I prefer the type with a wooden handle, as it won't get hot when you are stirring a sauce.

*Garlic press*: Invest in a garlic press for those times when you need a lot of minced garlic; it will make your life a lot easier. Most garlic can be pressed without peeling; ask a salesperson whether the brand that interests you can do so.

*Offset spatulas*: Most chefs would not be without an assortment in the kitchen, as these tools are great for spreading everything from sandwich fillings to frosting. Pick up a few different sizes.

*Cheese knives*: Cutting soft cheeses can sometimes be a headache, but a cheese knife (the blade has several cutouts) makes short work of soft cheeses. A cheese plane is also nice for slicing off cheese for munching.

*Instant-read thermometer*: If you are roasting meats or poultry, a meat thermometer will tell you when it has reached the right temperature. I recommend the type with a dial, which can be recalibrated, as opposed to the type with a digital readout. A third type, which is a little more expensive, has a probe that stays in the meat while it is roasting and a digital display that sits on the counter and beeps when the meat has reached the right temperature.

*Angled measuring cups*: Oxo makes a fabulous liquid measuring cup that is angled on the inside so that when you pour liquid into it, you can see exactly how much is in the cup without picking it up and checking the side measurement. These plastic cups come in 1-, 2-, and 4-cup sizes.

*Glass measuring cups*: I have a few large glass measuring cups that can be used in the micro-

wave, and they are terrific for whisking together dressings and other liquid preparations.

*Heatproof spatulas*: Many companies are now making spatulas that are heat-tempered to 1,000°F. The beauty of these spatulas is that they can be used instead of wooden spoons, and then they go right into the dishwasher. The spatulas come in a variety of different colors, sizes, and shapes.

*Knives*: Everyone will tell you that knives are as important as the ingredients you cook with, and I do think that if you don't have sharp, quality knives, it makes your work so much harder. Trying to slice a tomato with a dull knife is an exercise in frustration. I recommend that you buy a good paring knife, a serrated bread knife (which is also great for cutting tomatoes), a chef's knife or a santoku, which is a cross between a chef's knife and a cleaver, and, when you are a ready, a carving knife for roasted meats.

*Pots and pans*: My students are always asking me which cookware I recommend. My response is to buy the very best that you can afford, and buy only the pieces that you will use. Many manufacturers will put together sets of cookware and sell them at a discount, but you may never use that 1-quart saucepan or the 7-inch skillet. If you like the benefits of nonstick interiors, then by all means buy those, but for roasting and caramelization, nothing beats a stainless-steel interior. Copper is a great heat conductor, and although copper cookware is expensive, you do get what you pay for. You will need a couple of 10- to 12-inch sauté pans, a 6- to 8-quart stockpot, a 5- to 6-quart Dutch oven for braising, and a 2- to 3-quart saucepan or saucier (a rounded-bottom saucepan). A heavy-duty roasting pan with a V-shaped rack is a great investment: you can use it to roast meats, but it can also double as a mega–lasagna pan. These are the basics; once you get started you may decide that you would like a larger or smaller pan in each category. Make sure the cookware is heavy and can withstand lots of use. You want to buy these pieces only once because they may be expensive.

*Oven-to-table ware*: Over the years, manufacturers have gotten the message that people love to bake and serve in the same pan, so many manufacturers make freezer-to-preheated-oven-to-table ware, which comes in a myriad of colors and designs. A 13 x 9-inch pan is my desert-island piece of equipment. If I had just one, I could make anything from lasagna to potpies to bread pudding to chocolate cake. I recommend at least one 13 x 9-inch pan, a 9- to 10-inch deep-dish pie plate, and a 9-inch square baking dish. If you are afraid of buying a color that may not match everything else that you have, buy white or cream; then you can accent the table with color rather than trying to match everything.

*Platters*: Serving for a buffet will entail having plates of varying sizes to serve the food. If you don't want to make the investment in porcelain platters, you can work around that by buying disposable foil or black lacquer trays from catering supply stores or grocery stores. If you use the disposable type of tray, I recommend that you scatter field greens over the bottom, or use decorative vegetables around the outside to make the tray look attractive, or place paper doilies over them. Your regular dinner plates can be used to display food as well, but you will need nice large serving platters for things like roasted meats, antipasti, and fruit and cheese platters.

*Thermal carafes*: I always offer coffee to my guests, and I find that large coffee urns don't make the best coffee, so I have several thermal carafes that each hold 20 cups of coffee. I brew the coffee in my regular coffeemaker before the party begins and fill the carafes with the brewed coffee. Thermal carafes can also be used to keep water hot for tea.

*Stand mixer or hand mixer*: I have both a KitchenAid stand mixer and a hand mixer. If I have just a little bit to mix together I take out the hand mixer, but I am always using the KitchenAid for mixing doughs, mashing potatoes, and making bread. I still have the original KitchenAid that I got 20 years ago, and it's going strong, so although it may seem like a huge investment, over time it pays off.

*Immersion blender*: This nifty little tool is great for pureeing soups and sauces and making a quick milk shake. It is small and compact, and I love using it.

*Food processor*: This is another desert-island piece of equipment. It grates cheese; kneads bread doughs; mixes pie dough, cookie dough, and cake batter; purees soup; and slices and dices veggies and fruits. There isn't much that this machine can't do, and if I were limited to one small electric appliance for the kitchen, this would be it.

*Silicone baking liners*: Silicone is a beautiful thing, and these baking-sheet liners keep cookies from sticking to your cookie sheets. Anything baked on them just slides right off. The added bonus of no-stress cleanup in the dishwasher or with a dish detergent with a grease cutter, such as Dawn, is icing on the cake. Another great kitchen helper is the Roll'Pat, which is a larger silicone sheet that is great for rolling out pie doughs and puff pastry. I store the sheet rolled around my rolling pin, so it's always ready to rock and roll.

*Silicone rolling pin*: Hardly anything sticks to this heavy-duty pin, making for no-fuss cleanup. You'll love its ease of use. And it comes in a variety of gorgeous colors.

*Heavy-duty jelly-roll pans*: If you need new cookie sheets, I recommend that you buy jelly-roll pans that have a rim around the outside.

They are the same size as most cookie sheets, but you can use them for so many different baking projects, such as large recipes of brownies and bar cookies, as well as for large cakes and rolled soufflés.

*Butter slicer*: This gadget looks like a long egg slicer, and I use it to slice sticks of butter so that each guest can take an individual pat or two rather than lopping off half the stick, then leaving a tiny, messy bit for everyone else.

*Cutting boards*: Make sure to have a large heavy-duty plastic or wooden board with a well so that when you are carving meats, there is a place for excess juices, preventing them from running off the board and staining your counters and floor.

*Lap trays*: Invest in a dozen lap trays if you have a small entertaining space, so you can feed more than four people for dinner. Available at Cost Plus or Pier 1 Imports for about $5 apiece, these trays should be large enough to accommodate a dinner plate, flatware, and glassware, so that guests aren't balancing everything on their laps. The trays are also great to use for serving when you are not using them for eating dinner.

## Pantry Staples

These are the items I've found it's best to have on hand. Chances are you already have many of these items in your pantry ready to go when you want to have a party.

## HERBS AND SPICES

I tell my students that I have a 30-minute rule when it comes to fresh herbs. Fresh herbs will get lost in a dish that must cook for longer than 30 minutes, so if that's the case, I recommend dried herbs, whose strong flavor will hold up to long simmering. If you have fresh herbs that you would like to use, add them during the last 10 minutes of the cooking time, to refresh a sauce or to give a dish a just-made taste. I don't recommend that you buy "rubbed" herbs, as much of the essential oils are lost when the herb is ground. Buy those that are labeled "whole" on the jar. These are the dried herbs and spices in my spice drawer:

Sea salt

Whole black peppercorns for grinding

Basil

Oregano

Dill

Cayenne pepper

Red pepper flakes

Rosemary

Marjoram

Old Bay Seasoning

Colman's dry mustard

Thyme

Sage

Tarragon

Cumin

Chinese five-spice powder

Celery salt

Ground chiles: ancho and chipotle

Chili powder

Garlic salt

Seasoned salt

Creole seasoning

Ground ginger

Ground cinnamon

Cinnamon sticks

Whole nutmeg (grate using a nutmeg or microplane grater)

Whole cloves

Whole allspice berries

Whole bay leaves

Sweet Hungarian paprika

Poppy seeds

Sesame seeds

## DRY PANTRY

Dry pantry items are essentials that sometimes need refrigeration once opened. You will use them to put together many a meal long after the holiday. I keep most of these things on hand because they can mean the difference between a spur-of-the-moment party and run-of-the-mill takeout.

Oils: extra-virgin olive, regular olive, canola, vegetable

Vinegars: balsamic, white balsamic, red wine, white wine, champagne, sherry, cider, rice

Soy sauce

Hoisin sauce

Hot sauce: green, red, and chipotle

Ketchup

*Mustards: Dijon, whole-grain, Creole, yellow*

*Worcestershire sauce*

*Assorted dried pastas*

*Assorted rices*

*Canned plum tomatoes*

*Canned artichoke hearts*

*Canned beans: white, black, red, garbanzo*

*Chicken broth*

*Beef broth*

*Chipotle chiles in adobo sauce*

*Coconut milk*

*Prepared horseradish*

*Mayonnaise*

*Sun-dried tomatoes*

*Orange oil*

*Lemon oil*

*Pure vanilla extract*

*Vanilla bean paste*

*Peanut butter*

*Chocolate chips*

## The Tables

Now that you have figured out the guests, the menu, and your timetable, and filled in the gaps in your kitchen equipment and pantry, you can decide whether your party will be a seated affair or a buffet. This all depends upon your preference and your entertaining space. For the most part, I find that eight people seated at a table is the maximum number for good conversation and eating. When you get beyond eight, it's difficult to carry on a decent conversation, and passing food becomes unwieldy. When my guest count grows beyond eight, I prefer to set up the dining table or a kitchen counter as a buffet, and, depending upon the meal to be served, set up smaller tables or supply people with lap trays. If your guest count is more than eight and you still want to sit down and pass dishes at a large table, I recommend that you have two of each dish for the table, one at each end; so on Thanksgiving you would have platters of turkey and gravy boats at both ends of the table, as well as cranberries, potatoes, and so forth. This technique can work for large crowds, but it can be tricky if there are lots of children and/or older adults who aren't able to pass platters easily. For a large gathering, setting up a buffet and then having guests serve themselves is really more efficient, because you can swap out dishes that run low, and you can make sure that all your guests get what they need. At the table, have those items that people might want more of, such as rolls, butter, and condiments.

Remember to plan for highchairs and booster seats if they will be needed. Older adults, small children, or the physically challenged should go through the buffet line first, or seat them at the tables first, and ask someone to fill a plate for them. Older children can help their grandparents or younger relatives so that nothing is spilled and all your guests get what they want.

For cocktail parties and grazing parties, such as a New Year's Eve party, you won't need sit-down tables. In that case, move furniture to make more room to mingle; tripping over end tables and small furniture is not fun. Foods that do not need "traction," or a knife to cut them, don't require a table or lap tray, so plan accordingly. Visualize the food on the serving table, and then arrange the serving platters where you will place them during the party to make sure there is enough room for them to fit comfortably, and so that you can add an additional leaf to the table if needed. Place sticky notes where the serving platters should go so that you can easily replicate your plan, or draw a rough sketch. If any guests come early and ask to help, you can direct them to the sticky notes.

Linens, flatware, glassware, and china will all need to be cleaned before your party. If you don't have enough, then borrow or rent what you need. I've given you tips in some of the menus for how to make mismatched china and other tableware look as if it belongs together. If you are just starting out, buy large cream or white dinner plates; they match everything and are a good first investment for entertaining. You can find inexpensive all-purpose wineglasses at stores like Crate and Barrel or Ikea, and good stainless flatware as well. Save the boxes and store the tableware in them once they have been cleaned if space is at a premium. And please don't serve wine in plastic cups. It makes even expensive wines seem cheap. Many stores and catalogs now carry wine charms that hook onto the stems of glasses so that people will remember which glass is theirs. You can achieve the same purpose by tying different colored ribbons to the stems to coordinate with your decorating theme.

Linens are a matter of personal taste, but I find it is most practical to own several different lengths of hotel-type tablecloths in white. Then you can decorate with whatever colors you choose for the event. Accent white or cream tablecloths with colored napkins, flowers and vases, fabric runners, candles and candleholders, streamer ribbons, place cards, and other seasonal items.

Centerpieces for a seated dinner should be low, no more than 8 or 9 inches high, so that your guests can see one another across the table. I discourage you from using hurricane lamps or tall tapers at the table (but certainly use them elsewhere around the entertaining space), as they obstruct and distract you from your dining partners. Low candles, like votives or short pillars, are preferable. Make sure to have salt, pepper, butter, and rolls at each end of the table so that your guests can easily reach them. If you don't have the time or inclination to arrange flowers, think about using a pretty bowl filled with seasonal fruits or vegetables, shells, river rocks, or other items I suggest in conjunction with the menus, or simply order an arrangement from your local florist.

Here is where the rubber meets the road: there are some things you just won't have time to do, and there are plenty of servicepeople out there who are ready and willing to help you with arranging flowers, creating crudité platters, baking rolls, or even cooking part of your meal or serving it. If you go this route, be sure to add the ordering and pick-up or delivery dates to your do-ahead calendar, as well as the order confirmation numbers.

Remember when you hire anyone to make the responsibilities and compensation clear. Make sure to feed your helpers before the party, and tip them according to the service received. If they do a lousy job, you are not required to tip. If they do a good job, 15 percent is standard; 20 percent is for going above the standard you set; and 25 percent would be for the server who not only did what you asked, but also went above and beyond and tucked you into bed with cookies and milk after the party!

Set up your dining tables, place settings, and buffet tables up to five days ahead of time, and cover them with a sheet to keep them free of dust. Now you can cross off another chore that can be stressful right before the party. Make sure to wash all your serving dishes, and clean any silver or items that need polishing, way ahead of time.

For buffet service, arrange the plates at one end of the table, and then arrange the food: main course or courses, sauces, side dishes, salad, bread or rolls, butter, salt, pepper, and condiments. At the end of the line place flatware rolled in napkins for your guests to pick up as they leave the table, so that they won't have to hold forks and knives while they are trying to serve themselves.

For a sit-down dinner, set each place setting with the appropriate flatware, linen, glasses, and plates. If you are plating the dinner, then leave the dinner and salad plates in the kitchen. Depending upon how formal your meal is, you will need water glasses and wineglasses, and the flatware will be based upon what you are serving. Remember soup spoons if you are serving soup, salad forks, and dessert forks or spoons. Creative types can find lots of books and Internet sites that illustrate napkin folding; otherwise, simply roll the napkins and tie with ribbon or raffia.

Grazing parties will require lots of small cocktail plates and napkins for your guests to use, as well as toothpicks and skewers to pick up items. If you feel that forks will be needed, set these out on the table as well. Make sure to have plates for discarded toothpicks and forks on the table.

## The House

Some holidays, Thanksgiving in particular, are times for faraway relatives to come to visit, so either set up a guest room in your home or, if you don't have room for them to stay overnight with you, remember to make reservations ahead of time at a local hotel or inn. Also make accommodations for children by having age-appropriate toys, videos, or books on hand—no matter how much you love them, they are bored by adult conversation a lot of the time. I sometimes set up a room with games and toys and make it off-limits to the adults so that the children feel special and welcomed.

Clean the living spaces for your guests a couple of days before the party and then give them a quick once-over the night before. If you are having an outdoor party, clean the grill if you are using it so that it doesn't smoke, and make sure that any outdoor tables and chairs are clean. Clean the guest bathroom the day before the party and then go over it again quickly shortly before the party begins. Assign your spouse or an adult child the task of checking the bathroom every hour or so to replenish towels, tissues, and toilet paper. I usually have a basket in the bathroom filled with additional toilet paper and hand towels.

Make arrangements to board the dog or cat. This doesn't mean I don't love pets. What it does mean is that most animals have a problem when new people are introduced into their environment, and they may become a distraction for you and your guests by barking or jumping up on your guests. We once had a cat that was so upset by the odor of a guest's hairspray that halfway through dinner he jumped into her hair! Some animals will also help themselves to food from the table if no one is looking. Many people are allergic to animals, and many animals have a problem with children in the house. . . . It's just better to be a good host and pet owner, so make your guests the center of attention and board your animals. You, your pets, and your guests will be happier for it.

If you are storing coats in a closet, clear some room and make sure to have enough hangers. Or if you are using a bedroom to store coats, make sure that the bed is made and the room is picked up. (Another pet problem: I once attended a party at which the cat discovered a fur coat in a bedroom and picked it apart!)

Music is important for any party, and I recommend that you play background music that you like but nothing that will interfere with your guests' conversation. Some people do not hear well with a lot of ambient noise, so I'm an advocate of low-volume, comfortable music on the stereo. I've made some general suggestions to help set the tone for various gatherings, but of course your choice will depend on your personal taste. You can also burn a CD of your favorite music and play that, then give your guests a copy of the CD as a party favor.

Remember the camera! I can't stress enough how important it is to document these special occasions. You can put someone in charge of the camera or have several disposable cameras strategically placed for people to take photos as they wish. It's important to save the memories, and you may even want to keep a scrapbook of your parties, a record of the menus and your guests, as well as of purveyors who were especially good for future reference. This record can be as simple as a loose-leaf or spiral-bound notebook with pocket inserts to keep all your notes, lists, and calendars in one place. It helps to keep you organized, and that's the point of do-ahead planning! No one ever had a great party without a great plan, so just stick to it and follow my advice to help avoid stress and anxiety.

## Last Words

Holiday parties are all about celebration and remembrance: they should be fun, filling you with joy, excitement, and love for the people who will be coming and the knowledge that you will be creating happy memories. It's okay to have a few jitters—even the best actors and actresses get stage fright—but once you open the door and see your guests' smiling faces, and you return that smile and say, "I'm so glad you're here," you're off to a great start. Your success is assured: you've invited people you care about, you've prepared all your dishes ahead of time, and you're relaxed and ready to party! Make your guests feel welcomed and treasured, and serve delicious food without a lot of fuss and last-minute prep, and you'll enjoy your holiday parties all through the year.

Ring in the New

# A New Year's Eve Party and a Morning-After Brunch

# New Year's Eve Cocktails and Small Bites

To welcome the New Year, I've planned the ultimate, luxurious, pull-out-all-the-stops party. Picture everyone in elegant clothes, sipping champagne and eating your fabulous make-ahead buffet—you will be the star, feeling as fresh as a daisy because all your food was made ahead. New Year's is a time to celebrate the year gone by and the one to come, but it's also a time to celebrate friendship, and what better way than to give a party with fabulous food, beautiful décor, and bubbly drinks?

I've designed this cocktail party for about 20 people, but of course you may halve or double recipes according to your guest list. For a New Year's party, send out written invitations at least four to six weeks ahead of time. Most people make their New Year's plans early, so get a jump on them and plan ahead. The invitation should state that you'll serve cocktails and heavy hors d'oeuvres, the starting and ending time (midnight, of course, or you may invite people to stay over through breakfast the next day—and guess what?—the Diva has you covered for brunch, too!), and the dress code. You can certainly host a casual affair, but I think this celebration screams for fancy party clothes!

For New Year's Eve, I prefer a full bar, with champagne, and a bartender. You can't survive an elegant party if you are worrying about your guests' drink orders. With someone else to tend bar, you'll feel more relaxed, and it is one thing you won't have to worry about. A good bartender will walk around during the party when there is a lull and pick up soiled cocktail napkins, loose toothpicks, and empty cups and glasses. You might consider hiring the bartender for the after-party clean-up as well. Another option is to stock a limited bar and offer your guests "signature drinks," two or three special drinks that complement the theme of your event.

This buffet calls for elegance. Use white, black, and gold and/or silver: cloth linens, nice flatware, and lots of cloth or paper cocktail napkins scattered throughout the entertaining space. A black tablecloth accented with gold or silver platters and white flowers will give the room lots of sex appeal and class. If you choose not to use a black tablecloth, then use a white or cream tablecloth and dress it with black, gold, and silver accents. In either case, perk up these colors with a splash of red, with roses or carnations in the flower arrangements.

You will want votive candles everywhere, as well as pillars in different heights to give the rooms a beautiful glow. Turn off most lights, and allow the candlelight to be your mood maker. Fill the bottom of hurricane lamps with fruit, shells, or items of the season, and then arrange your pillar candles in the hurricanes to give them a festive look. For the table, a large, low flower arrangement in the center of the table is a dramatic statement and will give your table definition. Have flowers throughout the house, giving it a feeling of luxury and elegance. If you need to save money on flowers, use what my daughter, Carrie, and I call the "river rock trick"—many florists will help brides and hostesses save money by using river rocks in the bottom of glass vases to give the vase some definition, then using only a few flowers in the vase to create some drama. River rocks work in any size container, though keep in mind that a small vase calls for small rocks. In place of river rocks, you can use fresh cranberries, lemons, limes, shells, or colored marbles.

If it appeals to you, have the requisite party hats, noisemakers, and confetti on hand. You can make up a goodie bag for each guest containing these items as well as fortune cookies to open at the stroke of midnight for ringing in the New Year. Or you may use the streamers and noise-makers as table decorations, either arranged haphazardly on the tables or piled into a large bowl, for selection later by your guests.

For music, set an upbeat tone with Big Band, swing jazz, or contemporary pop or dance music. Although it's my custom not to have the television on during a party (except for the Super Bowl and Final Four), for this party you may want to watch the ceremonial dropping of the ball in Times Square to count down and celebrate the New Year. Here in California, we do the "canardly" New Year's party; we gather early, then watch the ball drop in New York, because we *can hardly* stay up till midnight!

## Do-Ahead Countdown

Choose whether to serve the Smoked Seafood Platter or The Diva's Smoked Seafood Dip. Then:

### ✳ 6 weeks ahead

Download shopping list and do-ahead calendar and fill them out

Shop for nonperishables and order any luxury items such as caviar

Make and freeze Rosemary Cranberry Sauce for Cranberry-Brie Bites

Make (but don't bake) and freeze Baked Saga Blue Cheese with Sherried Apricots

Make and freeze Mediterranean Artichoke Pesto Torte

Make and freeze Wendy's After Eight Brownies

Make and freeze Almond Toffee Bars

### ✳ 5 weeks ahead

Make (but don't bake) and freeze Shrimp Dillyicious Puffs

Make (but don't bake) and freeze Cranberry-Brie Bites

### ✳ 1 month ahead

Make and freeze pesto for Pesto Scallop Skewers

### ✳ 1 week ahead

Make Sesame-Soy Dipping Sauce for Spinach-Wrapped Chicken Bites

Toast and freeze bread for Crostini Bar

### ✳ 4 days ahead

Make Mustard-Tarragon Dip

Make Crab and Corn Rémoulade Dip

Make dipping sauces for Boiled Shrimp with Dipping Sauces

Make cream cheese mixture for Smoked Seafood Platter (if serving)

Make toppings for Crostini Bar

### ✳ 2 days ahead

Remove Shrimp Dillyicious Puffs, Cranberry-Brie Bites, Mediterranean Artichoke Pesto Torte, Baked Saga Blue Cheese with Sherried Apricots, crostini toasts, Wendy's After Eight Brownies, and Almond Toffee Bars from freezer and defrost in refrigerator

Make Spinach-Wrapped Chicken Bites

Make (but don't bake) Pesto Scallop Skewers

Make Boiled Shrimp

Make The Diva's Smoked Seafood Dip (if serving)

### ✳ 1 day ahead

Set the table and set up the bar

Prepare crudités or pick up arranged platter

### ✳ 2 hours ahead

Bake Shrimp Dillyicious Puffs

Bake Saga Blue Cheese with Sherried Apricots

Bake Cranberry-Brie Bites

Bake Pesto Scallop Skewers

Arrange crackers, crostini, and vegetables with appropriate spreads and dips

Start the coffee in large urn; otherwise, begin making pots to store in pump pots

Arrange the desserts by the coffee station with cream and sugar

### ✳ 30 minutes ahead

Arrange the Smoked Seafood Platter (if serving)

# Signature Drinks or a Full Bar?

Signature drinks are a lot of fun, and for this party you can choose to serve a "signature" cocktail or two to your guests, in addition to wine, beer, and soft drinks, without the expense and work of having a full bar. Such libations get the conversation flowing and invite your guests to become their own mixologists, with the proper ingredients and garnishes. Print up the recipes on cards to place by the glasses and alcohol.

For a classic party, to celebrate the old and ring in the new, nothing beats classic gin and vodka martinis, with a garnish bar that goes beyond the traditional pimiento-stuffed olive to include cheese-stuffed olives (blue, goat, and feta are great choices) as well as olives stuffed with garlic, jalapeños, anchovies, and almonds. The advantage of using a neutral spirit such as gin or vodka for your signature drinks is that you can have a couple of traditional mixers on hand, such as tonic water, Collins mix, and juice, for those who may want something different.

Champagne is, of course, a classic New Year's drink, and you can spin classic champagne cocktails in many directions: using a bit of Cointreau, Chambord, crème de cassis, amaretto, or Midori, you can change the color and complexion of these classic drinks. You can also make a classic champagne cocktail using a rosé champagne, and Champagne Cosmopolitan Cocktails (page 69) are always a winner during the holidays.

The other option is to organize a full bar, which can seem like a chore and a storage problem, but is certainly the swankiest way to go. Here is a basic bar setup for serving 20 people. Multiply upward or downward depending on your guest list. Remember to personalize it by taking your guests and their preferences into consideration.

*1 bottle vodka*

*1 bottle gin*

*1 bottle bourbon or whiskey*

*1 bottle Scotch*

*1 bottle rum*

*1 bottle tequila*

*1 to 2 bottles liqueurs, such as amaretto, sambuca, or Cointreau*

*2 cases beer and one 6-pack nonalcoholic beer*

*5 bottles red wine*

*5 bottles white wine*

*Dry vermouth*

*Sweet vermouth*

*Angostura bitters*

# Crudités with Tarragon-Mustard Dip

*Makes about 2 cups*

**With a little taste of Dijon mustard and the zing of fresh tarragon, this tangy dip is terrific with vegetables and can also be served with bite-size chunks of cooked chicken, steamed vegetables, poached salmon, or cooked shrimp.**

1¹/2 cups sour cream

¹/2 cup mayonnaise

¹/4 cup Dijon mustard

¹/4 cup finely chopped shallots

2 tablespoons chopped fresh
tarragon

2 teaspoons white wine
vinegar

¹/2 teaspoon freshly ground
black pepper

In a medium-size bowl, combine all the ingredients and stir to blend. **Diva Do-Ahead:** At this point, cover and refrigerate for at least 2 hours and up to 4 days.

# Crudités

Crudités are raw or blanched cut-up vegetables served with a dip before dinner or as a snack. If you are in a hurry, check to see whether your grocer has already done some of the work for you by looking for baby carrots and cut-up vegetables in the produce section or at the salad bar.

Arranging crudités in a basket or on a large ceramic platter can offer you a creative opportunity akin to flower arranging, or you can simply fan out leaves of endive, or choose two vegetables to arrange for a simpler platter. To expand on the natural theme, hollow out a vegetable such as a purple cabbage, a large bell pepper, or a large artichoke and pour the dip into it, then arrange the dipping vegetables around it. Make the presentation even more attractive by using leaves from cabbage, decorative kale, or a bag of prepared field greens for the base of the arrangement. Try garnishing the platter with bouquets of fresh herbs, pea shoots, or broccoli sprouts. Edible unsprayed flowers like nasturtiums, day lilies, or violets also add a designer touch. Arrange all green vegetables with a white dip, or red, white, and green vegetables with an Italian-inspired dip. Remember, it's not the number of veggies in the basket, but the color, size,

texture, and compatibility with the dip that are important. And don't forget to wash all vegetables in cold water before serving them. The following vegetables work well in crudité arrangements:

**Artichokes:** Cut the top 1 inch off globe artichokes and steam until tender, 20 to 30 minutes. Place on a platter with other vegetables and make sure to have a plate handy for the leftover leaves. Or steam baby artichokes for 15 to 20 minutes, quarter them lengthwise, and arrange on the platter.

**Asparagus:** Trim the tough bottoms, plunge into boiling salted water for 30 seconds, shock in ice water, pat dry, and refrigerate until ready to use. (I have some friends who serve pencil-thin spring asparagus raw.)

**Beans:** Trim the ends of tender green or yellow wax beans and pull off their tough strings. Then blanch in boiling salted water for 1 minute, shock in ice water, pat dry, and refrigerate until ready to use. Try presenting them standing upright in your arrangement by filling a hollowed-out bell pepper or positioning them among the other vegetables.

**Belgian endive:** Trim the bottom and separate the leaves, which make great "scoops" for lobster salad, shrimp salad, or chicken salad.

**Broccoli and cauliflower:** Some people like their broccoli and cauliflower raw, while others prefer them blanched for 1 minute in boiling salted water. Either method is fine; blanched broccoli has a brighter green color. Broccoli and cauliflower should be cut and separated into florets before blanching and serving.

**Carrots:** Your grocer sells "baby" carrots in bags, and I recommend using them to save time. If they look a little sad or dry, place them in a bowl of cold water in the refrigerator for 2 hours or overnight. Drain and pat dry before using. You can serve the carrots whole or cut them in half lengthwise. They add color and crunch to your arrangement and, if you are serving children, you can count on baby carrots to be their vegetable of choice.

**Celery:** Your supermarket may sell this vegetable already cut up. Celery doesn't do well once it is cut, but you can soak the precut variety in cold water for a few hours to perk it up, or buy hearts of celery. Trim them into 2-inch lengths, then cut each length into thin sticks. Store celery in zipper-top plastic bags for up to 36 hours to retain its crunch.

**Cucumbers:** I buy only European cucumbers, which have almost no seeds, meaning you get more usable cucumber for your dollar. You don't need to peel them, but do scrub the outside. Then trim the ends, slice into 2-inch lengths, and cut the lengths into quarters. Cut cucumbers can be stored, wrapped in paper towels (to absorb moisture) in zipper-top plastic bags, for up to 36 hours in the refrigerator.

**Jicama:** Peel and cut into 3 x 1-inch lengths and store in zipper-top plastic bags for up to 48 hours.

**Mushrooms:** Clean raw button mushrooms and serve whole, halved, or quartered, depending upon their size. You can clean them up to 24 hours ahead and store, wrapped in paper towels in zipper-top plastic bags, in the refrigerator. Most chefs will instruct you to wipe mushrooms clean, but I prefer to buy them already cleaned in the package or to spray them with water to remove the grit. Don't soak them, but rather place them in a colander and spray with water, then dry. Soaking will cause the mushrooms to become waterlogged and mushy.

**Peas:** Remove stems and tough strings from sugar snap peas and snow peas and blanch for 30 seconds in boiling salted water. Shock them in ice water to stop the cooking, pat dry, and refrigerate, wrapped in paper towels in zipper-top plastic bags for up to 24 hours. If the peas are especially tender (from your garden, maybe), then serve them raw.

**Peppers:** Green, yellow, orange, red, purple, and white bell peppers all add color and crunch to an arrangement. Seed the peppers and remove the ribs. Then cut peppers into strips about $3/4$ inch wide. Store, wrapped in paper towels in zipper-top plastic bags, for up to 24 hours in the refrigerator.

**Radishes:** Trim red and white radishes. Then cut them in half or serve them whole if they are small. You can clean and prepare the radishes the day before serving; keep them fresh in a bowl of cold water in the fridge until you are ready to use them, then pat dry and arrange.

**Tomatoes:** Tiny cherry tomatoes and pear-shaped orange and yellow tomatoes make great color and taste additions. You can leave on the stems or remove them; I leave them to give my guests something to hold onto when dipping.

**Zucchini and yellow squash:** Baby vegetables have become more common in super-markets, but they remain expensive to serve to a large group. I love to include whole baby zucchini, yellow squash, and pattypan squash in my vegetable arrangements. If baby squash are too costly, use the larger varieties. Cut zucchini into 2-inch lengths, then cut length-wise into quarters for nice long dippers. Small yellow summer squash and crooknecks can be cut into $1/2$-inch-thick rounds. The "crook" of the crookneck can be cut in half for dipping, too. Store squash, wrapped in paper towels in zipper-top plastic bags, for up to 36 hours in the refrigerator.

Nonveggie dippers include potato chips, tortilla or corn chips, crackers, bagel chips, pita wedges, and sliced baguettes. Check the chip and cracker aisles at your grocery store, and you will find everything you need. I recommend that you buy unflavored crackers or chips so that the flavor of the dip is what your guests will taste.

# Shrimp Dillyicious Puffs

*Serves 12 to 16*

*Tiny bay shrimp go a long way, so you will need only about 1/3 pound. Creamy, and flecked with pink shrimp, zesty lemon, and fresh dill, these little puffs will make you look like a four-star chef. If you want to add more color and flavor, sprinkle some chopped fresh dill and grated lemon zest on the work surface before you roll out the puff pastry.*

One 8-ounce package cream cheese, softened

2 teaspoons whole milk

1/3 pound bay shrimp, finely chopped

2 tablespoons chopped fresh chives

2 tablespoons chopped fresh dill or 1 tablespoon dried dillweed

2 teaspoons grated lemon zest

1/2 teaspoon Old Bay Seasoning

One 17.5-ounce package Pepperidge Farm frozen puff pastry, defrosted

1 large egg, beaten with 2 tablespoons water

**1.** With an electric mixer, beat together the cream cheese and milk until smooth, then stir in the shrimp, chives, dill, lemon zest, and Old Bay. **Diva Do-Ahead:** At this point, you can cover and refrigerate for up to 2 days.

**2.** Roll out each puff pastry sheet into a 16-inch square. Cut each square into 2-inch squares. (You will have 64 small squares.) Place a square into a muffin tin cup and spoon 1 teaspoon of the shrimp mixture into the center of the dough. Draw up the corners of the dough toward the center and twist together to seal it. Brush with a bit of the egg wash. (If you are freezing the pastries, don't brush with the egg wash.) Repeat until you have used up all the pastry.
**Diva Do-Ahead:** At this point, you can cover and refrigerate for up to 8 hours or freeze in the tins, then transfer to a zipper-top plastic bag and keep frozen for up to 5 weeks.

**3.** Preheat the oven to 400°F. Bake the puffs until golden brown, 12 to 14 minutes. If they are frozen, place on a baking sheet lined with parchment paper, aluminum foil, or a silicone baking liner; brush with the egg wash and bake at 375°F for 15 to 17 minutes, until golden brown. Serve warm or at room temperature.

## Diva Variation

If you don't have enough muffin tins, you can make turnovers. Place some of the filling in the center of a square, then fold the dough over into a triangular shape and crimp the edges together all the way around. Brush with the egg wash before baking.

# Cranberry-Brie Bites

*Serves 12 to 16*

**I've seen variations on this theme for the holidays, but the cranberry sauce never seemed to be savory enough to complement the creamy Brie. I came up with a zesty Rosemary Cranberry Sauce, which works beautifully with the rich cheese.**

One 1/2-pound wedge Brie cheese

One 17.5-ounce package Pepperidge Farm frozen puff pastry, defrosted

1 cup Rosemary Cranberry Sauce (page 28)

1 large egg, beaten with 2 tablespoons water

**1.** Cut the Brie into 1/2-inch-thick slices and cut each slice into strips 1 inch long.

**2.** Roll out each puff pastry sheet into a 16-inch square. Cut each square into 2-inch squares. (You will have 64 small squares.) Place a square into a muffin tin cup and spoon 1 teaspoon of the cranberry sauce in the middle of the dough. Lay a piece of Brie on top of the sauce. Draw up the corners of the dough toward the center and twist together to seal. Brush with a bit of the egg wash. (If you are freezing the pastries, don't brush with the egg wash.) Repeat until you have used up all the pastry. **Diva Do-Ahead:** At this point, you can cover and refrigerate for up to 8 hours or freeze in the tins, then transfer to a zipper-top plastic bag and keep frozen for 5 weeks.

**3.** Preheat the oven to 400°F. Bake the bites until golden brown, 12 to 14 minutes. If they are frozen, place on a baking sheet lined with parchment paper, aluminum foil, or a silicone baking liner; brush with the egg wash and bake at 375°F for 17 to 20 minutes, until golden brown. Serve warm or at room temperature.

# Rosemary Cranberry Sauce

*Makes about 3 cups*

*This piquant sauce is also delicious to serve for other holidays. Offer it as an accompaniment to roasted poultry or pork, use it as a glaze for ham, or spoon it over blocks of cream cheese to spread on crackers.*

2 tablespoons unsalted butter

1/2 cup chopped onion

2 tablespoons chopped fresh rosemary

One 12-ounce bag fresh cranberries, picked over for stems

1 1/2 cups sugar

1/2 cup water

Grated zest of 1 lemon

**1.** Melt the butter in a large saucepan over medium heat. Add the onion and rosemary and cook, stirring, until the onion softens, 3 to 4 minutes. Add the remaining ingredients, bring to a boil, and continue boiling until the cranberries begin to pop and the mixture begins to thicken, 4 to 6 minutes. Reduce the heat to medium-low and simmer for another 10 minutes, until the sauce is thickened and the cranberries have all popped, releasing their juices.

**2.** Remove from the heat and let cool to room temperature. **Diva Do-Ahead:** At this point, you can cover and refrigerate for up to 2 weeks or freeze for up to 2 months. Serve cold or at room temperature.

## Diva Quickie

For even quicker Brie bites, make this easy alternative to the Rosemary Cranberry Sauce: stir 1 teaspoon dried rosemary and 1 teaspoon grated lemon zest into one 15-ounce can of whole-berry cranberry sauce.

# Mediterranean Artichoke Pesto Torte

*Serves 16*

*This beautiful torte combines layers of garlicky artichoke pesto, roasted red pepper puree, and fla-vored goat cheese. Delicious on toasted baguette slices, cucumber slices, or crackers, it can be made several days ahead and refrigerated, or frozen for several weeks. You will find small tortes like this in the deli section of your grocery store for a small fortune. Instead of making this recipe in one large mold, you can layer the mixture into smaller ramekins to set out at different tables around the entertaining space. Any leftover pesto and puree is delicious tossed into pasta.*

## Goat Cheese Layer

Two 11-ounce packages goat
  cheese, softened
One 8-ounce package cream
  cheese, softened
2 cloves garlic, minced

## Artichoke Pesto

Two 4.5-ounce jars marinated
  artichoke hearts, drained
2 cloves garlic
$1/4$ cup packed fresh Italian
  parsley leaves
$1/2$ cup pine nuts
$1/2$ cup freshly grated
  Parmesan cheese
$1/4$ to $1/3$ cup olive oil, as
  needed

## Roasted Red Pepper Puree

Two 6-ounce jars roasted red
  peppers, drained
$1/4$ cup olive oil
2 tablespoons balsamic
  vinegar
Salt and freshly ground black
  pepper to taste

Marinated artichoke quarters
  or thin red bell pepper strips
  for garnish

**1.** Line a 4-cup decorative mold with plastic wrap so it extends over the sides by about 4 inches.

**2.** To make the goat cheese layer, with an electric mixer, beat the cheeses together in a large bowl until smooth. Add the minced garlic and blend until incorporated.

**3.** To make the pesto, in a food processor combine the arti-choke hearts, garlic, parsley, pine nuts, and cheese, and pulse to break up the artichokes. Add $1/4$ cup of the oil and pulse 3 to 4 more times. Add more oil if necessary to get a pesto-like consistency, though you still want chunks of artichoke. Trans-fer the pesto to a small bowl and wipe the inside of the food processor clean.

**4.** To make the puree, combine the red peppers, oil, and vinegar in the food processor and pulse 4 to 5 times, until almost smooth; there should still be red pepper bits in the mixture. Season with salt and pepper to taste.

*continued on next page*

# Mediterranean Artichoke Pesto Torte *continued*

**5.** Wet your hands with cold water and spread a ¹/₂-inch layer of the cheese mixture over the bottom of the mold. Top the cheese with a ¹/₂-inch layer of the artichoke pesto, then another layer of cheese, and then a ¹/₂-inch layer of the red pepper puree. Continue to layer in sequence, ending with the cheese. Bring the ends of the plastic wrap over the mold. Refrigerate for at least 1 hour to firm up the torte.

**Diva Do-Ahead:** At this point, you can refrigerate for up to 3 days or freeze for up to 6 weeks. Defrost in the refrigerator overnight before continuing. Freeze any remaining pesto or red pepper puree for future use.

**6.** When ready to serve, unmold the torte onto a serving platter, removing the plastic wrap, and garnish with the marinated artichoke hearts or red bell pepper strips or both. Serve cold or at room temperature.

# Baked Saga Blue Cheese with Sherried Apricots

*Serves 10 to 12*

**Creamy Saga blue is similar to Brie but with a pronounced band of blue cheese through the center, giving it lots of personality. It marries well with the sweet-tart taste of apricot preserves and the crispy puff pastry crown. Serve this appetizer with baguette slices, water crackers, or sliced European cucumbers.**

12 ounces Saga blue cheese

1 sheet Pepperidge Farm frozen puff pastry ($^{1}/_{2}$ of a 17.5-ounce package), defrosted and rolled out into a 15-inch square

$^{1}/_{2}$ cup apricot preserves

2 tablespoons cream sherry

1 large egg, beaten with 2 tablespoons milk, heavy cream, or water

**1.** Place the cheese in the center of the puff pastry.

**2.** In a small bowl, combine the preserves with the sherry and spread over the cheese. Bring the corners of the puff pastry toward the center of the cheese and twist together into a decorative knot. Cover with plastic wrap or slip into a 2-gallon zipper-top plastic bag and refrigerate for at least 1 hour so the puff pastry will relax. **Diva Do-Ahead:** At this point, you can refrigerate for up to 24 hours or freeze for up to 6 weeks. Defrost overnight in the refrigerator before continuing.

**3.** Preheat the oven to 350°F and place the puff pastry–wrapped cheese on a cookie sheet lined with parchment paper, aluminum foil, or a silicone baking liner. Brush with the egg wash.

**4.** Bake until the crust is golden, 35 to 45 minutes. Remove from the oven and let it rest for 15 minutes before serving.

## Diva Puff Pastry Tip

Here are two tricks for baking semisoft cheeses in puff pastry:

❋ Keep the cheese and pastry cold before baking.

❋ Make sure to let the wrapped cheese rest in the refrigerator for at least an hour before baking.

# Crab and Corn Rémoulade Dip

*Makes about 4 cups*

*Rémoulade is a spicy sauce that is used as a dipping sauce for cold seafood, or in seafood salads. This dip is positively addictive. You can serve it in a bowl with crackers or, for a more elegant presentation, dollop spoonfuls onto the ends of endive leaves and arrange on a platter.*

3/4 cup mayonnaise

1/4 cup Dijon or Creole mustard

2 tablespoons ketchup

1 tablespoon finely chopped cornichons or dill pickles

1 tablespoon chopped fresh Italian parsley

2 teaspoons finely chopped shallot

2 teaspoons finely chopped capers

1 teaspoon horseradish

1/2 teaspoon sweet paprika

1 pound lump crabmeat

1 cup chopped celery

8 ounces frozen white corn, defrosted

1/4 cup chopped chives for garnish

**1.** In a large bowl, whisk together the mayonnaise, mustard, ketchup, cornichons, parsley, shallot, capers, horseradish, and paprika. **Diva Do-Ahead:** At this point, you can refrigerate for up to 5 days.

**2.** Fold in the crabmeat, celery, and corn. Cover and refrigerate for at least 4 hours. **Diva Do-Ahead:** At this point, you can refrigerate for up to 36 hours. Garnish with chopped chives and serve chilled.

# Spinach-Wrapped Chicken Bites with Sesame-Soy Dipping Sauce

*Serves 10 to 12*

*These succulent bites of cooked chicken wrapped in bright green spinach will be gone in no time, so plan to have plenty of them on hand, along with cocktail toothpicks for spearing. The prep requires a little bit of time, but the result is well worth the effort.*

6 boneless, skinless chicken
   breast halves
2 cups chicken broth
$1/2$ cup soy sauce
1 quarter-size piece fresh
   ginger, peeled and chopped
1 clove garlic, minced
One 10-ounce bag baby
   spinach
2 quarts boiling water
Sesame-Soy Dipping Sauce
   (page 34)

**1.** Trim the chicken breasts of any fat and place them in a large sauté pan with the broth, soy sauce, ginger, and garlic. Bring to a boil, reduce the heat to medium-low, and gently simmer the chicken until cooked through, 15 to 20 minutes. Let cool in the broth.

**2.** Remove the chicken from the broth and cut into $1/2$-inch pieces. Discard the broth.

**3.** Place the spinach in a colander in the sink and pour the boiling water over it. Rinse with cold water and pat dry. Lay a spinach leaf on a cutting board and place a piece of chicken in the center. Roll the leaf around the chicken and secure with a toothpick. Repeat until all the chicken is wrapped. **Diva Do-Ahead:** At this point, you can cover and refrigerate for up to 2 days.

**4.** Arrange the wrapped chicken on a serving platter and place the dipping sauce in a small bowl in the center. Serve warm or at room temperature.

# Sesame-Soy Dipping Sauce

*Makes about 1 cup*

**This sauce is delicious with Spinach-Wrapped Chicken Bites, but it's equally good served with skewers of cooked beef, salmon, or shrimp.**

3/4 cup soy sauce

2 tablespoons toasted sesame oil

1 tablespoon rice vinegar

1 teaspoon peeled and grated fresh ginger

1 clove garlic, minced

2 scallions (white and tender green parts), thinly sliced on the diagonal

2 tablespoons sesame seeds

**1.** In a small bowl, combine the soy sauce, oil, vinegar, ginger, garlic, and scallions, stirring to blend. [Diva Do-Ahead: At this point, you can cover and refrigerate for up to 1 week.]

**2.** Stir in the sesame seeds just before serving.

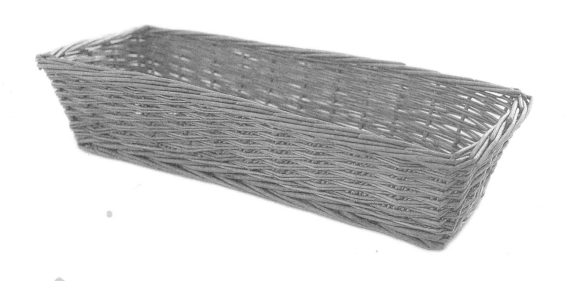

# Pesto Scallop Skewers

*Serves 10*

*This simple presentation is terrific for a cocktail party or appetizer buffet. I like to use small bay scallops because you can eat them in just one bite, but if you wish, you may cut large sea scallops into quarters. Panko crumbs are Japanese bread crumbs, which are coarsely ground and make a delicious crunchy coating. If you can't find them, substitute unflavored dry bread crumbs.*

1 cup basil pesto, homemade (page 36) or store-bought
1 1/2 pounds whole bay scallops, or sea scallops, quartered
Wooden skewers
1 1/2 cups panko

**1.** Pour the pesto into a zipper-top plastic bag or 13 x 9-inch baking dish. Add the scallops and toss to coat well. **Diva Do-Ahead:** At this point, you can cover or seal and refrigerate for up to 24 hours.

**2.** Soak wooden skewers in water for 1 hour. Preheat the oven to 400°F.

**3.** Put the panko on a shallow plate or baking dish. Remove the scallops from the pesto with a slotted spoon and roll them in the crumbs. Thread 1 or 2 scallops on each skewer. Lay them on a baking sheet lined with parchment paper, aluminum foil, or a silicone baking liner, making sure the skewered scallops don't touch. Bake until cooked through and the crumbs are golden, about 3 minutes. **Diva Do-Ahead:** At this point, you can let cool, cover, and refrigerate overnight. Bring to room temperature before continuing.

**4.** Arrange the scallops on a serving platter. Serve warm or at room temperature.

## Diva Variation

If you would like to serve these scallops as a main dish, marinate large sea scallops in the pesto, roll in the panko, then place in a baking dish and bake until cooked through, 8 to 12 minutes.

# Basil Pesto

*Makes about 3 1/2 cups*

2 cups fresh basil leaves

1 cup freshly grated Parmesan
 cheese

1/4 cup pine nuts

3 cloves garlic

1/2 cup olive oil

In a blender or food processor, process the basil, cheese, pine nuts, and garlic together until roughly chopped. With the machine running, gradually add the oil and process until smooth. Scrape down the bowl and process again for another 30 seconds. **Diva Do-Ahead:** At this point, you can pour into a jar, float 1/2 inch of olive oil on the top, and refrigerate for up to 5 days. Pour off the oil, and stir before using.

## How Much Sauce?

Most caterers figure on 2 tablespoons of sauce per person, but I'm more likely to make 3 tablespoons per person to avoid running out. However, if you have a few different sauces on the table, then it's okay to prepare 2 tablespoons of each sauce per person. When one runs out, the others can be used.

# Boiled Shrimp with Dipping Sauces

*Serves 10 to 12*

*This simple cooking method is foolproof—the shrimp always come out tender and succulent. Over-cooked shrimp are tough and unappetizing, so follow these directions and you will be right on the money. Remember that shrimp tend to be quite popular; I recommend at least three shrimp per person. Leftovers, if there are any, can be thrown into a salad, pasta, soup, or gumbo. Serve the shrimp with a choice of three delicious dipping sauces—a traditional cocktail sauce, one with an Asian flair, and one with a south-of-the-border flavor.*

4 cups water
2 tablespoons Old Bay
   Seasoning
1 lemon, quartered
2 pounds large or extra-large
   shrimp, peeled and deveined

**1.** Combine the water and Old Bay in a large saucepan. Squeeze the lemon into the water and add the rinds. Bring to a boil. Add the shrimp, cover, and remove from the heat. Let the shrimp remain in the water for 15 minutes.

**2.** Drain the shrimp, allow them to cool slightly, and peel. **Diva Do-Ahead:** At this point, you can let cool completely, transfer to a zipper-top plastic bag, and refrigerate for up to 2 days.

## Old-Fashioned Cocktail Sauce

*Makes 3 cups*

*Guests expect a version of this sauce at a seafood bar, so plan to make it, but also include the other two sauces.*

2 cups ketchup
3/4 cup chili sauce
3 tablespoons horseradish
1 tablespoon Worcestershire
   sauce
1 teaspoon freshly squeezed
   lemon juice
5 shakes hot sauce

In a large mixing bowl, stir together all the ingredients. Taste for seasoning, adding more horseradish or hot sauce if desired. Refrigerate for at least 4 hours to allow the flavors to blend. **Diva Do-Ahead:** At this point, you can refrigerate for up to 5 days. Serve cold.

# Spicy Peanut Sauce

*Makes 3 cups*

*With its Southeast Asian flavor, this sauce is also a terrific dipping sauce for satay or skewers, and it makes grilled chicken or pork very special. For a smooth sauce, use regular peanut butter, not natural-style.*

2 tablespoons vegetable oil

2 teaspoons peeled and grated
fresh ginger

1 clove garlic, mashed

2 tablespoons finely minced
jalapeño chile

1 cup chicken broth

1 cup smooth peanut butter

1 cup unsweetened coconut
milk

1/4 cup firmly packed light
brown sugar

2 tablespoons soy sauce

6 shakes hot sauce or to taste

**1.** In a medium-size saucepan, heat the oil, and add the ginger, garlic, and jalapeño, sautéing for 1 minute, until fragrant. Remove from the heat to prevent spattering; gradually pour in the broth, peanut butter, and coconut milk. Return to the stovetop over medium heat and whisk until smooth.

**2.** Add the brown sugar, soy sauce, and hot sauce, and bring to a boil. Simmer for 5 minutes. Remove from the stove and cool. Cover and refrigerate for at least 4 hours.

**Diva Do-Ahead:** At this point, you can refrigerate for up to 4 days. You may have to reheat gently to liquefy the sauce, but serve at room temperature.

## How Much Is Enough?

When buying shrimp for a buffet bar I will use large, extra-large, jumbo, or colossal shrimp because they make a dramatic statement on the table, but they can be very expensive. When you go to the market, you will see the shrimp labeled by size, but the number beside it is the most important one, 20/25, or 0 to 15. It refers to the number of shrimp in a pound, so if it says 0 to 15, that means there are about 15 per pound for colossal, 21 to 25 for jumbo, 26 to 30 for extra-large, and 31 to 35 for large. Large is the smallest size I would use for a seafood bar, but for salads and casseroles you can go to the bite-size medium, which are 36 to 40 to the pound. Let your budget be your guide; if shrimp will break the bank, then you may want to rethink this part of the menu.

# Bloody Margarita Cocktail Sauce

*Makes 3 cups*

*Spicy and thin, this cocktail sauce gets its kick from spiced tomato juice and tequila. It's also a nice addition to grilled chicken or other seafood.*

1 cup spicy tomato juice or
  Bloody Mary mix
$1/2$ cup ketchup
$1/2$ cup chunky salsa (your
  favorite brand and heat
  strength)
$1/2$ cup finely chopped celery
$1/4$ cup finely chopped
  scallions (white parts only)
$1/4$ cup finely chopped fresh
  cilantro
$1/4$ cup gold tequila
2 tablespoons fresh lime juice
$1/4$ teaspoon ground cumin
Salt and freshly ground black
  pepper to taste

In a mixing bowl, combine all the ingredients until blended. Taste for seasoning, adding salt and pepper as needed. Cover and refrigerate for at least 4 hours to allow the flavors to blend. **Diva Do-Ahead:** At this point, you can refrigerate for up to 4 days.

## Shell On or Off?

Shrimp can be expensive for a large group, so try buying the shrimp raw and cooking them yourself. If you have time to peel and devein them, buy them raw with shells (the cheapest way to buy them). Starting on the underside, remove the feelers. Then pull off the top shell and either leave the tail on or discard it. Some people like to keep the tail on so their guests have an instant "handle" for picking up the shrimp. Sometimes you can't save the tail shell because it will all come off with the top shell, so you'll have to offer toothpicks. Once the shell is removed, make a shallow cut with a sharp knife down the back of the shrimp and lift out the intestinal vein that runs down the back. Rinse the shrimp in cold water and keep refrigerated before cooking.

If you don't have time to peel, buy your shrimp already peeled and deveined (but still raw). If you buy frozen cooked shrimp, defrost them in a colander for 1 hour, then toss them with a sprinkle of Old Bay Seasoning and lemon juice and refrigerate until ready to serve.

# Smoked Seafood Platter

*Serves 12*

*A smoked seafood platter is a deliciously simple way to add to the seafood count at the table, and it's a luxuriously elegant appetizer. If you own a stovetop smoker, you can smoke your choices of seafood: shrimp, salmon, tuna, oysters, mussels, and clams. Make sure to have a large platter that will fit the seafood nicely with the garnishes.*

2 cups whipped cream cheese

1 tablespoon fresh dill, finely chopped

2 teaspoons freshly grated lemon zest

One 10-ounce bag mesclun or spring mix salad greens

One side of smoked salmon (about 10 ounces)

$1/4$ to $1/3$ pound assorted smoked fishes, bones removed (trout, albacore tuna, yellowtail, mussels, clams, and/or shrimp)

$1/2$ cup finely chopped red onion

$1/2$ cup small capers, drained

3 lemons, cut into wedges, for garnish

Dill sprigs for garnish

Assorted crackers, bagel chips, and cocktail rye and pumpernickel bread for serving

**1.** In a mixer, combine the cream cheese, dill, and lemon zest. Cover and refrigerate for up to 5 days. One day before serving, line a baking sheet with parchment paper, aluminum foil, or a silicone baking liner. Place the cream cheese mixture into a pastry bag fitted with a large star tip and pipe out mounds. If you don't have a pastry bag, shape the cream cheese into small golf ball–sized rounds, using a small scoop. **Diva Do-Ahead:** At this point, you can cover and refrigerate for up to 24 hours.

**2.** Just before serving, spread some of the greens on the bottom of a serving platter. Arrange the seafood on the platter and carefully lift the piped cream cheese off the baking sheet with an offset spatula and arrange around the seafood. Sprinkle the seafood and cream cheese with the red onion and capers, garnish the platter with lemon wedges and dill sprigs, and serve with assorted crackers and bread on the side.

## Diva Quickie

To save time, you might want to serve a smoked seafood dip (salmon, trout, clam) instead of the platter. The Diva's Smoked Seafood Dip (recipe follows) is a simple dip that is a real crowd-pleaser.

# The Diva's Smoked Seafood Dip

*Serves 8 to 10*

*This smoky dip studded with nuggets of smoked salmon and flavored with dill is simple to whip up for an elegant party or for a spur-of-the-moment get-together. It's also a great way to use up the smoked salmon that you may have gotten as a gift for the holidays.*

1 pound cream cheese, softened
1 cup sour cream
1 1/2 teaspoons horseradish
5 shakes hot sauce
Grated zest of 1/2 lemon
6 ounces smoked seafood, chopped or flaked (salmon, trout, and clams all work well)
2 tablespoons chopped fresh dill
Crackers or cucumber rounds for serving

**1.** In the bowl of an electric mixer, cream together the cream cheese and sour cream until smooth. Stir in the horseradish, hot sauce, and lemon zest, beating the mixture until they are incorporated.

**2.** Fold in the seafood and 5 teaspoons of the dill, stirring until blended.

**3.** Cover and refrigerate for at least 2 hours. **Diva Do-Ahead:** At this point, you can refrigerate for up to 2 days. Stir the dip and garnish with the remaining 1 teaspoon dill. Serve cold with crackers.

## Diva Variation

This dip is awesome used in place of the shrimp mixture in Shrimp Dillyicious Puffs (page 26).

# White Gloves and Caviar

Caviar is a luxurious and delicious item to have on your buffet table, but it is an investment, so remember to think about who is coming and whether or not they will enjoy it. True caviar is the preserved roe of the sturgeon and is a rare, expensive product. There are three primary varieties: sevruga, osetra, and beluga. There is currently a ban on imported beluga caviar, but your local purveyor should have plenty of high-quality American-produced caviars to recommend. It is essential to keep the caviar cold, and once you have opened the tin, it should be eaten right away. It is tradtionally served in a small crystal dish seated in crushed ice along with freshly toasted bread, then washed down with a small glass of iced vodka. Purists serve caviar with only bread and no condiments. Others prefer to serve sieved hard-cooked egg yolks, sieved hard-cooked egg whites, lemon wedges, red onion, and crème fraîche on the side.

# Crostini Bar

*Serves 12*

*Crostini are small toasts with toppings that are usually served family-style at the table as an antipasto. I love crostini because you can make simple toppings ahead of time (see the recipes on pages 44–45). After a little last-minute arranging, you have a wonderful appetizer with lots of color, texture, and flavor.*

**Toasts**

2 thin baguettes, sliced
  1/2 inch thick

**1.** Preheat the oven to 350°F. Arrange the bread on baking sheets.

**2.** Bake the bread for 10 minutes, until it is no longer soft and begins to color slightly.

**3**. Allow the toast to cool to room temperature. **Diva Do-Ahead:** At this point, you can store in zipper-top plastic bags at room temperature for 1 day or freeze for up to 3 weeks.

*Diva Variation*

Rub the toasted bread with a clove of garlic after removing from the oven (but not if you are freezing the toasts—the garlic loses flavor when frozen).

## Diva Tip

One regular baguette will yield twenty to twenty-four 1/2-inch slices.

# Roasted Eggplant Topping

*Makes about 2 cups*

*Roasting eggplant and garlic brings out their sweetness, and this spread, with its spike of balsamic vinegar, is delicious served as a topping for toasted breads.*

2 large purple eggplants
(about 1¹/2 pounds), stems
removed and sliced in half
lengthwise

¹/4 cup extra-virgin olive oil

4 cloves garlic, unpeeled

¹/2 cup finely chopped fresh
Italian parsley

2 tablespoons balsamic
vinegar

5 shakes hot sauce

1 teaspoon salt

¹/2 teaspoon freshly ground
black pepper

**1.** Preheat the oven to 400°F. Line a baking sheet with aluminum foil or a silicone baking liner.

**2.** Drizzle the cut sides of the eggplant with some of the oil and arrange them cut side down along with the garlic. Roast for 20 minutes, until the tip of a knife inserted into the eggplant goes in easily. Remove from the oven and cool.

**3.** When the eggplant is cool, scoop out the tender inside and place in a food processor. Squeeze the garlic from its skin and add to the work bowl.

**4.** Pulse the mixture on and off 5 to 6 times, until eggplant is chopped. Remove to a mixing bowl. Stir in the parsley, vinegar, hot sauce, any remaining olive oil, salt, and pepper. Taste for seasoning and add more salt or pepper if necessary. **Diva Do-Ahead:** At this point, you can cover and store in the refrigerator for up to 4 days. Remove from the refrigerator 1 hour before serving and stir to blend. Serve immediately.

# Sweet Pepper and Parmigiano Topping

*Makes about 2 cups*

*Sweet tender Italian green frying peppers and nutty Parmesan cheese pair up for another delicious topping for toasted breads or crackers. It's also great on sandwiches or burgers. Use authentic imported Parmigiano-Reggiano for this recipe.*

2 tablespoons olive oil

6 thin green sweet Italian frying peppers, cored and cut into 1/2-inch rounds

2 large sweet yellow onions, finely sliced into half-moons

1/4 cup tomato puree

1 teaspoon sugar

1 teaspoon salt

1 teaspoon freshly ground black pepper

1/4 cup finely chopped fresh Italian parsley

2 ounces Parmigiano-Reggiano cheese, finely chopped

**1.** In a large skillet, heat the oil, add the peppers and onions, and sauté for about 3 minutes, until they cook down a bit, stirring so that they don't brown.

**2.** Sprinkle the mixture with the tomato puree, sugar, salt, and pepper, and cook until the tomato has almost evaporated and the peppers are softened, about 10 minutes. Stir in the parsley. Remove the mixture to a small bowl. Allow to cool to room temperature and then stir in the cheese. **Diva Do-Ahead:** At this point, you can cover and refrigerate for up to 4 days. Serve at room temperature.

# Gorgonzola-Walnut Topping

*Makes about 2 cups*

*This topping, made with creamy blue Gorgonzola and toasted walnuts, is terrific on top of toasted bread. Also try it as a spread for crackers and serve some nice red grapes on the side.*

1 1/2 cups crumbled Gorgonzola cheese

1/4 cup mascarpone cheese

2 teaspoons ruby port

1/2 cup finely chopped toasted walnuts (page 114)

**1.** In a small bowl, stir together the two cheeses and the port until they are combined. **Diva Do-Ahead:** At this point, you can cover and refrigerate for up to 4 days.

**2.** One hour before serving, stir in the walnuts. Serve at room temperature.

# Wendy's After Eight Brownies

*Makes about twenty-four 2-inch brownies*

*My friend Wendy Morgan is always giving me great tips for entertaining, and when she served this simply scrumptious brownie, I knew it would be the perfect dessert for our New Year's Eve buffet. Rich brownie batter sandwiches After Eight Mints, giving you a mint chocolate brownie to die for— and the chocolate frosting sends it over the top!*

### Brownies

3/4 cup (1 1/2 sticks) unsalted butter
4 ounces unsweetened chocolate
1 3/4 cups sugar
3 large eggs
1 cup all-purpose flour
24 After Eight Mints

### Frosting

1 cup sugar
1/3 cup whole milk
5 tablespoons unsalted butter
One 6-ounce package semi-sweet chocolate chips

**1.** To make the brownies, preheat the oven to 350°F. Coat the inside of a 13 x 9-inch baking dish with nonstick cooking spray.

**2.** In a medium-size saucepan, melt the butter and chocolate together, stirring until the chocolate is melted. Remove from the heat. Stir in the sugar until blended, then stir in the eggs one at a time, beating well after each addition.

**3.** Stir in the flour until it disappears. Pour half of the batter into the prepared pan. Cover the top of the batter with the mints and dollop the remaining batter over the top of the mints. Using an offset spatula that has been dipped into hot water, spread the batter as evenly as possible. The batter may not reach the sides of the pan but will spread once it bakes.

**4.** Bake the brownies for 25 to 30 minutes, until a skewer inserted into the center comes out with a few crumbs. Remove to a cooling rack.

**5.** To make the frosting, in a small saucepan heat together the sugar, milk, and butter. Bring to a boil and boil for 1 minute. Remove from the heat and stir in the chocolate chips, stirring until the chips are melted. Pour the hot frosting over the warm brownies.

**6.** Cut the brownies while they are still warm. Allow to cool completely, then remove them from the pan. **Diva Do-Ahead:** At this point, you can cover tightly with plastic wrap and store in the refrigerator for 2 days or freeze for 2 months. Bring to room temperature for serving.

# Almond Toffee Bars

*Makes about 40 squares*

**These decadent bars have a buttery crust that is covered with a layer of melted almond roca, a buttercrunch almond-chocolate candy. At Christmastime I make my own almond roca and use the small bits to bake atop the bars, but you can purchase almond roca and chop it up into bits, or chop up Heath bars. These squares freeze well, but if someone knows they are in the freezer, they won't last long!**

2 cups all-purpose flour

3/4 cup light brown sugar

1 cup (2 sticks) unsalted butter, cut into small pieces

1 large egg yolk

1 tablespoon Frangelico liqueur (optional)

2 cups chopped almond roca candy or Heath bars

**1.** Preheat the oven to 350°F. Coat the inside of a 13 x 9-inch baking dish with nonstick cooking spray.

**2.** Place the flour and brown sugar in the work bowl of a food processor; pulse on and off to distribute the dry ingredients.

**3.** Drop the butter onto the dry ingredients and pulse on and off about 6 times, until the mixture is crumbly. Scrape down the sides, add the egg yolk and the Frangelico, if using, and pulse on and off another 4 times.

**4.** Press the dough into the prepared pan and bake for 20 minutes, until the crust is a light golden brown.

**5.** Turn off the oven, scatter the almond roca over the crust, and return the pan to the oven for 10 minutes, or until the almond roca is melted. Remove from the oven to a cooling rack and allow to cool completely before cutting into squares. **Diva Do-Ahead:** At this point, you can store in airtight containers at room temperature for 4 days or freeze for 6 weeks.

# A New Year's Day Brunch for 12

A New Year's Day brunch is a great time to have friends and neighbors over. Everyone is relaxed and mellow, and this menu is a sure-fire winner for your friends and family to enjoy in an informal setting.

If you have a special cocktail that you like to serve on New Year's, have that mixed in pitchers for your guests to serve themselves; otherwise, Bloody Marys and Mimosas are a perfect match with this delicious brunch. Although I've suggested this brunch for New Year's Day, it works in most seasons, and you should feel free to use the recipes for other events that you wish to celebrate with a midday meal.

Table decorations should be colorful and celebratory—lots of rich, deep colors. A cream or white tablecloth accented with deep burgundy, blue, or green, set off with lighter shades of the same color in the napkins or flowers will make your table look warm and sumptuous. Fill small vases with tiny shells, colored marbles, dried black-eyed peas (traditional at New Year's for good luck), or river rocks, and then place one or two flowers into the vase—it will look like a lot more than the sum of its parts. Lay down pine boughs or ferns, then center a pineapple amid other fruits with wired ribbon twisted throughout, and you have a beautiful, festive winter centerpiece. Or you may simply arrange seasonal fruits in an attractive bowl to decorate your table.

Because this brunch is a casual get-together, I suggest serving it as a buffet or a family-style meal, giving you the opportunity to serve everything at once. Your guests can graze on whatever they like. Depending upon how many guests you have, you may want to set up additional tables, or have lap trays for people to balance their plates on. I have designed this celebration so that it

doesn't require what I call "traction," when you need both a knife and fork to eat the meal.

If you serve a buffet, try to stagger the heights of your dishes for visual interest. Serve the coffee-cake on a cake stand. Use a sturdy box underneath the tablecloth and place the platter of scones on top of that to add dimension so that the table doesn't look quite so flat. Line up the plates at one end of the table and place the flatware rolled in napkins, tied with ribbon or raffia, at the other end of the table. It's easier to navigate a buffet line if you have to concentrate just on handling a plate and not the utensils, too! Set up a small area with condiments, such as butter, salt and pepper, and jam away from the buffet table so that people aren't slowing down the food line by stopping for them.

Because brunch is a morning meal (and the morning after what may have been a big night), have some smooth jazz playing in the background—Wynton Marsalis or Miles Davis is perfect.

## Do-Ahead Countdown

* **6 weeks ahead**

  Download shopping list and do-ahead calendar and fill them out

  Shop for nonperishables

  Make and freeze Raspberry Sauce

  Make (but don't bake) and freeze Sausage and Egg Strudels

  Make and freeze Spicy Nuts for salad

* **1 month ahead**

  Make (but don't bake) and freeze White Cheddar Scones

  Make and freeze Blueberry-Almond Coffeecake

* **2 weeks ahead**

  Make Apple Vinaigrette

* **4 days ahead**

  Prepare Bloody Mary base as well as any garnishes

* **3 days ahead**

  Remove Raspberry Sauce, nuts, and coffeecake from freezer and defrost in refrigerator

* **2 days ahead**

  Make (but don't bake) Peaches-and-Cream Grand Marnier Bread Pudding

* **1 day ahead**

  Set the table

  Remove the scones and strudels from freezer and defrost in refrigerator

  Toss potatoes for Roasted Red Potatoes with oil and seasonings

* **2 hours ahead**

  Prepare apples and celery for salad

  Preheat the oven

* **1 hour ahead**

  Roast the potatoes

* **45 minutes ahead**

  Bake bread pudding

  Bake strudels

  Bake scones

* **10 minutes ahead**

  Rewarm coffeecake

* **5 minutes ahead**

  Toss salad

# Brunch-Time Bloody Marys

*Serves 12*

*This is my daughter Carrie's favorite Bloody Mary, for which she and her boyfriend, Eric Mand, have become famous. She recommends that you set up a Bloody Mary bar and mix as your guests get thirsty. Fill a pitcher full of the basic "Bloody" mix and set out some pint glasses and a good supply of ice. I've suggested lemon slices and celery stalk stirrers for garnishes. You might also want to put out extra spices and sauces so that people can adjust the flavoring to their taste. Other fabulous garnishes to consider are cooked shrimp perched on the rim, pickled okra, pickled green beans or asparagus spears, and lime slices.*

One 64-ounce bottle V8 juice or tomato juice (we like Sacramento)

One 32-ounce bottle Clamato

2/3 cup Worcestershire sauce

1/4 cup horseradish

10 shakes hot sauce

1 tablespoon celery salt

1/4 teaspoon freshly ground black pepper, plus more for garnish

Juice of 1/2 lemon

Ice cubes

One 750-milliliter bottle vodka

Celery stalks for garnish

Lemon slices for garnish

**1.** In a 3- to 4-quart pitcher, stir together the V8, Clamato, Worcestershire, horseradish, hot sauce, celery salt, pepper, and lemon juice. Cover and refrigerate for at least 4 hours. **Diva Do-Ahead:** At this point, you can cover and refrigerate for up to 4 days.

**2.** For each drink, fill an 8-ounce glass with ice, pour in 2 ounces of vodka, and fill the glass with the Bloody Mary mix. Stir to blend. Garnish the drinks with a celery stalk, freshly ground black pepper, and a lemon slice.

# Classic Mimosas

*Serves 12*

*This lovely champagne and orange juice drink can be made in a nonalcoholic version as well. It is a terrific starter for brunch and also lends itself to a serve-yourself bar. A fresh whole strawberry or a few raspberries in the bottom of each glass is a beautiful garnish. This is not truly a do-ahead drink, but as long as everything is chilled, you will be ready to rock and roll at a moment's notice.*

1 gallon chilled orange juice
Three 750-milliliter bottles
　chilled champagne

Pour $1/2$ cup orange juice into a wineglass or champagne flute. Top off with champagne and serve immediately.

## Diva Variations

**Virgin Mimosa:** Substitute 7UP or another lemon-lime soda for the champagne.

**Wine Mimosa:** Substitute white wine for the champagne.

**Cantaloupe Mimosa:** Puree 2 cups chopped cantaloupe (about $1/2$ cantaloupe) with $1/2$ cup orange juice and top off with champagne for a deliciously different mimosa.

# Peaches-and-Cream Grand Marnier Bread Pudding with Raspberry Sauce

*Serves 12*

*Your guests will love this bread pudding. Simply elegant, and bursting with peaches and mascarpone cheese, it is served with a piquant raspberry sauce to give it the flavor of a peach Melba dessert. A great do-ahead, this brunch pudding can be made either in a casserole dish or in individual muffin cups.*

6 large eggs

1 cup heavy cream

1 1/2 cups granulated sugar

1 teaspoon ground cinnamon

1/4 cup Grand Marnier, triple sec, or orange juice

One 8-ounce loaf French bread, torn into 1/2-inch pieces

4 cups coarsely chopped, peeled, and pitted ripe peaches or two 16-ounce bags frozen sliced peaches, defrosted, drained, and chopped

2 cups mascarpone cheese

1/2 teaspoon ground nutmeg

1/4 cup (1/2 stick) unsalted butter, melted

Confectioners' sugar for garnish

2 cups Raspberry Sauce (recipe follows)

**1.** Coat a 13 x 9-inch baking dish or two 12-cup muffin tins with nonstick cooking spray.

**2.** In a medium-size bowl, whisk together the eggs, cream, 1 cup of the granulated sugar, 1/2 teaspoon of the cinnamon, and Grand Marnier.

**3.** Place the bread in a large bowl and pour the egg custard over it, stirring to blend.

**4.** In another large bowl, stir together the peaches, mascarpone, and nutmeg. Pour half of the bread mixture into the prepared baking dish, top with all of the peach and mascarpone mixture, and spread the remaining bread over the top. If you are using muffin tins, place about 1 tablespoon of the bread mixture in the bottom of each cup and then top with some of the peach mixture and the remaining bread mixture. Cover and refrigerate for at least 2 hours. **Diva Do-Ahead:** At this point, you can refrigerate for up to 2 days.

**5.** Preheat the oven to 375°F. Remove the casserole or muffin tins from the refrigerator.

**6.** In a small bowl, mix together the remaining 1/2 teaspoon cinnamon and the remaining 1/2 cup granulated sugar and sprinkle over the bread pudding. Brush with the melted butter and bake until golden and the peaches are bubbling around the sides, 35 to 40 minutes. (Bake the muffins for 15 to 20 minutes until puffed and golden.)

**7.** Remove from the oven, sift confectioners' sugar over the top, and serve warm with the Raspberry Sauce.

# Raspberry Sauce

*Makes about 4 cups*

*This brilliant red sauce will complement your bread pudding, or even plain old vanilla ice cream. It's also delicious over pancakes and waffles. Keep a batch stored in your freezer for sauce emergencies!*

Two 10-ounce bags frozen
　raspberries, defrosted
1/2 cup sugar
2 tablespoons lemon juice or
　Grand Marnier

In a medium-size saucepan, stir together the raspberries, sugar, and lemon juice. Bring the mixture to a boil and simmer for about 5 minutes, stirring frequently, until the sauce begins to thicken. Remove from the heat and pour through a sieve into a large measuring cup, pressing down on the seeds. Discard the seeds and allow the sauce to cool. **Diva Do-Ahead:** At this point, you can refrigerate for up to 2 weeks or freeze for up to 2 months. The sauce can be served warm, at room temperature, or cold.

## Diva Tip

Fresh raspberries can be very expensive, and sometimes you will get the box home only to discover that the bottom layer is moldy. For sauces, I recommend that you use frozen raspberries, so that you can be assured that you will be able to use all the raspberries in the package.

# White Cheddar Scones

*Makes 16 large or 24 small scones*

**These savory scones are delicious when tucked into a breadbasket on your brunch buffet table.**

3<sup>3</sup>/4 cups all-purpose flour

1<sup>1</sup>/2 tablespoons baking powder

1<sup>1</sup>/2 cups finely shredded sharp white cheddar cheese

6 shakes of hot sauce

2<sup>1</sup>/2 cups heavy cream

2 large egg yolks

2 tablespoons whole milk or heavy cream

**1.** Preheat the oven to 425°F. Line a baking sheet with parchment paper, aluminum foil, or a silicone baking liner.

**2.** Whisk the flour and baking powder together in a large bowl. Add the cheese and stir to blend. Stir the hot sauce into the cream, then drizzle the cream into the flour mixture and stir until the dough is rough but begins to hold together.

**3.** Turn the dough out onto a lightly floured work surface and knead it about 8 times, until it starts to become smooth. Divide in half and pat each half into a circle about 8 inches in diameter. Cut each circle of dough into wedges—8 for large scones or 12 for smaller ones. Or, using a biscuit cutter, cut the scones into 2-inch rounds. Transfer to the prepared baking sheet. **Diva Do-Ahead:** At this point, you can freeze the wedges. Once they are frozen, transfer to a zipper-top plastic bag and freeze for up 6 weeks. Defrost for 30 minutes before continuing.

**4.** Whisk together the egg yolks and milk in a small bowl and brush the wash over the tops of the scones. Bake until golden brown, 16 to 18 minutes. Remove from the baking sheets and serve warm.

## Freezing Scones

Baked scones can be frozen for about 1 month in zipper-top plastic bags, but they lose something when they are reheated. I love to serve them freshly baked out of the oven, so I prefer to freeze the rolled-out wedges of uncooked dough. That way, I can put them in the fridge the night before to defrost and bake them in the morning, or take them out of the freezer and let them defrost for 30 minutes on the counter, then bake them.

However, if freezing the baked scones is the way you want to go, here's how. Defrost them overnight in the refrigerator. Preheat the oven to 350°F and place the scones on a lined baking sheet. Place a pan of boiling water on the bottom rack of the oven and warm the scones for about 10 minutes, until heated through. The water will provide moisture and the scones should turn out nicely.

# Sausage and Egg Strudels

*Serves 12*

*Elegant, crisp phyllo dough encases a deliciously creamy scrambled egg, sausage, and Swiss cheese mixture to give you a beautiful brunchtime entrée. Phyllo is not difficult to work with, but you need to keep it covered, or else it will dry out. Make sure to brush it liberally with butter and sprinkle bread crumbs between the layers to absorb the liquid in the filling so that the pastry doesn't get soggy.*

## Sauce

3 tablespoons unsalted butter

3 tablespoons all-purpose flour

1 1/2 cups whole or 2 percent milk

1/2 cup shredded Swiss cheese

1/4 cup freshly grated Parmesan cheese

1/2 teaspoon salt

Pinch of cayenne pepper

Pinch of ground nutmeg

## Filling

3/4 pound bulk pork sausage (I like Jimmy Dean)

8 large eggs

1 teaspoon dried thyme

1/2 teaspoon freshly ground black pepper

2 tablespoons unsalted butter

2 tablespoons chopped fresh Italian parsley

## Phyllo

1 pound phyllo dough (see page 58), defrosted

1 cup (2 sticks) unsalted butter, clarified (see page 59)

1/2 cup plain dry bread crumbs

**1.** To make the sauce, in a medium-size saucepan, melt the butter over medium heat, then add the flour, whisking until smooth. Cook until white bubbles begin to form on the top. Cook for another minute, then gradually add the milk, whisking until smooth and the sauce begins to boil. Remove from the heat and stir in the two cheeses, salt, cayenne, and nutmeg. Set aside in a large bowl or storage container to cool.

**2.** To make the filling, in a 10-inch skillet, cook the sausage, breaking it up with a fork, until it is no longer pink. Drain the sausage in a colander.

**3.** In a large bowl, beat together the eggs, thyme, and pepper until blended. Add the sausage.

**4.** Melt the butter in a 10-inch skillet over medium-high heat, then add the egg mixture and cook, stirring with a fork, until just set but still moist. Add the eggs and parsley to the

*continued on next page*

## Sausage and Egg Strudels *continued*

cheese sauce. **Diva Do-Ahead:** At this point, you can cover and refrigerate for up to 2 days.

**5.** Remove the phyllo from the package, unroll, and place on a clean kitchen towel. Cover with another kitchen towel to keep it from drying out.

**6.** Line a baking sheet with parchment paper, aluminum foil, or a silicone baking liner. Arrange a phyllo sheet on a clean work surface, keeping the others covered. Liberally brush the phyllo with clarified butter and sprinkle with some of the bread crumbs. Fold the sheet in half lengthwise. Brush the surface with butter and sprinkle with crumbs. Spoon ⅓ cup of the filling 1 inch in from a short end of the pastry sheet. Fold the edge of the pastry over the filling and brush with butter. Fold the sides of the pastry in toward the middle and brush with butter and sprinkle with crumbs. Starting at the end with the filling, fold the dough over the filling, then turn in the sides toward the middle, and roll up to form a package shaped more or less like an egg roll. Brush the top and bottom with butter and arrange on the prepared sheet. Repeat to make 12 packages. **Diva Do-Ahead:** At this point, you can cover and refrigerate for up to 2 days or freeze for up to 6 weeks; once the packages are frozen, they can be transferred to zipper-top plastic bags or storage containers, layers separated by plastic or waxed paper.

**7.** Preheat the oven to 375°F. Bake until puffed and golden, about 15 minutes. Frozen phyllo packets can go straight from the freezer into the oven, but will take a little longer to bake, 20 to 30 minutes. Let cool for 5 minutes before serving.

## Phyllo Sheet Sizes

Phyllo is sold in large (18 x 14-inch) sheets, the size used for the recipes in this book, but also in smaller (14 x 9-inch) sheets. If you use the smaller sheets for this recipe, follow the instructions in step 6 but don't fold the sheet in half before creating the egg-roll shape.

## Diva Variations

- Substitute turkey sausage for the pork sausage.
- Substitute 1 1/2 cups flaked cooked salmon for the sausage.
- Substitute one 16-ounce package frozen chopped spinach, defrosted and squeezed dry, for the sausage.
- Substitute 1 1/2 cups diced smoked turkey for the sausage.

## Another Diva Variation

If you would prefer to make 2 large rolls, rather than individual servings, line a baking sheet with a piece of parchment or foil that is twice the length of the baking sheet, letting the excess overlap evenly on either side. Arrange 1 sheet of phyllo, brush with clarified butter, and sprinkle with bread crumbs. Repeat with 4 more sheets of phyllo. Center half of the egg mixture lengthwise down the center of the phyllo (it should be 3 to 3 1/2 inches wide), fold the short top and bottom ends onto the eggs, then fold in the sides to seal, and brush all the phyllo with butter. Repeat with 5 more layers of phyllo and the other half of the egg mixture to make another roll. Refrigerate until the rolls are firmed up, about 2 hours, then carefully turn the rolls seam side down, using the foil to help you roll.

**Diva Do-Ahead:** Wrap the rolls and refrigerate for up to 2 days, or freeze for up to 6 weeks, defrosting before proceeding. Bake the rolls for 20 to 25 minutes, until they are golden brown. Remove from the oven, allow them to rest for 5 to 10 minutes, then slice into 1 1/2-inch slices with a serrated knife. Use a long, wide spatula to transfer the slices to your serving platter or individual plates.

# Clarified Butter

Clarified butter is butter that has been melted and the milk solids and whey removed. To clarify butter, melt it in a small saucepan and skim all the foam off the top. Pour the butter into a container, leaving any water and milk solids in the bottom of the pan. Refrigerate butter until ready to use.

It is important to use clarified butter in phyllo dough preparations because the water and milk solids will make the phyllo soggy rather than crispy when it bakes. Many markets now sell clarified butter (check the dairy aisle), if you don't want to go to the trouble of making it yourself.

# Roasted Red Potatoes

*Serves 12*

*Tiny new potatoes roasted at a high temperature become caramelized on the outside and sweet on the inside. You can roast these potatoes the day before and then reheat them in a hot skillet on the stovetop or in the oven. I found that refrigerating the coated potatoes before baking resulted in a crisper crust than when I roasted them immediately after coating. Vary the herbs to suit your preferences; here I suggest thyme to complement the flavor in the egg strudels, but oregano, marjoram, and rosemary are also great choices. Leftovers make terrific potato salad and frittatas, or you can add them to soups.*

3 pounds red or white
potatoes, left whole if small
(1 inch), halved or quartered
if larger

1/3 cup olive oil

2 teaspoons chopped fresh
thyme, plus sprigs for
garnish

2 teaspoons salt

1 1/2 teaspoons freshly ground
black pepper

Coarse salt for garnish

**1.** Place the potatoes, oil, thyme, salt, and pepper in a large mixing bowl and toss with your hands to coat the potatoes. Cover with plastic wrap and refrigerate for at least 3 hours. **Diva Do-Ahead:** At this point, you can refrigerate for up to 24 hours.

**2.** Preheat the oven to 400°F. Line a baking sheet with aluminum foil or a silicone baking liner.

**3.** Transfer the potatoes to the baking sheet and bake for 45 to 55 minutes, turning them every 15 minutes or so, until they are tender, brown, and crispy. Remove from the oven. **Diva Do-Ahead:** At this point, you can let the potatoes cool, then transfer to an ovenproof serving bowl, cover, and refrigerate for up to 24 hours. Reheat, covered with foil, for 10 minutes at 350°F, then uncover and heat another 5 minutes. Or reheat thoroughly in a large skillet. Serve warm or at room temperature, garnished with thyme sprigs and a sprinkle of coarse salt.

## Skin On or Off?

Leaving the skins on these potatoes is usually my preference, because they offer some nice color, but if there is a greenish tinge to the potato skin, you need to remove it. The green is a toxin, which must be removed (just peel it away); then the potatoes will be perfect. The green results from exposure to light and is not harmful if removed.

# Spinach Salad with Apples, Spicy Nuts, and Apple Vinaigrette

*Serves 12*

*This beautiful salad has a little something different in each bite: bright green spinach, tart apples, and crunchy, spicy nuts, all bound together with a slightly sweet apple and poppy seed dressing. All the components can be prepared ahead and then tossed together just before serving. If you'd like to serve this dish another time as a more substantial salad, add cut-up cooked chicken or roasted pork.*

1/4 cup apple juice

2 tablespoons cider vinegar

2 tablespoons light brown sugar

2 tablespoons Dijon mustard

3/4 cup canola oil

2 tablespoons poppy seeds

2 Gala apples, cored and chopped

1 tablespoon lemon juice

1 cup chopped celery

Three 10-ounce bags baby spinach

1 cup Spicy Nuts (page 62)

**1.** Whisk together the apple juice, vinegar, brown sugar, mustard, and oil. **Diva Do-Ahead:** At this point, you can cover and refrigerate for up to 2 weeks. Whisk to reblend and add the poppy seeds before serving.

**2.** Combine the apples and lemon juice, tossing to coat. Add the celery. **Diva Do-Ahead:** At this point, you can cover and refrigerate for up to 6 hours.

**3.** In a large salad bowl, toss together the apples, spinach, and the dressing until the spinach is coated. Garnish with the nuts and serve immediately.

# Spicy Nuts

*Makes 2 cups*

**Simple to prepare, these nuts are the Diva's secret weapon to perk up an ordinary salad. Or if you want to serve Spicy Nuts as a nibble before dinner, use nut halves instead of chopped nuts. These nuts also add zest to a cheese spread: roll a ball of cheese spread in Spicy Nuts, refrigerate to firm up, and serve with crackers.**

2 tablespoons unsalted butter
3 tablespoons sugar
1 teaspoon seasoned salt
1/2 teaspoon Lawry's garlic salt
1/8 teaspoon cayenne pepper
2 cups chopped pecans or
   walnuts

**1.** Melt the butter in a large nonstick skillet over medium heat. Add 2 tablespoons of the sugar, the seasoned salt, garlic salt, and cayenne, and stir until the spices emit some aroma, 1 to 2 minutes. Add the nuts and toss until well coated, about 4 minutes.

**2.** Remove from the heat and place the nuts in a glass bowl. Sprinkle the remaining 1 tablespoon sugar over the nuts and toss until coated. **Diva Do-Ahead:** Store the nuts in zipper-top plastic bags in the refrigerator for up to 2 weeks or in the freezer for up to 2 months.

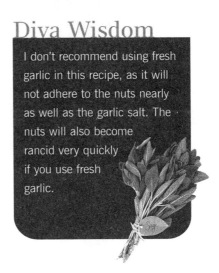

## Diva Wisdom

I don't recommend using fresh garlic in this recipe, as it will not adhere to the nuts nearly as well as the garlic salt. The nuts will also become rancid very quickly if you use fresh garlic.

# Blueberry-Almond Coffeecake

*Makes one 10-inch cake*

*This wonderful coffeecake, studded with blueberries and topped with streusel and almonds that toast beautifully in the oven, may become your favorite morning snack.*

### Streusel

1/2 cup granulated sugar
1/2 cup all-purpose flour
3/4 teaspoon ground cinnamon
1/4 teaspoon ground nutmeg
1/4 cup (1/2 stick) unsalted
 butter, melted

### Cake

1/2 cup (1 stick) unsalted
 butter, softened
3/4 cup light brown sugar
2 large eggs
1 cup buttermilk
1 teaspoon pure vanilla extract
1/2 teaspoon grated lemon zest
1 1/2 cups all-purpose flour
3/4 teaspoon baking powder
1/4 teaspoon baking soda
1/4 teaspoon salt
1 cup fresh or frozen and
 not defrosted blueberries
 (or raspberries, blackberries,
 or a combination)
1 cup sliced almonds

**1.** To make the streusel, combine the dry ingredients in a small bowl. Gradually stir in the melted butter with a fork until crumbs form. Set aside.

**2.** Preheat the oven to 375°F. Coat the inside of a 10-inch springform pan with nonstick cooking spray.

**3.** To make the cake, in the large bowl of an electric mixer, cream together the butter and sugar, adding the eggs one at a time, until blended. Add the buttermilk, vanilla extract, and lemon zest, beating until the mixture is combined.

**4.** Add the flour, baking powder, baking soda, and salt, beating on low speed until blended.

**5.** With a spatula, carefully fold in the berries until they are distributed throughout the batter. Pour the batter into the prepared pan, sprinkle the streusel over the top, and cover with the almonds.

**6.** Bake for 35 to 45 minutes, until a skewer inserted into the center comes out clean. Cool 15 minutes on a wire rack before removing the sides of the pan and serving. **Diva Do-Ahead:** The cooled cake can be frozen for up to 1 month. Defrost overnight on the counter, and rewarm, loosely tented with foil in a preheated 350°F oven, for 10 minutes. Or bake 3 days ahead and store at room temperature in an airtight container.

## Diva Variation

My friends Ellen and Dan Einstein, who own Sweet 16th, a bakery in Nashville, Tennessee, double this recipe and bake it in a 13 x 9-inch baking pan for the same amount of time.

A Fine Romance

# A Valentine's Day Sweetheart Dinner

Going out to a restaurant on Valentine's Day is vastly overrated. Restaurants are jammed, servers are harried, and the evening often ends up being a more disappointing than romantic experience! This menu is fancy enough to be served in a restaurant, but so much more relaxed and intimate. I've designed this menu for four people. If you choose to have additional couples over, you can easily double the recipes. And, of course, you may cut them in half if you want to reserve the night for just you and your sweetheart.

No matter how many guests you choose to host, this menu is a perfect way to say I love you. Of course you can make it all ahead of time! Starting off with ruby-colored Champagne Cosmopolitan Cocktails and then a light, creamy corn soup served with heart-shaped crostini as a first course, the dinner progresses to individual Wellingtons. I've given you a choice of beef, poultry, or seafood to serve as an entrée. Arranged like a wrapped gift on the dinner plate in a pool of scrumptious sauce, these main courses will become part of your entertaining repertoire for other special dinners, too. A colorful spinach salad accented with fresh

raspberries and a poppy seed dressing rounds out the meal. Your knockout punch is molten chocolate cakes with a caramel center served in a pool of caramel sauce. You can expect a marriage proposal or a renewal of vows after this dinner!

For your table decorations, a white or cream tablecloth accented with red and pink decorations would be spectacular with accents of gold or silver, possibly in charger plates, ribbons to wrap cutlery, and wired ribbon to weave down the length of the dinner table. Also tie gold or silver ribbons to the stems of wineglasses at each place setting and attach small hearts or heart-shaped wine charms to the ribbons. Strew heart-shaped confetti or candy conversation hearts down the center of the table or fill votive holders with hearts, and in the middle place a gorgeous long, low centerpiece with roses in your choice of color.

Votive candles for lots of sexy low lighting are musts. Floating candles are another beautiful accent for your table: pour cranberries or red marbles into the bottom of a low shallow container, fill it with water, and float white votive candles on the water (tinting the water red with food coloring will also work if you don't have cranberries or marbles). Pillar candles with bases wrapped in coordinating velvet colors also make a beautiful accent for your entertaining space. One trick the Diva has learned is to recycle those fabric bags that people use to give wine as gifts. You will collect a lot of velvet ones over the holidays, and they can be used as candleholders for tall pillars. Place a candle in the bag, and then allow the bag to "pool" around the bottom of the pillar—it looks very chic. Finally, decorate your table with appropriately sweet party favors, such as small chocolate champagne bottles and individual heart-shaped chocolate truffles or chocolate-dipped strawberries wrapped in cellophane bags tied in ribbon to coordinate with your color scheme. For a retro party favor, fill cellophane bags with candy conversation hearts.

To help set the mood with music, stock up on romantic standards such as Frank Sinatra and Nat King Cole, or sultry singers such as Etta James and Diana Krall.

# Do-Ahead Countdown

✳ **1 month ahead**

Download shopping list and do-ahead calendar and fill them out

Shop for nonperishables

Make and freeze Heart-Shaped Crostini

Make (but don't bake) and freeze Beef Wellingtons (if serving)

Make and freeze Pinot Noir Butter Sauce base (if serving)

Make (but don't bake) and freeze Individual Molten Chocolate-Caramel Cakes

✳ **1 week ahead**

Make Caramel Sauce

✳ **4 days ahead**

Make mix for Champagne Cosmopolitan Cocktails

Make Creamy Corn Bisque with Fresh Chives

Make Lemon-Dill Velouté Sauce for Salmon Wellingtons (if serving)

Make Poppy Seed Vinaigrette

✳ **2 days ahead**

Make (but don't bake) Chicken Wellingtons (if serving)

Remove Beef Wellingtons and sauce base from freezer and defrost in refrigerator (if serving)

Remove chocolate cakes from freezer and defrost in refrigerator

✳ **1 day ahead**

Set the table and set up the bar

Make (but don't bake) Salmon Wellingtons (if serving)

Clean spinach for salad

✳ **That morning**

Cover cakes and set on counter at room temperature (up to 8 hours before baking)

Measure ingredients for Dilled Hollandaise Sauce, ready to go for last-minute blending

Chop chives for soup

✳ **2 hours ahead**

Place Lemon-Dill Velouté or Pinot Noir Sauce in saucepan to reheat

Preheat oven

Place crostini on baking sheet to reheat

Place Creamy Corn Bisque in pan to reheat

Bring Poppy Seed Vinaigrette to room temperature

✳ **1 hour ahead**

Toast the bread

✳ **30 minutes ahead**

Reheat the soup

Remove Beef Wellingtons (if serving) from refrigerator

Remove Salmon Wellingtons (if serving) from refrigerator

✳ **Doorbell rings**

Bake Wellingtons

Remove Individual Molten Chocolate-Caramel Cakes from refrigerator

✳ **Just before serving**

Finish Dilled Hollandaise Sauce (if serving)

Finish Pinot Noir Butter Sauce (if serving)

Warm Lemon-Dill Velouté Sauce (if serving)

Toss the Spinach Salad with Fresh Raspberries with the Poppy Seed Vinaigrette

✳ **45 minutes to 1 hour into the party**

Bake cakes and rewarm caramel sauce

# Champagne Cosmopolitan Cocktails

*Makes 8 cocktails*

*Cosmopolitans are a vodka and cranberry juice drink that were made famous by the television show* **Sex and the City.** *Your sweetheart dinner demands something rosy in color, and substituting bubbly champagne for the vodka makes these drinks extra-special for your Valentine's party. You can mix up the base ahead of time and open the chilled champagne just before serving. I've designed this recipe to make eight drinks because no one wants to end up with an open bottle of leftover champagne!*

1¹/₂ cups Cointreau

1¹/₂ cups cranberry juice
cocktail

¹/₂ cup freshly squeezed lime
juice

16 fresh raspberries

One 750-milliliter bottle
chilled champagne

In a large pitcher, mix together the Cointreau, cranberry juice, and lime juice. Refrigerate until chilled. **Diva Do-Ahead:** At this point, you can refrigerate for up to 4 days. When ready to serve, pour 2 tablespoons of the juice mixture into each champagne flute, add 2 raspberries per glass, and fill with champagne. Serve immediately.

## Diva Wisdom

Remember that icing champagne will get it colder in less time than refrigerating the bottles, so stick the bottles into a cooler filled with ice rather than loading up the fridge when you need space to store your do-ahead items.

# Creamy Corn Bisque with Fresh Chives and Heart-Shaped Crostini

*Serves 4*

*This smooth and creamy soup is the perfect first course for your Wellington meal: light yet flavorful. If you would like to jazz it up a bit, sprinkle the top of the soup with some lump crabmeat, finely chopped sun-dried tomatoes, or crumbled goat cheese, or lay a thin slice of Brie on top to melt into the soup.*

2 tablespoons unsalted butter

$1/2$ cup finely chopped onion

$1/4$ cup finely diced carrots

$1/4$ cup finely diced celery

$1/4$ teaspoon dried thyme

Pinch of cayenne pepper

$1^1/2$ tablespoons all-purpose flour

$2^1/2$ cups chicken or vegetable broth

3 cups white corn, cut from the cob or frozen and defrosted

$1/2$ teaspoon salt

$1/4$ teaspoon freshly ground black pepper

$1/2$ cup heavy cream

2 tablespoons chopped fresh chives

Heart-Shaped Crostini (recipe follows)

**1.** Melt the butter in a medium-size saucepan and add the onion, carrots, celery, thyme, and cayenne, stirring until the vegetables are coated. Sauté over medium heat for about 4 minutes, until the vegetables soften.

**2.** Add the flour and stir until it begins to bubble in the bottom of the pan.

**3.** Slowly add the chicken broth and whisk until the mixture is smooth. Add 2 cups of the corn and bring to a boil. Simmer the soup for 6 to 7 minutes, until the vegetables are tender. Add the salt and pepper.

**4.** Take the pan off the heat and, using an immersion blender, puree the soup. Or let the soup cool slightly, then puree in batches in a blender or food processor. **Diva Do-Ahead:** At this point, you can cover and refrigerate for up to 4 days.

**5.** Add the cream and the remaining 1 cup corn and reheat to serving temperature. Serve garnished with chopped chives and crostini.

# Heart-Shaped Crostini

*Makes about 10 crostini*

*These darling heart-shaped crisps are the perfect garnish for the corn bisque, but they are also great on their own, to serve with drinks before dinner. You will have some left over and, because they freeze well, you can keep them on hand for unexpected company.*

1/4 cup (1/2 stick) unsalted butter, softened

2 tablespoons olive oil

1 clove garlic, minced

1/2 teaspoon dried thyme

1/2 teaspoon sweet paprika

One 8-ounce loaf sturdy white bread, sliced about 1/2 inch thick

**1.** In a small mixing bowl, blend together the butter, oil, garlic, thyme, and paprika. **Diva Do-Ahead:** Cover and refrigerate for up to 1 week or freeze for 1 month. Bring to room temperature before using.

**2.** Using a 1 1/2- to 2-inch heart-shaped cookie cutter, cut hearts from the bread, reserving the leftover crusts for croutons or bread crumbs.

**3.** Preheat the oven to 375°F. Line a baking sheet with parchment paper, aluminum foil, or a silicone baking liner. Spread a thin layer of the softened butter over each slice of bread and place butter side up on the baking sheet. Bake the crostini for 7 to 10 minutes, until the bread is crisp and the butter has turned golden brown. Remove from the oven and allow to cool completely. **Diva Do-Ahead:** At this point, you can store the crostini in zipper-top plastic bags at room temperature for up to 2 days or freeze for 1 month. Defrost the bread at room temperature.

# Chicken Wellingtons Stuffed with Crab and Mushrooms, with Dilled Hollandaise Sauce

*Serves 4*

*This elegant entrée of chicken with crab and mushrooms baked in puff pastry can be assembled a day ahead, then popped into a hot oven just before serving. A Chardonnay (not too oaky) or Sauvignon Blanc would pair nicely.*

4 skinless, boneless chicken breast halves, tenders removed (reserve for another purpose)

$1/2$ teaspoon salt

$1/4$ teaspoon freshly ground black pepper

1 tablespoon unsalted butter

$1/2$ tablespoon olive oil

$1/4$ pound sliced button mushrooms

2 tablespoons mayonnaise

$1/4$ pound lump crabmeat, picked over for shells and cartilage

1 teaspoon Worcestershire sauce

$1/2$ teaspoon Old Bay Seasoning

1 tablespoon chopped fresh chives

All-purpose flour for rolling the pastry

1 sheet Pepperidge Farm frozen puff pastry ($1/2$ of a 17.5-ounce package), defrosted

1 large egg

1 tablespoon whole milk or heavy cream

Dilled Hollandaise Sauce (page 74)

**1.** Sprinkle the chicken on both sides with the salt and pepper. In a large skillet, heat the butter and oil over medium-high heat until the butter is melted, then cook the chicken until browned on both sides but not cooked through, about 3 minutes per side. Remove from the pan and set aside to cool.

**2.** In the same pan, sauté the mushrooms until they begin to color and the liquid in the pan has evaporated, about 7 to 10 minutes. Transfer the mushrooms to a mixing bowl to cool.

**3.** In a small bowl, combine the mayonnaise, crabmeat, Worcestershire, Old Bay, chives, and the cooled mushrooms.

**4.** To assemble the Wellingtons, on a lightly floured work surface, roll out the puff pastry into a 20-inch square. Cut into quarters, so that you have four 10-inch squares. Arrange 1 chicken breast in the center of each square and top with 2 tablespoons of the crab mixture. Gather the ends of the puff pastry together (it's okay to stretch the dough) toward the center and twist into a knot. Transfer the Wellingtons to a rimmed baking sheet lined with parchment paper, aluminum foil, or a silicone baking liner. Cover and refrigerate for at least 2 hours to firm up the pastry. **Diva Do-Ahead:** At this point, you can refrigerate for up to 2 days.

**5.** Preheat the oven to 400°F. Remove the Wellingtons from the refrigerator 30 minutes before baking to bring to room temperature. In a small dish, beat the egg with the milk, then brush the tops of the Wellingtons with the egg wash, being careful it doesn't drip onto the baking sheet; if it does, the pastry won't rise as dramatically. Bake until the pastry is golden brown, 20 to 25 minutes.

**6.** Remove the Wellingtons from the oven and serve in a pool of Dilled Hollandaise Sauce.

# Dilled Hollandaise Sauce

*Makes about 2 cups*

*Although you can begin this recipe ahead of time, it's best to finish it just before serving. This is very simple to do if you have everything measured and the butter is hot. Dilled Hollandaise Sauce is also delicious with asparagus, artichokes, eggs, seafood, and roasted beef tenderloin. Typically white pepper is used for hollandaise, but I find that in most people's cupboards the black pepper is fresher.*

6 large egg yolks

1/4 cup chopped fresh dill

2 tablespoons freshly squeezed lemon juice

1 teaspoon salt

1/2 teaspoon freshly ground black pepper

1 pound (4 sticks) unsalted butter, melted and hot

**1.** In a blender or food processor, blend or process the egg yolks, dill, lemon juice, salt, and pepper until well combined. **Diva Do-Ahead:** At this point, you can cover and refrigerate for up to 8 hours.

**2.** Just before serving, with the machine running, slowly pour in the hot butter through the lid or feed tube and blend until the sauce thickens. Serve immediately, or keep warm for up to 1 hour in a thermal container or in the top of a double boiler set over simmering water.

## Diva Alert

Raw egg yolks have the potential to carry salmonella bacteria. Use fresh eggs, and to make sure that the eggs in this recipe are cooked, heat the butter until it is bubbling, then add it to the egg mixture in the blender. Your eggs should reach salmonella instant-kill stage at 160°F on an instant-read thermometer if you have heated the butter enough. Keeping the hollandaise warm over boiling water will also maintain a safe temperature for the sauce, ensuring that everyone remains healthy.

# Beef Wellingtons Stuffed with Mushrooms, with Pinot Noir Butter Sauce

*Serves 4*

*This recipe is a splurge of time and money, but you will know it was well worth the effort when you take the finished dish from the oven and bring it to the table. Puff pastry is sold frozen in your supermarket, so these Wellingtons are simple to put together and give you that all-important do-ahead edge: you can assemble them up to 1 month before and freeze. Just pop the frozen Wellingtons into the oven about 45 minutes before you're ready to serve. Open a bottle of Pinot Noir or Syrah to complement the meal.*

1 tablespoon unsalted butter

2 tablespoons finely chopped
 shallots

$1/2$ teaspoon salt, plus more
 for seasoning

$1/8$ teaspoon freshly ground
 black pepper, plus more for
 seasoning

$1/2$ teaspoon dried thyme

$1/4$ pound white button
 mushrooms, finely chopped

1 teaspoon Pinot Noir

Four 4- to 5-ounce filet
 mignons

1 tablespoon olive oil

1 sheet Pepperidge Farm
 frozen puff pastry ($1/2$ of a
 17.5-ounce package),
 defrosted

All-purpose flour for rolling the
 pastry

1 large egg

1 teaspoon water

Pinot Noir Butter Sauce
 (page 77)

**1.** In a large skillet over medium heat, melt the butter. Add the shallots, $1/2$ teaspoon salt, $1/8$ teaspoon pepper, and the thyme and cook, stirring, until the shallots are translucent, 3 to 5 minutes. Add the mushrooms and cook, stirring a few times, until all the mushroom liquid has evaporated. Add the wine and deglaze the pan by scraping the browned bits off the bottom. Let the wine completely evaporate. Transfer the filling to a bowl, cover, and refrigerate until cold.

**Diva Do-Ahead:** At this point, you can cover and refrigerate for up to 2 days.

**2.** Sprinkle the filets evenly on both sides with salt and pepper. Heat the oil in a large skillet over medium-high heat and brown the filets for 2 minutes on each side. (The meat will still be red inside, but the outside should be nicely

*continued on next page*

browned.) Remove from the pan and let cool to room temperature. **Diva Do-Ahead:** At this point, you can cover and refrigerate for up to 24 hours.

**3.** To assemble the Wellingtons, on a lightly floured work surface, roll out puff pastry to about ¼ inch thick and trim to form a 16-inch square. Cut the square into quarters. **Diva Do-Ahead:** At this point, you can cover, in a single layer or with waxed paper between layers, and refrigerate for up to 24 hours.

**4.** Place a piece of puff pastry on a flat work surface. Arrange 1 filet in the center of each square and top with 2 table-spoons of the mushroom mixture. Gather the ends of the puff pastry together and twist into a knot. Transfer the Wellingtons to a baking sheet lined with parchment paper, aluminum foil, or a silicone baking liner. Repeat with the remaining pastry pieces, filets, and filling. Refrigerate for at least 2 hours to firm up the pastry. **Diva Do-Ahead:** At this point, you can cover and freeze for up to 1 month.

**5.** Preheat the oven to 400°F. Remove the Wellingtons from the refrigerator 30 minutes before baking to bring to room temperature. Beat the eggs with the water in a small dish and brush the pastry with the egg wash. Bake the Wellingtons until an instant-read thermometer inserted into the center of a filet registers 120°F, about 20 minutes. If baking frozen Wellingtons, bake for 15 minutes, then reduce the oven temperature to 350°F and bake to an internal temperature of 120°F, about another 25 minutes. Remove from the oven and serve in a pool of Pinot Noir Butter Sauce.

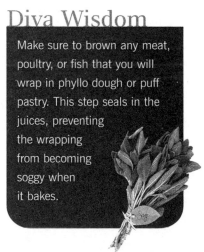

## Diva Wisdom

Make sure to brown any meat, poultry, or fish that you will wrap in phyllo dough or puff pastry. This step seals in the juices, preventing the wrapping from becoming soggy when it bakes.

# Pinot Noir Butter Sauce

*Makes about 1 1/3 cups*

*This deeply flavored sauce is a great match for your Beef Wellingtons, but you can also serve it with grilled steaks, lamb, or salmon to jazz them up. If you would prefer to use a different wine, Zinfandel, Merlot, Burgundy, or Cabernet Sauvignon are all excellent choices.*

6 tablespoons (3/4 stick) unsalted butter, softened

1/2 cup finely chopped shallots

2 tablespoons chopped fresh thyme

3 cups Pinot Noir

1 cup beef broth

2 teaspoons salt

1 1/2 teaspoons freshly ground black pepper

1/4 cup all-purpose flour

**1.** In a saucepan, melt 2 tablespoons of the butter, and add the shallots and thyme, sautéing until the shallots are translucent and beginning to turn light golden, 4 to 5 minutes.

**2.** Add the wine, broth, salt, and pepper, and simmer for 30 minutes, until the mixture has reduced by one-third. **Diva Do-Ahead:** At this point, you can strain the sauce, cool to room temperature, and refrigerate for up to 5 days or freeze for up to 6 weeks.

**3.** Bring the sauce to a boil. Make a paste out of the flour and remaining 4 tablespoons butter in a small bowl. Slowly stir some of the flour mixture into the sauce, until the sauce reaches the desired thickness. Serve immediately, or keep warm on the stove over low heat for up to 1 hour.

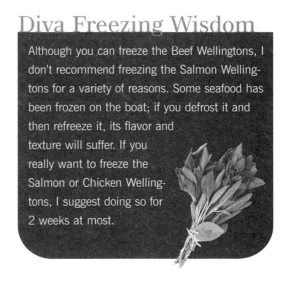

## Diva Freezing Wisdom

Although you can freeze the Beef Wellingtons, I don't recommend freezing the Salmon Wellingtons for a variety of reasons. Some seafood has been frozen on the boat; if you defrost it and then refreeze it, its flavor and texture will suffer. If you really want to freeze the Salmon or Chicken Wellingtons, I suggest doing so for 2 weeks at most.

# Salmon Wellingtons Stuffed with Crab and Asparagus, with Lemon-Dill Velouté Sauce

*Serves 4*

*This delicious package of salmon topped with crabmeat and asparagus spears wrapped in crackly phyllo dough is served in a pool of dilled sauce. You can use either the 18 x 14-inch or 14 x 9-inch phyllo sheets; the larger sheet will create a more substantial pastry knot. Accompanied by a Sauvignon Blanc or a dry Riesling and a spinach salad, this beautiful entrée will become one of your favorites for do-ahead entertaining. The Wellingtons can be made one day ahead, and then baked while you are serving the bisque. Lemon halves wrapped in cheesecloth and tied with chives make a nice garnish on the side, along with snipped dill and any remaining lump crabmeat strewn into the sauce on the plate.*

1 1/2 tablespoons unsalted butter

1/2 tablespoon olive oil

3/4 teaspoon Old Bay Seasoning

Four 4- to 5-ounce salmon fillets, skin removed

8 asparagus spears, trimmed to fit the length of the salmon filets and ends peeled

1/4 teaspoon salt

Pinch of freshly ground black pepper

1/2 pound phyllo dough, defrosted

3/4 cup (1 1/2 sticks) unsalted butter, clarified (see page 59)

1/2 cup dry bread crumbs

1/4 pound lump crabmeat, picked over for shells and cartilage

Lemon-Dill Velouté Sauce (page 80)

Dill sprigs for garnish

2 whole lemons cut in half, wrapped in cheesecloth and tied with chives, or lemon wedges

**1.** In a medium-size sauté pan, melt 3/4 tablespoon of the butter with the oil over medium-high heat. Sprinkle the Old Bay Seasoning over the fillets.

**2.** When the foam from the heated butter subsides, add the salmon and cook on one side for 3 minutes, until golden. Turn the salmon and cook another 2 to 3 minutes, until the golden on that side as well. Remove the salmon from the pan, drain on paper towels, and allow to cool to room temperature.

**3.** Wipe out the pan, and add the remaining ³/₄ tablespoon butter. Toss the asparagus in the pan with the salt and pepper, and cook for 2 minutes to soften. Remove from the pan and allow to cool.

**4.** To assemble the Wellingtons, unwrap the phyllo and cover it completely with a clean kitchen towel. Lay 1 piece of phyllo on a flat surface and brush with clarified butter. Sprinkle with some of the bread crumbs, and continue to layer until you have 4 sheets of phyllo buttered and sprinkled with crumbs. Arrange 1 salmon fillet in the center of the phyllo and top with 2 tablespoons of crabmeat and 2 asparagus spears. Gather the ends of the phyllo toward the center and twist into a knot. Brush the phyllo all over with clarified butter. Transfer the package to a baking sheet lined with parchment paper, aluminum foil, or a silicone baking liner. Assemble the remaining packages. **Diva Do-Ahead:** At this point, you can cover and refrigerate the Wellingtons for up to 24 hours.

**5.** Preheat the oven to 400°F. Remove the Wellingtons from the refrigerator 30 minutes before baking to bring to room temperature. Bake the Wellingtons for 15 to 20 minutes, or until the pastry is golden brown and an instant-read thermometer inserted into the salmon registers 165°F. Remove the salmon from the oven and serve in a pool of the Lemon-Dill Velouté Sauce, garnished with sprigs of dill, lemon halves wrapped in cheesecloth, and any remaining lump crabmeat.

## Working with Phyllo

Phyllo is quite simple to work with if you keep it covered and work quickly. Don't let it scare you, as it can be a great way to wrap lots of different fillings. Leftover phyllo can be refrigerated for up to 7 days, then used as a crust for chicken potpie or a top crust for your favorite berry, apple, or peach pie.

# Lemon-Dill Velouté Sauce

*Makes 3 cups*

**This lemony sauce flecked with dill is delicious with seafood or chicken. The sauce can be made four days ahead of time, then reheated for serving.**

2 tablespoons unsalted butter

2 tablespoons all-purpose flour

1 1/2 cups vegetable or seafood broth

1 cup heavy cream

Zest of 1 lemon

2 tablespoons freshly squeezed lemon juice

1/4 cup chopped fresh dill

Salt and freshly ground black pepper to taste

**1.** In a medium-size saucepan, melt the butter and whisk in the flour. When white bubbles form on the bottom of the pan, whisk the flour mixture for at least 2 to 3 minutes. Gradually add the broth, whisking until the mixture is smooth and comes to a boil.

**2.** Stir in the cream, lemon zest, lemon juice, and dill, and season with salt and pepper if necessary. Serve immediately. **Diva Do-Ahead:** At this point, you can cool to room temperature and refrigerate for up to 4 days. Gently warm over low heat before serving.

# Spinach Salad with Fresh Raspberries and Poppy Seed Vinaigrette

*Serves 4*

**An elegant and simple salad, this slightly sweet pairing lends a nice balance to a savory, rich meal. If raspberries aren't looking especially nice at your grocer, substitute sliced strawberries or dried cranberries.**

1/4 cup rice vinegar

2 tablespoons sugar

2 tablespoons chopped red onion

1/2 teaspoon Dijon mustard

1 tablespoon poppy seeds

1/2 cup vegetable oil

One 10-ounce bag baby spinach

1/2 cup fresh raspberries

**1.** In a medium-size bowl, whisk together the vinegar, sugar, red onion, mustard, poppy seeds, and oil until blended.

**Diva Do-Ahead:** At this point, you can cover and refrigerate for up to 4 days.

**2.** When ready to serve, assemble the salad. Combine the spinach and raspberries in a large salad bowl and toss with some of the dressing, adding more to taste. Serve immediately. Refrigerate any leftover dressing.

# Individual Molten Chocolate-Caramel Cakes with Diva Caramel Sauce

*Serves 8*

*Served warm from the oven, these chocolate cakes have a surprise caramel center and a divine caramel sauce to float in. A diva's best friend, the batter can be made up and refrigerated for eight hours before serving. I have even frozen the batter in the ramekins, then defrosted and baked them, and the cake has been a great success. For this reason I have created this recipe to make eight miniature cakes: Freeze whatever you don't want to bake and pull it out another time to wow guests with no effort at all.*

**For the ramekins**

1/4 cup unsalted butter, softened

1/2 cup confectioners' sugar

**For the cakes**

1/2 cup (1 stick) unsalted butter

8 ounces bittersweet or semi-sweet chocolate, coarsely chopped

4 large eggs

1 large egg yolk

1 teaspoon pure vanilla extract or vanilla bean paste (see page 171)

1/3 cup granulated sugar

2 tablespoons all-purpose flour

8 Kraft caramels

Diva Caramel Sauce (recipe follows)

**1.** Generously butter eight 6-ounce ramekins and dust with confectioners' sugar. Set aside on a baking sheet.

**2.** To make the cakes, in a medium-size saucepan melt the butter and chocolate over low heat, stirring once or twice until smooth. Set the chocolate aside to cool slightly.

**3.** In the bowl of an electric mixer fitted with a whisk, beat the eggs, egg yolk, vanilla extract, and sugar until the volume nearly triples, about 5 minutes. The color will be very light and the mixture will drop from the beaters in a thick stream.

**4.** Whisk in the cooled chocolate and then sprinkle the flour over the mixture and fold in until incorporated.

**5.** Ladle or pour the mixture into the prepared ramekins and place a caramel into the center of the batter. **Diva Do-Ahead:** At this point, you can cover and refrigerate the cakes for up to 8 hours or freeze for 1 month.

**6.** When you are ready to bake the cakes, bring them to room temperature for 30 minutes, preheat the oven to 400°F, and bake for 12 to 13 minutes. Run a paring knife around the inside edges of the ramekins to loosen cakes. Invert onto serving plates, cool for 1 minute, and lift off ramekins. Serve in a pool of caramel sauce.

## Diva Caramel Sauce

*Makes about 3 1/2 cups*

*True caramel is made with sugar that caramelizes on the bottom of the pan, and it's much too fussy for me to even attempt. This sauce, although not a true caramel, tastes like the real thing, and you can make it ahead of time and then reheat it. It's fabulous with the molten cakes but just as delicious over vanilla ice cream or cake, or sandwiched between layers of pudding in a parfait glass.*

1/2 cup (1 stick) unsalted butter

2 cups firmly packed light brown sugar

2 cups heavy cream

**1.** Melt the butter in a large saucepan over medium-high heat.

**2.** Stir in the brown sugar and continue stirring until it dissolves. Add the cream and cook, stirring constantly, until the sauce boils. **Diva Do-Ahead:** At this point, you can let cool, cover, and refrigerate for up to 1 week. Warm over medium heat or on 50 percent power in the microwave before serving. Serve hot.

## Other Ideas for Stuffing Molten Cakes

- Chocolate truffles
- Chocolate-covered cherries
- Raspberry truffles
- Fresh raspberries (3 or 4 per cake)
- Squares of white chocolate
- Chocolate mint truffles

# Tell Thy Son
# A Passover Seder

All holidays are days for remembering, whether it is our war dead on Memorial Day, our country's independence on the Fourth of July, or the Pilgrims' celebration of their first year in their new country on Thanksgiving. We celebrate holidays to remember those who came before us and to pass down our own traditions to those who will celebrate after us. Passover is a solemn holiday with its remembrance of the Jews' slavery in Egypt, God's protection on the night of Passover, and the Exodus from Egypt. Special foods are served, prayers said, and rituals followed. It is a time for the family to be together to remember.

Although I am not Jewish, many friends have invited me to their Passover Seders and explained the rituals, including the special foods that are served. With their counsel I came up with delicious do-ahead foods that follow the traditions and guidelines that govern this holiday.

Passover is an eight-day holiday that begins with a Seder on the night of the fifteenth day of the Hebrew month of Nisan, which occurs in the later part of March or in early April. The celebration of this holiday varies in places around the world, but certain foods are always presented on a Seder plate: bitter herbs, usually horseradish, to remember the difficult conditions that the Jews endured; haroset, traditionally made of chopped fruits, nuts, wine, and spices, to recall the building mortar used by the slaves in Egypt; matzo, or unleavened bread, to symbolize the night the Israelites fled Egypt with no time to allow their bread to rise; a roasted lamb shank, to recall the lambs that were sacrificed on the night of the Exodus from Egypt; greens, usually sprigs of parsley or celery tops, dipped in salt water to remember the tears of the Israelite slaves; and roasted hard-boiled eggs, a symbol of rebirth and sacrifice. Wine is also an important part of the Seder, and adults are required to drink four glasses of kosher wine.

For your table, you will need to decorate around the ritual requirements of this dinner, but certainly you can have flowers on the table, as long as they are no higher than 8 to 9 inches so that you can see across the table. This dinner does require your best china, linens, glassware, and silver, so coordinate any flowers, candles, or other decorations with the colors of your tableware. The décor should be in keeping with the seriousness of the celebration. At each place set a Haggadah, the booklet that contains the story of Passover, to be recited together as part of the Seder.

For this "fleishig" (i.e., meat, not dairy) Passover Seder I've devised a delicious do-ahead dinner for about eight people. Begin with two simple spreads to serve with matzo before dinner or at the table with soup. A luscious roasted vegetable soup is a delicious beginning to the meal, and the beef brisket with plums and apricots is succulent and tender. To absorb some of the delicious sauce, roasted smashed red potatoes with olive oil and rosemary fill the bill. A red cabbage and apple sauté makes a nice side dish, providing a piquant accompaniment as well as color. For dessert, there are chocolate meringues with fresh raspberries and a gorgeous ruby red raspberry sauce. And because you can prepare the entire meal in advance, you will be able to relax and enjoy this holy night with family and friends.

## Do-Ahead Countdown

* **1 month ahead**

  Download shopping list and do-ahead calendar and fill them out

  Shop for nonperishables

  Make and freeze Braised Brisket with Apricots and Plums

  Make and freeze Raspberry Sauce for the meringues

* **4 days ahead**

  Roast vegetables for Roasted Vegetable Soup

  Make Red Cabbage and Apple Sauté

* **2 days ahead**

  Make Roasted Eggplant Dip

  Make Smoked Salmon Spread

  Make Roasted Vegetable Soup

  Remove brisket from freezer and defrost in refrigerator if frozen, or make brisket

  Make Chocolate Meringues and store airtight at room temperature

* **1 day ahead**

  Set the table

  Make Roasted Red Smashed Potatoes with Olive Oil and Rosemary

  Prepare the berry mixture for the meringues

* **4 hours ahead**

  Make Haroset

  Remove Raspberry Sauce from freezer and defrost

# Smoked Salmon Spread

*Serves 8*

*This simple spread made with smoked salmon, hard-boiled eggs, and mayonnaise is a great starter for any occasion, but it gives this Passover table a little color and a lot of flavor.*

6 ounces smoked salmon, finely chopped

1/2 cup mayonnaise

4 large hard-boiled eggs, peeled and finely chopped

2 scallions (white and tender green parts), finely chopped

2 teaspoons finely chopped fresh dill

Salt and freshly ground black pepper to taste

In a medium-size mixing bowl, stir together the salmon, mayonnaise, eggs, scallions, and half of the dill. Taste for seasoning and add salt and pepper if desired. **Diva Do-Ahead:** At this point, you can cover and refrigerate for up to 2 days. Sprinkle the remaining dill on top and serve cold with matzo.

# Roasted Eggplant Dip

*Makes about 2 cups*

*This spicy dip combines roasted garlic, eggplant, and tomatoes, along with a few seasonings to give you a dip to serve with matzo or fresh crudités. You can serve it as an hors d'oeuvre with drinks before dinner, or scoop a bit of it and the salmon spread onto small appetizer plates and serve with matzo at the table. A creamy Chardonnay will work nicely with both this dip and the salmon spread.*

1 large purple eggplant
(about 3/4 pound),
cut in half lengthwise
1/2 cup extra-virgin olive oil
6 cloves garlic
4 canned plum tomatoes,
drained and halved
lengthwise
1 teaspoon salt
Pinch of red pepper flakes
2 scallions (white and tender
green parts), chopped
1/4 cup chopped fresh Italian
parsley

**1.** Preheat the oven to 400°F. Line a baking sheet with parchment paper, aluminum foil, or a silicone baking liner.

**2.** Rub the cut side of the eggplant with some of the olive oil, and arrange the eggplant cut side down on the baking sheet. Arrange the garlic and the tomato halves on the sheet and sprinkle with some of the oil and the salt and red pepper flakes.

**3.** Bake the eggplant for 30 minutes, or until it is soft when pierced with the tip of a sharp knife. Remove the pan from the oven and allow to cool for about 30 minutes.

**4.** When the eggplant is cool enough to handle, scoop out the flesh and put it into the work bowl of a food processor. Squeeze the garlic from its skin into the bowl. Add about 2 tablespoons of the olive oil and process until the mixture is smooth. Add the tomatoes and pulse on and off until the tomatoes are chopped.

**5.** Transfer the mixture to a bowl and stir in the scallions and half of the parsley. Taste for seasoning and add more salt or red pepper if desired. **Diva Do-Ahead:** At this point, you can cover and refrigerate for up to 2 days. Be aware that the garlic will intensify in flavor as time passes.

**6.** Bring the dip to room temperature, sprinkle with the remaining parsley, and drizzle with the remaining olive oil before serving.

# Haroset

*Makes about 3 cups*

*Haroset is one of the ritual foods of the Passover Seder, and its versions are numerous. In the book of the Song of Songs, the ingredients mentioned include chopped pomegranates, dates, figs, and nuts blended with vinegar. These days kosher wine is used instead. This simple dish reminds the Seder participants of the mortar that was used by the Israelite slaves in Egypt and is served not only at the Seder, but throughout the Passover holiday as a snack with matzo. I've taken a little bit of the old and made it new using pomegranate juice along with a few spices to liven up the chopped fruits and nuts. If you have a food processor, you can make quick work of this dish by chopping all the ingredients together. Coat the blade of your knife or the work bowl blade with nonstick cooking spray to keep the sticky fruits under control.*

3 Granny Smith apples, peeled, cored, and finely chopped

6 dried figs, finely chopped

6 pitted dates, finely chopped

6 dried apricots, finely chopped

1 1/2 cups slivered almonds, toasted (see page 114), and coarsely chopped

1/2 cup golden raisins

1/2 cup pomegranate juice

1/2 teaspoon ground cinnamon

1/8 teaspoon ground ginger

**1.** In large bowl, combine the apples, figs, dates, apricots, almonds, and raisins.

**2.** Sprinkle the juice, cinnamon, and ginger over the fruits. Toss the ingredients until they are well blended. **Diva Do-Ahead:** At this point, you can cover and refrigerate for up to 4 hours. Serve at room temperature.

## Diva Note

Pom brand pomegranate juice is available in the produce section or fresh juice section of most grocery stores. If it is not available, you can substitute kosher wine.

# Roasted Vegetable Soup

*Serves 8*

*Instead of traditional matzo ball soup, which too many leaden matzo balls have given a bad rap, I decided on a roasted vegetable soup for this menu. It's a very nice beginning to the Passover meal and will also satisfy any vegetarians in the crowd. Not too heavy yet full of flavor from the roasted vegetables, this soup is perfect whenever you crave a nice, comforting bowl.*

4 medium-size red or Yukon Gold potatoes, peeled and diced

4 medium-size carrots, peeled and diced

1 parsnip, peeled and diced

4 medium-size shallots, quartered

2 cloves garlic, minced

1 teaspoon dried thyme

1 teaspoon salt

1/2 teaspoon freshly ground black pepper

1/2 cup olive oil

1 leek (white and some of the tender green part), finely chopped

3 ribs celery, finely chopped

Four 15.5-ounce cans vegetable broth

1/4 cup chopped fresh Italian parsley

**1.** Preheat the oven to 400°F. Line a rimmed baking sheet with aluminum foil or a silicone baking liner. Place the potatoes, carrots, parsnip, shallots, garlic, thyme, salt, and pepper on the baking sheet, sprinkle with all but 2 tablespoons of the oil, and mix with your hands until the vegetables are coated.

**2.** Bake the vegetables for 15 to 20 minutes, until the potatoes are almost tender (they should give a bit when the tip of a knife is inserted). Remove from the oven and set aside.

**Diva Do-Ahead:** At this point, you can transfer the vegetables and all the juices to a bowl, cover, and refrigerate for up to 2 days. Bring to room temperature before proceeding.

**3.** In a large stockpot over high heat, add the roasted vegetables and the remaining olive oil, and sauté the leek and celery until they begin to soften, about 4 minutes. Add the broth, bring to a boil, and simmer for 10 minutes. Taste the soup, adding additional salt and pepper if desired.

**Diva Do-Ahead:** At this point, you can let soup cool to room temperature, cover, and refrigerate for up to 2 days. Add the parsley just before serving. Serve hot.

## Diva Variation

For Roasted Vegetable Chicken Soup, substitute chicken broth for the vegetable broth and add 1 cup of diced cooked chicken when adding the broth to the vegetables.

# Braised Brisket with Apricots and Plums

*Serves 8 to 10*

*Brisket is the ultimate do-ahead entrée, because it tastes even better the next day. Brisket has a deep beefy flavor, and this recipe includes red wine and fruit that combine to make a deliciously balanced sauce. If you would like a thicker sauce, puree the fruit with an immersion blender, which will thicken it without using flour. Serve this dish with Pinot Noir or Syrah (either of which you can use in the recipe as well).*

1½ teaspoons salt

1 teaspoon freshly ground black pepper

3 cloves garlic, minced

¼ cup olive oil

One 6-pound beef brisket, trimmed of fat

2 large sweet onions, thinly sliced

2 teaspoons dried thyme

1 cup red wine

½ cup firmly packed light brown sugar

¼ cup Dijon mustard

2 cups beef broth

1 cup dried apricots, halved

½ cup dried plums, halved

½ cup chopped fresh Italian parsley

**1.** Preheat the oven to 300°F. In a small bowl, make a paste of the salt, pepper, garlic, and 1 tablespoon of the oil. Rub all over the meat.

**2.** Heat 2 tablespoons of the oil over high heat in a large roasting pan or Dutch oven that will fit the brisket. Brown the brisket on both sides, taking care not to burn the garlic. Remove the brisket from the pan and add the remaining 1 tablespoon oil. Sauté the onions and thyme until the onions begin to soften, about 2 minutes. Add the wine, sugar, and mustard and bring to a boil.

**3.** Return the brisket to the pan and pour in the broth. Add the apricots and dried plums to the pan. Cover the roasting pan with aluminum foil and braise the brisket for 3 to 4 hours, until fork-tender. **Diva Do-Ahead:** At this point, you can refrigerate the brisket and its sauce for up to 2 days or freeze for up to 1 month.

**4.** Remove the brisket from the sauce and allow the meat to rest for 15 minutes.

**5.** On the stovetop, bring the sauce in the roasting pan to a boil and boil for about 10 minutes to reduce and concentrate the flavors. Slice the brisket thinly against the grain. **Diva Do-Ahead:** At this point, you can refrigerate the sliced meat and sauce overnight, then reheat, covered, in a 300°F oven for 15 to 20 minutes. Arrange the brisket on a serving platter, stir the parsley into the sauce, spoon some over the meat, and arrange the fruit down the center of the meat. Serve additional warm sauce on the side.

## Slow Cooker Savvy

You can prepare this recipe in a 6-quart slow cooker. Prepare the recipe through step 2, then place all the ingredients in the slow cooker and continue with the recipe. Cook on high for 4 hours, then turn down to low and cook for 4 more hours.

# Roasted Red Smashed Potatoes with Olive Oil and Rosemary

*Serves 8*

*These red potatoes become crispy and sweet when roasted at a high temperature. Then smashing them in a sauté pan with olive oil and rosemary gives them even more flavor. This dish pairs perfectly with the brisket but can be used as a simple side dish for any roasted meat or poultry.*

3 pounds small red potatoes, halved

$2/3$ cup olive oil

$1^1/2$ teaspoons salt

$1/2$ teaspoon freshly ground black pepper

1 tablespoon chopped fresh rosemary

**1.** Preheat the oven to 400°F. Line a baking sheet with parchment paper, aluminum foil, or a silicone baking liner. Arrange the potatoes on the baking sheet, pour $1/2$ cup of the oil over them, and sprinkle with the salt and pepper. Toss the potatoes so that they are coated with the oil and seasonings. **Diva Do-Ahead:** At this point, you can cover and refrigerate for up to 24 hours.

**2.** Roast the potatoes for 45 to 50 minutes, until crisp and tender, turning them once during the cooking process.

**3.** Remove from the oven and heat the remaining oil in a large skillet. Add the rosemary and sauté for 1 minute. Add the potatoes and smash them in the pan, using a wooden spoon or heavy spatula. Turn them to expose their flesh to the flavored oil. Continue to cook the potatoes, turning to prevent them from sticking, for about 10 minutes. Serve immediately. **Diva Do-Ahead:** At this point, you can cool and refrigerate for up to 24 hours, then reheat, covered, in a 300°F oven for 20 minutes before serving.

## Diva Variation

Roast 6 cloves of peeled garlic with the potatoes, and then smash them in the skillet, too.

# Red Cabbage and Apple Sauté

*Serves 8*

*Red cabbage is often overlooked as a side dish, but I think the sweet and piquant flavor in this dish provides a really nice balance on the dinner plate, especially with the delicious brisket entrée. Crisp Granny Smith apples and chopped walnuts add crunch, color, and texture. This dish is also delicious with roasted poultry.*

1/4 cup vegetable oil

3 large Granny Smith apples, peeled, cored, and sliced into 1/2-inch-thick wedges

1 large red onion, thinly sliced into half-moons

1 large head red cabbage, cored, quartered, and thinly sliced

1/2 cup balsamic vinegar

1/4 cup firmly packed light brown sugar

1 teaspoon salt

1 cup chopped walnuts, toasted (see page 114)

**1.** In a wide stockpot, heat the oil over medium heat and sauté the apples and onion for 6 to 8 minutes, until the onion is translucent and the apples begin to soften.

**2.** Add the cabbage, vinegar, sugar, and salt, stirring to combine. Cover and simmer for about 20 minutes until the cabbage is softened. **Diva Do-Ahead:** At this point, you can cool, cover, and refrigerate for up to 4 days. Serve the cabbage warm or at room temperature, garnished with the walnuts.

# Chocolate Meringues Filled with Fresh Raspberries

*Makes 12 meringues*

*Meringues are egg whites and sugar whipped until stiff and shiny, then baked until they are firm. These meringues, with a hint of chocolate and a raspberry filling, are even more elegant. The meringues can be made two days ahead and stored in an airtight container. If you are feeling creative, use a pastry bag to pipe the meringues onto the baking sheets; otherwise, a tablespoon and offset spatula work just fine. A word to the wise: Do not attempt to make meringues on a humid or rainy day, as they will turn out gummy and unappetizing. Although this recipe makes 12 meringues, they may not all be equally gorgeous—so it's good to have a few extra on hand. I'm of the mind that any extra dessert is always a bonus!*

6 large egg whites

3/4 teaspoon cream of tartar

11/4 cups plus 2 tablespoons sugar

3 tablespoons Dutch-processed cocoa powder, sifted

6 cups raspberries or your choice of mixed berries

1 tablespoon freshly squeezed lemon juice

Raspberry Sauce (see page 55)

**1.** Preheat the oven to 225°F. Line 2 baking sheets with parchment paper or aluminum foil coated with nonstick cooking spray or silicone baking liners.

**2.** In the bowl of an electric mixer fitted with the balloon whisk attachment, beat the egg whites and cream of tartar until the whites begin to look foamy.

**3.** Sprinkle in 11/4 cups sugar about 1/4 cup at a time, beating well after each addition. Add the cocoa powder and beat until stiff peaks form.

**4.** Working with about 1/2 cup of the meringue at a time, mound the mixture into rounds about 3 inches in diameter and 1 inch high. Using the back of a spoon that has been dipped into water, make a depression in the center of each mound. (Alternatively, you can spread a thin 3-inch circle of meringue onto the baking sheet, then use a pastry bag fitted with a large star tip to pipe two to three layers of meringue around the base to make a bowl.)

**5.** Bake the meringue shells for 75 to 90 minutes, until they feel firm to the touch. Turn off the heat and allow the meringues to cool completely in the oven. **Diva Do-Ahead:** At this point, you can remove the meringues from the baking sheets and store at room temperature in an airtight container for up to 2 days.

**6.** In a small bowl, combine the berries, the remaining 2 tablespoons sugar, and the lemon juice. **Diva Do-Ahead:** At this point, you can cover and refrigerate for up to 24 hours.

**7.** To assemble each dessert, pool 2 to 3 tablespoons of the Raspberry Sauce onto a dessert plate. Top with a meringue, bowl side up, and fill with the berry mixture. Serve drizzled with additional raspberry sauce, if desired.

# Easter's on Its Way
# Two Dinners

# A Traditional Easter Dinner (or Brunch)

This simple buffet for 10 to 12 guests will make you the star at your Easter family get-together when everyone sees you so relaxed. The dishes can all be made ahead of time and then warmed in the oven before serving.

For this number of people, I recommend that you arrange a separate buffet area as well as tables that are set for people to sit down and eat. Whether you make the kitchen counter your buffet line and then have everyone eat in the dining room, or use the dining room table as your buffet service and then set up tables around the house, it's really up to you and the configuration of your entertaining space. If you live someplace that's warm in April, plan an outdoor meal. There have been too many times, however, when I've tried to serve an outdoor Easter meal at my mom's house near Boston, only to have it snow! So the Diva recommends that you always have a backup plan.

Because Easter is traditionally the beginning of spring in many parts of the country, use spring-time decorations, such as bunnies, lambs, tulips, and, of course, tinted hard-cooked eggs for the kids. If you plan to have an Easter egg hunt, I recommend hiding plastic eggs filled with candies rather than the hard-cooked eggs; otherwise, you may find them fermenting in your forgotten hiding places next July!

Set up your buffet table with pastel linens and a spring-themed arrangement in the center of the table. Tulips, daffodils, lilacs, irises, and lilies are all great choices for floral centerpieces. Asparagus stalks make a pretty arrangement when cut the same height to stand in a straight-sided vase. Add some flowers, and you have a very pretty and unusual arrangement. Wheatgrass also makes a pretty centerpiece, and you can intersperse it with small colored eggs for more of an Easter look. You can arrange some of the kids' smaller stuffed bunnies and chicks on the table, and small cellophane bags of colorful jellybeans make sweet party favors at each place setting. Wide pastel grosgrain ribbons used as streamers, anchored with double-stick tape going down the center of the table, nicely complement the spring-time theme, as does a recording of Vivaldi's *Four Seasons* or Aaron Copland's *Appalachian Spring* on the stereo.

# Do-Ahead Countdown

* **1 month ahead**

  Download shopping list and do-ahead calendar and fill them out

  Shop for nonperishables

  Make and freeze the base for Virgin Pineapple Coolers

  Make and freeze Quick Blueberry Sauce

  Make and freeze Easter Bunny Cake and frosting separately

* **2 weeks ahead**

  Make Maple-Bourbon Glaze

* **4 days ahead**

  Make (but don't bake) Corn, Bacon, and Cheddar Strata

  Make Creamy Fresh Herb Dressing

* **3 days ahead**

  Remove Virgin Pineapple Coolers and Quick Blueberry Sauce from freezer and defrost in refrigerator

  Make (but don't bake) Lemon-Blueberry Bread Pudding

  Make (but don't bake) Pineapple Stuffing

* **2 days ahead**

  Hard-boil eggs for salad

  Cook bacon for salad

  Defrost cake and frosting

* **1 day ahead**

  Set the table

  Prepare Roasted Asparagus

  Assemble and frost cake

* **Day of**

  Clean raspberries or strawberries for Bellini garnish

  Chill Prosecco and peach nectar for the Bellinis and the soda for Virgin Pineapple Coolers

  Make the Apple Slaw

* **3 to 4 hours ahead**

  Remove ham from refrigerator, glaze, and bake as directed

* **2 hours ahead**

  Reheat asparagus (if not serving at room temperature)

* **90 minutes ahead**

  Bake Lemon-Blueberry Bread Pudding

  Bake Corn, Bacon, and Cheddar Strata

* **1 hour ahead**

  Bake Pineapple Stuffing

* **Right before serving**

  Toss Field Greens with Creamy Fresh Herb Dressing

  Carve ham, if necessary (if spiral-sliced, arrange on platter)

  Add pecans to Apple Slaw

# Bellini alla Venezia

*Serves 10 to 12*

*An Easter celebration calls for something bubbly, so delight your guests with this luscious combination of peach nectar mixed with an Italian sparkling wine called Prosecco. Harry's Bar in Venice made the Bellini famous. Although Harry's has become a tourist attraction since the days of Ernest Hemingway, Orson Welles, and Humphrey Bogart, this drink still stands the test of time. Chill the peach nectar along with the Prosecco, and let your guests mix their own. A fresh strawberry or a few fresh raspberries in the bottom of the glass make a nice garnish. Peach nectar is sold in the fresh juice section of your grocery store, or, if all else fails, it is also available canned.*

12 small fresh whole strawberries or ¹/₂ cup fresh raspberries (optional)
1 quart chilled peach nectar
Two 750-milliliter bottles chilled Italian Prosecco

Place a strawberry or a few raspberries in the bottom of each champagne glass, if desired. Fill each glass halfway with chilled peach nectar, then top off with Prosecco.

## Diva Variation
For a Virgin Bellini, substitute 7UP or another lemon-lime soda for the Prosecco.

## Diva Bellini History

The Bellini at Harry's Bar is a delicate pink. The bartenders there juice white peaches, then add the pits to the juice to color it.

# Virgin Pineapple Coolers

*Makes 10 coolers*

*Tall, cool, tropical-tasting coolers are a great starter for brunch, and these fruity drinks will be a hit with young and old alike. To add a little spice for the adults, dark rum is a great addition! You will need to make this recipe in four batches in the blender, then store the mixture in the refrigerator in pitchers.*

One 32-ounce bottle
   pineapple-coconut juice
8 ripe bananas, peeled and
   sliced
2 cups fresh orange juice
2 cups sliced strawberries
Crushed ice
1 liter lemon-lime soda or
   plain sparkling water
1 pineapple (optional), peeled,
   cored, and cut into 10
   spears for garnish
10 small tropical drink
   umbrellas for garnish

**1.** In a food processor or blender, place 8 ounces of the pineapple-coconut juice, 2 bananas, $1/2$ cup of the orange juice, and $1/2$ cup of strawberries. Blend until smooth. Pour into a zipper-top plastic bag or pitchers and repeat 3 more times. **Diva Do-Ahead:** At this point, you can refrigerate for up to 4 days or freeze for up to 2 months. Defrost before proceeding.

**2.** To serve, fill each 8-ounce glass half full with crushed ice, add $1/2$ cup of the fruit mixture, and fill the rest of the glass with soda. Serve garnished with pineapple spears, if using, and little umbrellas.

# Lemon-Blueberry Bread Pudding with Quick Blueberry Sauce

*Serves 12*

*The tart taste of lemon zest contrasts with the sweet blueberries in this puffed and golden pudding, which is a delicious accompaniment to the glazed ham and other items on your buffet table. Use either fresh or frozen berries and prepare the pudding at least one day ahead of time to let the bread soak in the custard. Serve the Quick Blueberry Sauce in a gravy boat on the side.*

1¼ cups granulated sugar

Zest of 1 lemon

½ teaspoon lemon oil or
  1 teaspoon lemon extract

⅛ teaspoon ground nutmeg

8 large eggs

1½ cups heavy cream

9 cups challah or other egg
  bread, crusts removed, torn
  into chunks (about 1 pound)

2 cups fresh blueberries,
  picked over for stems, or
  frozen blueberries (do not
  defrost)

⅛ teaspoon ground cinnamon

Sifted confectioners' sugar for
  garnish

Quick Blueberry Sauce (recipe
  follows)

**1.** Coat a 13 x 9-inch baking dish with nonstick cooking spray.

**2.** In a large bowl, whisk together 1 cup of the sugar, the lemon zest, lemon oil, nutmeg, eggs, and heavy cream until blended. Add the bread to the bowl, pushing it down into the mixture to absorb the liquid. Add the blueberries and stir to combine. Pour into the prepared dish. Cover and refrigerate for at least 12 hours. **Diva Do-Ahead:** At this point, you can refrigerate for up to 3 days. Allow pudding to come to room temperature before continuing.

**3.** Preheat the oven to 350°F. Combine the remaining ¼ cup sugar and cinnamon and sprinkle over the pudding. Bake until puffed and golden brown, 45 to 50 minutes. Remove from the oven and let rest for 10 minutes before serving, garnished with a dusting of confectioners' sugar. Serve the blueberry sauce alongside.

## Diva Variation

This pudding is also terrific made in muffin tins. If you would like to make muffin-size bread puddings, prepare the bread pudding through the addition of the blueberries but then scoop it into muffin tins that have been coated with nonstick cooking spray. The batter will fill 12 to 16 muffin cups. Refrigerate as directed, sprinkle with the cinnamon-sugar mixture, and bake in a preheated 350°F oven for 25 to 30 minutes, or until puffed, golden, and cooked through. Serve warm.

# Quick Blueberry Sauce

*Makes about 3 1/2 cups*

**This quick sauce is perfect to serve with the bread pudding, but it's also delicious over pound cake, ice cream, or pancakes, and it freezes beautifully! Try it with other berries as well.**

1 cup sugar
2 tablespoons cornstarch
2 tablespoons water
1/4 cup freshly squeezed lemon juice
2 cups blueberries

**1.** In a large saucepan over high heat, stir together the sugar, cornstarch, water, and lemon juice until blended.

**2.** Add the blueberries and cook until the mixture begins to thicken and boil. Remove from the heat and allow to cool.
**Diva Do-Ahead:** At this point, you can refrigerate the sauce for up to 4 days or freeze for up to 1 month. Defrost in the refrigerator before serving at room temperature.

## Diva Tip

Substituting lower-fat products in bread puddings or stratas will give you additional liquid, which will throw off the baking time. You can use an egg substitute instead of whole eggs, and whole milk instead of heavy cream, but bake the pudding 10 to 15 minutes longer.

## Diva Wisdom

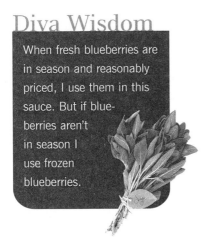

When fresh blueberries are in season and reasonably priced, I use them in this sauce. But if blueberries aren't in season I use frozen blueberries.

# Corn, Bacon, and Cheddar Strata

*Serves 10*

*Stratas are simply bread, eggs, and milk combined with flavorings and baked. This combination of sweet white corn, bacon, and white cheddar cheese is a perfect pairing with this ham dinner, or you can serve it as a side dish with another entrée. This strata can be made in a 13 x 9-inch baking dish or in individual ramekins or muffin cups. The strata can be baked ahead and frozen, or prepped ahead and then baked just before serving, giving you more time to relax and enjoy your company.*

6 tablespoons (3/4 stick) unsalted butter

3 cups white corn, cut from the cob or frozen and defrosted

4 scallions (white and some of the tender green parts), chopped

8 large eggs

2 cups whole milk

1 teaspoon salt

1 teaspoon dry mustard

6 shakes hot sauce

One 1-pound loaf good-quality white bread (any tough crusts removed), sliced 1/2 inch thick

12 strips bacon, cooked and crumbled

3 cups shredded white cheddar cheese

**1.** Coat the inside of a 13 x 9-inch casserole dish with non-stick cooking spray.

**2.** In a large sauté pan, heat 2 tablespoons of the butter and sauté the corn and scallions for 2 to 3 minutes. Set aside in a large bowl.

**3.** In another bowl, whisk together the eggs, milk, salt, dry mustard, and hot sauce until blended. Stir in the reserved corn mixture.

**4.** Arrange a layer of bread, wedging it in to fit into the bottom of the prepared baking dish. Melt the remaining 4 tablespoons butter in the microwave. Brush the bread with some of the butter and sprinkle with half the bacon and half the cheese. Pour half of the egg mixture over the bread.

**5.** Arrange the remaining bread over the cheese, brush with butter, and pour the remaining egg mixture over the bread, tilting the pan to get the egg mixture to the bottom of the casserole dish. Sprinkle with the remaining bacon and cheese. Cover and refrigerate for at least 8 hours. **Diva Do-Ahead:** At this point, you can refrigerate for up to 4 days.

**6.** When ready to bake, preheat the oven to 350°F. Remove the casserole from the refrigerator 45 minutes prior to baking to allow it to come to room temperature. Bake the casserole, uncovered, for 30 to 40 minutes, or until it is puffed and golden. **Diva Do-Ahead:** If you would like to freeze the baked casserole, bake it for 25 minutes, cool to room temperature, then cover and freeze for up to 1 month. Defrost in the refrigerator, then bake, covered, at 325°F for 15 to 20 minutes, until warmed through. **Serve warm or at room temperature.**

## Diva Variation

For individual servings, coat the inside of twelve 4-ounce ramekins or muffin cups with nonstick cooking spray. Tear the bread into small pieces and soak it in the egg-corn mixture in a large bowl for 8 hours. Scoop into the muffin cups and top with the bacon and cheese. Bake in a preheated 350°F oven for 15 to 20 minutes, until puffed and golden brown.

## Easy Add-Ins

Substitute 1 1/2 cups diced smoked ham for the bacon.

Substitute 1 1/2 cups shredded pepper Jack cheese for half of the cheddar.

Add 1 medium-size tomato, thinly sliced, as a middle layer.

Add 1 1/2 cups diced cooked chicken as a middle layer.

Substitute mozzarella cheese for the cheddar and layer 1 cup prepared pesto (see page 36) in the middle.

# Field Greens with Creamy Fresh Herb Dressing

*Serves 10*

*This colorful salad features a fresh herb dressing that will replace that ranch-style dressing you've been making from the package as your family's favorite. This salad also helps to get rid of some of the colored hard-cooked eggs you've made to celebrate Easter!*

Three 10-ounce bags field greens, baby spinach, or romaine lettuce

6 large hard-cooked eggs, peeled and sliced

1 medium-size red onion, thinly sliced and separated into rings

1 1/2 cups Creamy Fresh Herb Dressing (recipe follows)

12 strips bacon, cooked and crumbled

2 cups croutons, homemade or store-bought

**1.** In a large salad bowl, combine the field greens, 3 of the sliced eggs, and the red onion.

**2.** Toss the mixture with about 1 cup of the dressing. Add the bacon and croutons, adding more dressing and tossing again to coat the leaves. Sprinkle the top of the salad with the remaining sliced eggs for garnish and serve the remaining dressing on the side.

# Creamy Fresh Herb Dressing

*Makes about 2 1/2 cups*

*Creamy white, flecked with fresh herbs, and spiked with some garlic and lemon zest, this tangy dressing is a winner over spinach or field greens. It's also delicious as a dressing for pasta or potato salads, or to spoon over baked potatoes or steamed veggies.*

2 cups regular or low-fat
  mayonnaise

1/2 cup whole or 2 percent
  milk

2 tablespoons freshly squeezed
  lemon juice

3 tablespoons chopped fresh
  Italian parsley

2 tablespoons chopped fresh
  chives

1 tablespoon chopped fresh
  oregano

2 teaspoons chopped fresh
  tarragon

2 cloves garlic, mashed

1 teaspoon salt

1/2 teaspoon freshly ground
  black pepper

2 tablespoons lemon zest

In a glass mixing bowl, whisk together the ingredients until blended. Cover and refrigerate for at least 2 hours. **Diva Do-Ahead:** At this point, you can refrigerate for up to 4 days. When ready to serve, whisk to combine.

# Maple-Bourbon Glazed Ham

*Serves 10 to 12*

*Ham is the quintessential main course for Easter, and this beautifully glazed version is slathered with a maple syrup and Kentucky bourbon glaze for a delicious aroma and flavor. Hams in your supermarket will come in whole or half sizes, and the half will be either a shank or butt portion. Both portions are delicious; the shank may be a little easier to carve, but you can eliminate carving altogether by buying a spiral-sliced ham. Your choice will depend upon your budget, because spiral-sliced hams are at least twice the price of unsliced ham. Since hams are already fully cooked, they just need to be warmed in the oven. A final glazing and optional torching with raw sugar will give your ham the "fancy ham store" look. I suggest serving this ham with a Merlot or a rich Pinot Gris.*

One 6- to 8-pound fully cooked, bone-in, spiral-sliced or unsliced ham
Maple-Bourbon Glaze (recipe follows)

**1.** Preheat the oven to 300°F. Line a large roasting pan with aluminum foil or a silicone baking liner.

**2.** Remove the ham from its packaging and drain off any juices. Place the ham in the prepared pan, flat side down, making sure to remove the little plastic disk covering the bone, and cover the ham and pan completely with aluminum foil. Bake until an instant-read thermometer inserted in the center registers 120°F, about 2 1/2 hours.

**3.** Increase the oven temperature to 400°F and remove the aluminum foil from the pan. Pour the glaze over the ham and bake uncovered, basting every 10 minutes with the pan juices, until the glaze is set, another 20 to 30 minutes.

**4.** Remove the ham from the oven and allow it to rest for 15 minutes before carving, if necessary. Serve the ham drizzled with some remaining glaze.

### Diva Variation

To get that glossy look with the crackly glaze, press 1 to 2 cups of raw sugar onto the ham after you remove it from the oven. Fire up your crème brûlée torch and torch the sugar, being careful not to burn it. Heat the sugar until it begins to caramelize and turn a dark golden brown. Allow the ham to rest for 15 minutes, then carve and drizzle any remaining glaze over the slices.

# Maple-Bourbon Glaze

*Makes 2 cups*

**Not your mom's sticky sweet pineapple and clove glaze, this smoky, kicked-up glaze will give your Easter ham a real personality. Try it as a glaze for ribs or pork loins, too.**

1<sup>1</sup>/2 cups pure maple syrup

1/4 cup molasses

1/4 cup bourbon

2 tablespoons Dijon mustard

1/2 teaspoon ground allspice

1/4 teaspoon freshly ground
   black pepper

Stir all the ingredients together in a medium-size bowl until blended. **Diva Do-Ahead:** At this point, you can refrigerate in an airtight container for up to 2 weeks.

## Ham: What to Buy

Make sure to buy a cured ham (not a fresh ham, which is raw pork). Check the contents and make sure there are not a lot of added ingredients, such as "imitation smoke," gelatin, or water. These additives actually take away from the rich taste of the ham. Avoid the type of ham, usually canned, that is compressed into a loaf shape. Although easy to carve, it lacks flavor.

# Pineapple Stuffing

*Serves 8 to 10*

*My friend Martha Mand is always sharing great recipes with me, and this one has become my daughter's favorite on Easter. Because pineapple and ham are a match made in culinary heaven, this side dish is a natural for our traditional Easter dinner.*

1/2 cup (1 stick) unsalted
  butter, softened
3/4 cup sugar
6 large eggs
One 20-ounce can pineapple
  chunks, drained
8 ounces sturdy white bread,
  torn into 1/2-inch pieces

**1.** Coat the inside of a 13 x 9-inch baking dish with nonstick cooking spray. In a large mixing bowl using an electric mixer, cream the butter and sugar until fluffy. Add eggs one at a time, beating well after each addition. Fold in the pineapple and bread pieces.

**2.** Pour the mixture into the prepared pan, cover, and refrigerate for at least 4 hours. **Diva Do-Ahead:** At this point, you can refrigerate for up to 3 days. Remove the stuffing from the refrigerator 45 minutes before baking to allow it to come to room temperature.

**3.** Preheat the oven to 350°F. Bake for 45 to 50 minutes, until puffed and golden. Serve warm or at room temperature.

# Roasted Asparagus

*Serves 10*

*Roasted asparagus is simple to prepare, yet it makes an elegant presentation for any buffet dinner. The asparagus can be roasted earlier in the day and then served at room temperature or tossed quickly in a hot skillet just before serving to warm it. If you do roast the asparagus earlier, you can then separate the stalks into bundles of three and tie each with chives to arrange on a serving platter, already portioned for your guests.*

2 pounds asparagus, trimmed
   of tough stem ends
$1/4$ cup olive oil
$1^1/2$ teaspoons salt
1 teaspoon freshly ground
   black pepper

**1.** Preheat the oven to 400°F. Line a baking sheet with aluminum foil or a silicone baking liner.

**2.** Arrange the asparagus in a single layer on the sheet. Sprinkle with the oil, salt, and pepper, then roll the asparagus in the mixture until coated. Bake until crisp-tender, 4 to 5 minutes (pencil-thin asparagus will take about 3 minutes, thicker asparagus a bit longer). **Diva Do-Ahead:** At this point, you can set the asparagus aside at room temperature for up to 2 hours or let cool, cover, and refrigerate overnight. Serve warm or at room temperature.

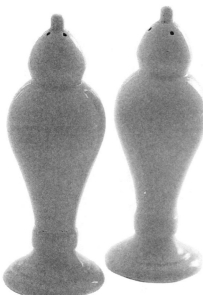

# Apple Slaw

*Serves 10*

*This colorful slaw is a perfect accompaniment to the baked ham, but you can also bring it to your next potluck dinner to serve along with fried chicken or grilled or pulled pork. Filled with apples and toasted pecans and tossed with a lime and honey vinaigrette, this is not your mother's coleslaw, but I think she'll like it just the same! The Spicy Nuts (page 62) are also delicious in this slaw.*

1 medium-size head green cabbage, shredded or thinly sliced

4 large, sweet, firm apples, like Gala or Jonathan, cored and julienned (leave peel on)

1 cup thinly sliced celery

1 cup seedless red grapes, cut in half

1/2 cup vegetable or canola oil

2 tablespoons freshly squeezed lime juice

2 tablespoons honey

2 tablespoons poppy seeds

1/8 teaspoon cayenne pepper

1 cup chopped pecans, toasted (see box at right)

**1.** In a large mixing bowl, combine the cabbage, apples, celery, and grapes.

**2.** In a small bowl, whisk together the oil, lime juice, honey, poppy seeds, and cayenne. Pour the dressing over the cabbage mixture and toss until combined. **Diva Do-Ahead:** At this point, you can cover and refrigerate the slaw for up to 12 hours. Add 3/4 cup of the pecans to the slaw and toss again. Garnish with the remaining pecans and serve.

## Toasting Nuts

For small quantities of nuts, I find the stovetop method of toasting to be easier than the oven. If you have 1 cup or less of nuts to toast, place them in a large dry skillet on the stovetop over medium heat. Stir the nuts to prevent them from burning. After about 4 minutes, you will begin to smell the nuts, and that will be your signal (before they actually turn brown) that you are getting close. Once you smell the nuts, it's important to watch them closely so that they don't burn. Once they begin to color, remove them from the pan to stop the cooking process. Allow to cool, then store in a zipper-top plastic bag in the freezer for up to 2 months, or in the refrigerator for up to 1 week.

If you have more than 1 cup of nuts, preheat the oven to 350°F and arrange the nuts in a single layer on a baking sheet lined with parchment paper, aluminum foil, or a silicone baking liner. Bake for 10 minutes, stirring once during the cooking time. Remove from the baking sheet and allow to cool. Store as directed above.

# Easter Bunny Cake

*Serves 12 to 14*

*Every Easter I make this cake for my children—even though they are both adults now, they still love to have this treat from childhood. You can make the cake and frosting a month ahead and freeze them separately, then assemble the cake the day before serving. You will need a large white cardboard rectangle to place the cake on, which you can buy from a gourmet retailer or a cake decorating or craft store. In a pinch a large cookie sheet or an inverted sheet pan will work; simply cover it with aluminum foil.*

2 cups cake flour

1 3/4 cups sugar

1 teaspoon baking powder

1/2 teaspoon baking soda

1/2 teaspoon salt

3/4 cup (1 1/2 sticks) unsalted butter, softened and cut into 1/2-inch bits

1 cup buttermilk

4 large eggs

1 tablespoon pure vanilla extract or vanilla bean paste (see page 171)

Creamy Vanilla Frosting (recipe follows)

Licorice whips for decorating

Jellybeans for decorating

3 cups sweetened flaked coconut

Green food coloring

Red food coloring

**1.** Preheat the oven to 375°F. Coat two 9-inch round baking pans with nonstick cooking spray.

**2.** In the food processor, combine the flour, sugar, baking powder, baking soda, and salt, and pulse 2 to 3 times. Distribute the butter over the flour mixture and pulse until the mixture resembles small peas.

**3.** Pour the buttermilk into a 2-cup measuring cup, add the eggs and vanilla extract, and beat with a fork to break up the eggs. With the food processor running, pour this mixture through the feed tube and process for about 45 seconds. Scrape down the sides, then process again for another 30 to 45 seconds, until blended. Alternatively, place the dry ingredients in the large bowl of an electric mixer, and distribute the butter over the dry ingredients. Beat on low until the dry ingredients begin to incorporate the butter. With the mixer running, slowly pour in the buttermilk mixture, beating for 2 minutes, scraping down the sides after 1 minute.

**4.** Divide the batter equally between the 2 prepared pans. Smooth the tops, without pressing down on the batter. Bake until golden and a skewer inserted into the center comes out

*continued on next page*

clean, 25 to 30 minutes. Transfer the pans to a cooling rack and let cool for 10 minutes. Remove from the pans and cool completely on the racks. **Diva Do-Ahead:** At this point, you can wrap the cake with plastic wrap and refrigerate for 2 days or freeze for up to 2 months. Defrost before continuing.

**5.** Cut off the sides of 1 cake in the shape of 2 tapered ovals to resemble rabbit ears, leaving the center to look like a bow tie. Arrange the other cake in the center of an 18 x 15-inch cardboard rectangle. Place the 2 ovals above the whole cake circle, to resemble ears, and arrange the bow tie underneath the circle.

**6.** Frost the tops and sides of the cake. Arrange licorice whips for whiskers and jellybeans for eyes and nose in the center circle. Tint 1 cup of the coconut with 2 drops of green food coloring, and sprinkle the coconut over the bow tie. Sprinkle with a few jelly beans to look like polka dots. Tint another 1 cup of the coconut with 1 drop of red food coloring and sprinkle the coconut inside the "ears" of the rabbit. Sprinkle the remaining 1 cup of the untinted coconut over the rabbit's face. **Diva Do-Ahead:** At this point, you can cover the cake with plastic wrap and store at room temperature for up to 24 hours.

# Creamy Vanilla Frosting

*Makes about 5 cups (enough to frost two 9-inch layers)*

4½ cups confectioners' sugar

1 cup (2 sticks) unsalted
   butter, cut into small cubes

1 teaspoon pure vanilla extract

1 to 2 tablespoons whole milk

**1.** In a food processor, pulse the sugar on and off to eliminate any lumps.

**2.** Distribute the butter over the sugar, add the vanilla extract and 1 tablespoon of the milk, and process until smooth, scraping down the sides of the bowl if necessary.

**3.** If the frosting is a bit thick, add a few drops more of the milk and process again. **Diva Do-Ahead:** At this point, you can remove the frosting from the work bowl and store in an airtight container in the freezer for up to 1 month or in the refrigerator for up to 1 week. Bring to room temperature before frosting the cake. Alternatively, if you are using an electric mixer, cream the butter, then add the sugar 1 cup at a time, until the frosting begins to come together. Add the vanilla and a bit of the milk, beating until the frosting is of spreading consistency.

## Diva Variation I

Use different flavored extracts: Orange, lemon, almond, and maple flavorings all work with this frosting. If you would like to make a chocolate frosting for a chocolate bunny, substitute ½ cup Dutch-processed cocoa powder for ½ cup of the confectioners' sugar. Espresso or coffee substituted for the milk in this variation will give you mocha frosting.

## Diva Variation II

This cake can easily be made into cupcakes, either the miniature size (the recipe makes about 90) or regular (about 36). Bake minis for 12 minutes, and regular-size cupcakes for 17 to 20 minutes. Frost and arrange on tiered cake plates for your guests to serve themselves. Garnish with tinted or untinted coconut, jellybeans, or your favorite sprinkles in springtime colors.

# A Mediterranean Easter Dinner

For those of you who aren't fond of ham or who are looking for something a little different, this Mediterranean-inspired dinner for eight to ten people is just the ticket to serve for Easter, or any other special-occasion spring dinner. You can find lamb racks year-round at your market, and wholesale clubs like Costco and Sam's price them quite reasonably.

Because this menu is a little more sophisticated than the Easter meal featuring ham, I suggest more elaborate table decorations. Again, low flower arrangements and votives should go on the table, along with sprays of rosemary or other Mediterranean herbs (oregano, tarragon, garlic chives, marjoram, basil) in small vases. These nosegays not only look great, but they also give the table a delicious fragrance. Tie your cloth napkins with thin pastel ribbons and serve this meal on your best china.

You will need to set your table for a sit-down dinner as your guests will need to cut meat from bones, and that will require traction. So plan a plated dinner at your dining room table or a buffet with tables set for people to dine at. Although the menu includes sangria before dinner, which you can certainly serve throughout the meal, I suggest serving other wine choices as well just in case someone wants to switch.

## Do-Ahead Countdown

* **2 months ahead**

  Download shopping list and do-ahead calendar and fill them out

  Shop for nonperishables

  Make and freeze mint pesto for lamb

  Make (but don't bake) and freeze crust for Rustic Apricot-Strawberry Crostata

* **1 month ahead**

  Make (but don't bake) and freeze Goat Cheese Mashed Potatoes

* **3 days ahead**

  Make Red Wine–Citrus Vinaigrette

  Remove mint pesto, Goat Cheese Mashed Potatoes, and crust for crostata from freezer and defrost in refrigerator

* **2 days ahead**

  Grill or broil eggplant for Eggplant Napoleons

* **1 day ahead**

  Set the table

  Make base for Blush Sangria

  Make Cucumber, Garlic, and Feta Dip

  Make Goat Cheese and Olive Spread

  Make Eggplant Napoleons

  Prepare crudités and pita for dip

  Marinate racks of lamb (and bake today if you'd like, then reheat tomorrow)

  Combine the jams for the crostata

* **Day of**

  Make Cucumber-Mint Salsa

  Bake Goat Cheese Mashed Potatoes

  Toss field greens with Red Wine–Citrus Vinaigrette

  Assemble and bake Rustic Apricot-Strawberry Crostata

# Blush Sangria

*Serves 10*

*Fruity and refreshing, this beverage is a great choice for a Mediterranean dinner. I like it ice-cold in chilled wineglasses, without the usual addition of club soda, but if you want to stretch your wine dollar, fill double rocks glasses half full with sangria, then fill the rest of the way with club soda for a sparkly and light refresher.*

1 cup superfine sugar

2 1/2 cups hot water

2 limes, thinly sliced

2 oranges, thinly sliced

Ice cubes

1 1/2 cups triple sec

Three 750-milliliter bottles dry rosé wine

1 cup hulled and halved strawberries, for garnish

1 cup fresh pineapple chunks, for garnish

**1.** Put the sugar in a medium-size heatproof bowl and pour the water over it, stirring to dissolve the sugar. Add the limes and oranges. Cover and let sit at room temperature for at least 4 hours. **Diva Do-Ahead:** At this point, you can refrigerate overnight.

**2.** Fill 3 large pitchers each with a tray of ice cubes. Pour 3/4 cup of the sugar syrup into each one and add some of the sliced fruit. Add 1/2 cup of the triple sec and 1 bottle of wine to each and stir gently.

**3.** To serve, place a strawberry half and a pineapple chunk in each wine glass and pour the sangria over them.

# Cucumber, Garlic, and Feta Dip with Crudités and Pita

*Serves 8 to 10*

*This spicy yogurt dip is delicious to serve before your lamb dinner, and if you have any left over, use it as a sauce for lamb in pita bread the next day. For fresh vegetable options for the crudités, see page 23. I prefer to use fresh pita cut into wedges, but you can substitute pita chips if you'd like.*

1 1/2 cups plain yogurt

2 cloves garlic, minced

2 cups peeled and grated European cucumber (about 1/2 cucumber)

1 tablespoon finely chopped fresh dill

1/2 cup crumbled feta cheese

1 tablespoon freshly squeezed lemon juice

Dill sprigs for garnish

Crudités of your choice

Ten 6-inch pita rounds, cut into wedges

In a large mixing bowl, stir together the yogurt, garlic, cucumber, dill, feta, and lemon juice until blended. Cover and refrigerate for at least 2 hours. **Diva Do-Ahead:** At this point, you can refrigerate overnight. Stir the dip before serving, garnished with dill sprigs, with fresh vegetables and pita wedges.

## Diva Decorating Tip

Place the dip in a small round bowl, center it on a round platter, and arrange the pita and crudités around the outside of the platter to resemble flower petals.

# Goat Cheese and Olive Spread

*Serves 8 to 10*

*Some hors d'oeuvres appear almost too easy to be true, but this one delivers both taste and visual appeal, not to mention that it's great to find a recipe this simple but so good. The smooth goat cheese is topped with a chunky mixture of olives, sun-dried tomatoes, and capers flavored with balsamic vinegar and fresh basil. I'm indebted to my friend Jan Stapp, an incredible cook, for her inspiration.*

Two 11-ounce logs goat cheese, softened

4 ounces cream cheese, softened

1/2 cup finely chopped pimiento-stuffed olives

1/2 cup finely chopped pitted Kalamata olives

1/4 cup finely chopped celery

1/4 cup finely chopped drained capers

1/4 cup finely chopped drained sun-dried tomatoes packed in oil

1/3 cup olive oil

3 tablespoons balsamic vinegar

2 tablespoons finely chopped fresh basil

2 tablespoons finely chopped fresh Italian parsley

Baguette slices, crackers, or pita chips for serving

**1.** In a medium-size mixing bowl, combine the goat cheese and cream cheese until blended. **Diva Do-Ahead:** At this point, you may wrap in plastic wrap and refrigerate for up to 3 weeks. Allow to come to room temperature before proceeding. Pat the mixture into a 10-inch pie plate or similar serving dish.

**2.** In a small mixing bowl, combine the olives, celery, capers, and sun-dried tomatoes, tossing to blend. Sprinkle the mixture with the oil, vinegar, and half of the basil and parsley, stirring to combine. **Diva Do-Ahead:** At this point, you can cover and refrigerate for up to 3 days. Using a slotted spoon, transfer the mixture to the top of the goat cheese. **Diva Do-Ahead:** At this point, you can cover with plastic wrap and refrigerate overnight.

**3.** Sprinkle the top with the remaining basil and parsley and serve with baguette slices, crackers, or pita chips.

# Eggplant Napoleons

*Serves 8 to 10*

*These elegant yet simple vegetable stacks are perfect party food because you can grill or broil them ahead of time, then layer and refrigerate until you are ready to serve. They are a wonderful accompaniment to grilled or roasted meats or poultry but can also be served as a first course. If your tomatoes are not beautiful, then I recommend roasting them first (see page 285).*

1/2 cup olive oil

2 teaspoons salt

1 teaspoon freshly ground
   black pepper

2 cloves garlic, minced

2 large purple eggplants
   (about 1 1/2 pounds), ends
   trimmed and cut crosswise
   into 1/2-inch-thick slices

2 medium-size vine-ripened
   tomatoes, thinly sliced

1/2 cup packed finely chopped
   fresh basil leaves

1 pound fresh mozzarella
   cheese, cut into 1/2-inch-
   thick slices

Extra-virgin olive oil for
   drizzling

**1.** In a small bowl, stir together the olive oil, salt, pepper, and garlic.

**2.** Build a hot charcoal fire or preheat the broiler or gas grill for 10 minutes. If using the broiler, line a baking sheet with aluminum foil.

**3.** Brush the eggplant with the oil mixture, place on the prepared sheet or the grill, and broil or grill until softened, 3 to 4 minutes per side. **Diva Do-Ahead:** At this point, you can let cool, cover, and refrigerate for up to 2 days. Bring to room temperature before continuing.

**4.** To assemble a napoleon, place an eggplant slice on a flat surface, cover with a slice of tomato, some of the basil, and a slice of mozzarella. Continue to make the napoleons in this way until the ingredients are used up. Save any leftover basil for garnish. **Diva Do-Ahead:** At this point, you can cover and refrigerate for 24 hours. Bring to room temperature before continuing.

**5.** Serve the napoleons on a large platter, drizzled with extra-virgin olive oil and garnished with any leftover basil.

# Mint Pesto–Crusted Lamb Racks with Cucumber-Mint Salsa

*Serves 8*

*Lamb and mint are an age-old culinary combination, and this crusted rack of lamb makes a spectacular presentation, not only in terms of flavor, but also in the richly burnished color of the finished dish. Serve the lamb cut into individual chops on a bed of cool Cucumber-Mint Salsa. The lamb can be roasted the day before, then gently warmed in the oven just before serving, eliminating some of the last-minute timing issues you might otherwise have with roasting. For wine, serve an Italian Sangiovese or Primitivo.*

1 cup packed fresh mint
  leaves
4 cloves garlic
1 tablespoon rice vinegar or
  white vinegar
1/4 cup olive oil
2 tablespoons fresh oregano
  leaves
1 teaspoon salt
1/8 teaspoon cayenne pepper
Four 1-pound racks of lamb,
  trimmed
Cucumber-Mint Salsa
  (page 126)

**1.** In the work bowl of a food processor, combine the mint, garlic, vinegar, oil, oregano, salt, and cayenne, processing until smooth. **Diva Do-Ahead:** At this point, you can freeze the pesto in an airtight container for up to 2 months. Defrost before proceeding.

**2.** Make 1/2-inch slits all over the racks of lamb and transfer to large zipper-top plastic bags.

**3.** Pour the pesto evenly over the racks and turn to coat. Seal the bags and marinate in the refrigerator for 12 hours. **Diva Do-Ahead:** At this point, you can refrigerate for up to 24 hours.

**4.** Preheat the oven to 400°F. Remove the racks from the bags and place in a roasting pan, fat side up.

**5.** Roast the lamb for about 25 minutes, or until an instant-read thermometer inserted into the thickest part of the meat registers 140°F. **Diva Do-Ahead:** If you would like to roast the racks ahead of time, roast them to 125°F and remove them from the oven. Allow to cool to room temperature,

*continued on next page*

then wrap in aluminum foil and refrigerate for up to 2 days.
One hour before serving, preheat the oven to 350°F and
place the racks in a baking dish for 30 minutes to come to
room temperature. Bake the racks for 15 to 20 minutes,
until they are heated through. Allow the meat to rest for 10
minutes before serving with the salsa.

## Cucumber-Mint Salsa

*Makes about 2 cups*

*Pale green in color, cool and minty in flavor, this salsa is beautiful as a bed for a lamb rack, or alongside roasted lamb. Although this is a do-ahead recipe, I recommend that you make the salsa the day you wish to serve it, as the cucumbers lose some of their crunch by the next day.*

1 European cucumber, cut into
 1/2-inch dice

2 scallions (white and some
 tender green parts), chopped

1/2 cup packed fresh mint
 leaves, finely chopped

2 tablespoons canola oil

1 tablespoon rice vinegar

1/4 cup chopped fresh Italian
 parsley

1 tablespoon sugar

1/2 teaspoon salt

Pinch of cayenne pepper

**1.** In a small mixing bowl, stir together the cucumber, scallions, mint, oil, vinegar, parsley, sugar, salt, and cayenne.

**2.** Cover the bowl with plastic wrap and refrigerate for at least 2 hours. **Diva Do-Ahead:** At this point, you can refrigerate for up to 8 hours. Toss again and serve cold.

The Diva Says

When boiling potatoes, I use a pasta pot with the colander insert; that way I can remove the potatoes from the water and drain them over the stove before I put them in the bowl.

# Goat Cheese Mashed Potatoes

*Serves 10*

*These make-ahead potatoes, with smooth goat cheese and tangy Parmesan cheese, are a perfect accompaniment for the racks of lamb. The potatoes puff up in the oven like a soufflé. You can prepare them in a large baking dish or in individual 4-ounce ramekins.*

8 medium-size baking potatoes, peeled and cut into chunks

6 tablespoons ($3/4$ stick) unsalted butter, softened

$1/2$ cup freshly grated Parmesan cheese

$1/2$ cup regular or low-fat sour cream (do not use nonfat)

One 11-ounce log goat cheese

$1/3$ cup chopped fresh chives (optional)

Salt and freshly ground black pepper to taste

**1.** Boil the potatoes in salted water to cover until tender. Drain.

**2.** Preheat the oven to 350°F. Rub a 13 x 9-inch baking dish with 2 tablespoons of the butter. Sprinkle $1/4$ cup of the Parmesan into the dish and tip the dish so the cheese is evenly distributed and adheres to the butter.

**3.** Put the potatoes in a large bowl and add the sour cream, goat cheese, 2 tablespoons of the remaining butter, and the chives, if using. Season with salt and pepper. Using an electric mixer, beat the potatoes until smooth.

**4.** Transfer to the prepared dish, dot with the remaining 2 tablespoons butter and sprinkle with the remaining $1/4$ cup Parmesan cheese. **Diva Do-Ahead:** At this point, you can cover and refrigerate for 2 to 3 days or freeze for up to 1 month. Bring to room temperature before continuing. Bake the potatoes until golden, about 25 minutes. Serve hot.

*Diva Variation*

To prepare these potatoes in ramekins, divide the whipped potato mixture evenly among ten 4-ounce ramekins. Bake for 15 to 20 minutes, until puffed and golden.

## Slow Cooker Savvy

These potatoes can be "baked" in a 4-quart slow cooker if you have a removable ceramic insert. Butter the insert and dust it with the Parmesan cheese as directed in step 2. Follow the recipe through step 3, filling the insert with the mashed potatoes. Cover and cook on low for 4 to 6 hours, until heated through. An extra dusting of Parmesan and butter just before serving makes them look divine.

# Field Greens with Red Wine–Citrus Vinaigrette

*Serves 8 to 10*

*The beautiful salad dressing is wonderful on field greens with orange or red grapefruit segments and a few toasted pine nuts tossed in. Refrigerate any leftover dressing for up to one week.*

1 1/2 cups olive oil

1/2 cup red wine

1/2 cup fresh orange juice

3 tablespoons freshly squeezed lemon juice

2 tablespoons minced fresh sage

1 1/2 teaspoons orange zest

1 1/2 teaspoons salt

1 teaspoon freshly ground black pepper

2 cloves garlic, minced

1 red grapefruit

2 navel oranges

Three 10-ounce bags field greens

1/2 cup toasted pine nuts (see page 114)

**1.** In a medium-size bowl, whisk together the oil, red wine, orange juice, lemon juice, sage, orange zest, salt, pepper, and garlic until blended. **Diva Do-Ahead:** At this point, you can cover and refrigerate for up to 3 days.

**2.** Slice off the bottoms and tops of the grapefruit and oranges. Stand each fruit on a flat end, and, using a boning knife or thin flexible knife, cut down the sides, removing the peel and white pith. Slice the grapefruit into 1/2-inch slices, then cut each slice into quarters. Slice each orange into 1/2-inch slices.

**3.** Place the field greens and grapefruit and orange segments into a large salad bowl and toss with some of the dressing. Sprinkle the salad with the pine nuts and serve additional dressing on the side.

# Rustic Apricot-Strawberry Crostata

*Serves 8 to 10*

*When I visited my family in Italy, my cousin Vera made a crostata to keep us fueled during the annual Festa di Ceri, a race through the town of Gubbio that lasts all day and into the night. My cousin Igor could be counted on to find the ones she'd hidden for later consumption. Crostatas are Italian jam tarts, and Vera makes hers with apricot jam. Igor likes his made with Nutella!*

2 2/3 cups all-purpose flour

1 1/3 cups granulated sugar

1 1/4 cups (2 1/2) sticks chilled unsalted butter, cut into small pieces

3 large egg yolks

3/4 cup apricot jam

3/4 cup strawberry jam

2 tablespoons freshly squeezed lemon juice (or more to taste)

Additional granulated sugar to taste (optional)

1/2 cup confectioners' sugar

Vanilla ice cream for serving (optional)

**1.** Place the flour, sugar, and butter into a food processor and pulse on and off until the mixture resembles coarse crumbs.

**2.** Stir the egg yolks together and, with the machine running, pour in the egg mixture and blend until the dough begins to come together but doesn't quite form a ball.

**3.** Press half the dough into a 10-inch tart pan with a removable bottom and refrigerate the rest for about 20 minutes. **Diva Do-Ahead:** At this point, you can freeze the dough in the tart pan and the remaining dough, wrapped in plastic wrap, for up to 2 months. Defrost before proceeding.

**4.** In a small mixing bowl, stir together the jams and lemon juice, tasting to see if the mixture needs more sugar or lemon juice. Spread into the tart shell and refrigerate until ready to bake. **Diva Do-Ahead:** At this point, you can refrigerate for up to 8 hours. Bring the crostata to room temperature before proceeding.

**5.** Preheat the oven to 400°F. Roll out the remaining dough, using some of the confectioners' sugar as you would flour. Cut the dough into 3/4-inch strips and make a lattice pattern over the jam (you don't need to weave the dough, just arrange it in a crisscross pattern). Sprinkle the tart with more confectioners' sugar and bake for 10 minutes. Lower oven temperature to 375°F and bake an additional 20 to 25 minutes, until tart is golden brown. Remove from oven and cool for 20 minutes. Remove tart from the pan and cut into slices. Serve warm, plain, or with vanilla ice cream.

Feeding the Hand
That Feeds You

# A Mother's
# Day
# Breakfast

Mother's Day in the United States is thought to have originated in 1872, when Julia Ward Howe, who wrote the lyrics for "Battle Hymn of the Republic," suggested an International Mother's Day to celebrate motherhood and peace. Most early celebrations were religious gatherings. In the late 1800s a mother in West Virginia urged her Methodist congregation to celebrate Mother's Day, and her daughter Anna Jarvis made it her mission in life to have Mother's Day declared a national holiday. President Woodrow Wilson signed the declaration in 1914.

For Mother's Day I've devised a simple, perfect meal that everyone in the family can help with: even the smallest child can layer fruit into parfait glasses! The entire menu can be made ahead of time; you'll just need to reheat the scones and bake the strata (while Mom's still sleeping, of course) to be on your way to feting Mom in style. And the servings are adaptable to scale up or down according to the size of your family.

If you want to serve Mom breakfast in bed, use a wicker or wooden breakfast-in-bed tray with a beautiful cloth placemat in spring colors, a bud vase with her favorite blooms, and a napkin tied with coordinating ribbon. Serve this meal on your best china, and be sure to bring a small pitcher of coffee or tea along as well, depending on what your mother likes to drink in the morning.

If your mom isn't the breakfast-in-bed type, set the table with a festive air, using a bright table-cloth and bouquets of spring flowers, like lilacs and roses or sweet peas and stargazer lilies. And include a tiara at her place (many toy and party stores carry tiaras)—after all, Mom deserves to be queen for a day!

## Do-Ahead Countdown

✱ **2 months ahead**

Download shopping list and do-ahead calendar and fill them out

Shop for nonperishables

Measure out and freeze fruit for Strawberry Smoothies

Make and freeze Maple Granola

✱ **6 weeks ahead**

Make (but don't bake) Heavenly Blueberry Scones

✱ **1 month ahead**

Make and freeze Orange Mascarpone Crème

✱ **1 day ahead**

Make (but don't bake) and refrigerate Goat Cheese, Prosciutto, and Artichoke Heart Strata

Remove Maple Granola from freezer and defrost

✱ **Day of**

Set the table or ready a breakfast-in-bed tray

Make Strawberry Smoothies

Bake Heavenly Blueberry Scones

Bake Goat Cheese, Prosciutto, and Artichoke Heart Strata

Prepare Fresh Fruit Parfaits with Orange Mascarpone Crème

# Strawberry Smoothies

*Makes 4 smoothies*

*A flavor-packed beginning to breakfast, these smoothies combine tart lime sherbet, bright red berries, and pineapple for a tropical blast to wake up Mom on her special day. Measure out the frozen fruit into zipper-top plastic bags, then label and freeze for up to two months. Have the liquids ready to go in the fridge and then let the blender rip!*

1 cup lime sherbet or lemon sorbet

1 cup orange juice

2 cups plain yogurt

2 cups frozen pineapple chunks

4 cups frozen strawberries

Fresh berries and pineapple spears for garnish (optional)

Place the ingredients (except the garnish) in a blender container in the order they are listed (you may need to divide the ingredients and make two batches). Blend on high speed until pureed. Pour into tall glasses, and serve garnished with fresh berries and pineapple spears, if desired. If fresh pineapple and berries aren't in season, small tropical drink umbrellas make a nice statement, too!

# Maple Granola

*Makes about 8 1/2 cups*

*Crunchy and filled with delicious goodies, this granola will wake up even the sleepiest mom on her day. This recipe makes a lot, but you can freeze it for up to two months. Serve this granola in cereal bowls with milk, or you can layer it in the Fresh Fruit Parfaits with Orange Mascarpone Crème (page 138).*

6 cups quick-cooking oats

1 1/3 cups chopped pecans or almonds

1/2 cup sweetened flaked coconut

1/2 cup sesame seeds

1/2 cup golden raisins

1/2 cup canola oil

1/2 cup maple syrup

1/2 cup firmly packed light brown sugar

2 tablespoons water

2 teaspoons pure vanilla extract

**1.** Preheat the oven to 300°F. Line 2 jelly-roll pans with parchment paper, aluminum foil, or silicone baking liners. In a large bowl, toss together the oats, pecans, coconut, sesame seeds, and raisins until combined.

**2.** In a medium-size saucepan, heat the oil, maple syrup, brown sugar, and water until it comes to a boil. Stir in the vanilla extract. Pour the liquid over the oat mixture and stir to coat.

**3.** Divide the granola between the 2 pans, spreading it into single layers. Bake for 35 to 45 minutes, until golden brown, stirring every 10 to 15 minutes. Cool the granola to room temperature and stir it to break up any chunks.

**Diva Do-Ahead:** At this point, you can store at room temperature in an airtight container for up to 1 week or freeze in zipper-top plastic bags for up to 2 months. Defrost at room temperature for about 2 hours.

# Heavenly Blueberry Scones

*Makes 12 scones*

*These delectable melt-in-your-mouth scones are a difficult wake-up call to resist. The dough can be made ahead and frozen, then defrosted overnight in the refrigerator and baked fresh in the morning. I prefer to bake the scones the day I want to serve them, but you can freeze leftover baked scones in zipper-top plastic bags and reheat them, after they have defrosted, in a 350°F oven for about five minutes.*

2 1/2 cups all-purpose flour
1/3 cup granulated sugar
1 tablespoon baking powder
3/4 teaspoon salt
1/2 cup dried blueberries
1 1/2 cups heavy cream
2 egg yolks mixed with
   2 tablespoons milk, cream,
   or water
1/2 cup raw sugar (optional)

**1.** Preheat the oven to 400°F. Line a baking sheet with parchment paper, aluminum foil, or a silicone baking liner.

**2.** Place 2 1/4 cups of the flour, the sugar, baking powder, and salt in a sifter or strainer and sift into a large mixing bowl. Add the blueberries to the dry ingredients and toss to blend.

**3.** A few tablespoons at a time, add the heavy cream, stirring with a wooden spoon, until the dough just comes together.

**4.** Scatter the remaining 1/4 cup flour on a board or work surface and turn the dough out, kneading it two or three times, until it comes together in a smooth mass. **Diva Do-Ahead:** At this point, you can slip the dough into a zipper-top plastic bag and refrigerate for 2 days or freeze for 6 weeks. Defrost before continuing.

**5.** Roll the dough out into a large circle 1/2 inch thick and cut the circle into 12 wedges. Transfer the wedges to the prepared baking sheet, brush with the egg wash, and sprinkle with the raw sugar, if desired. Bake for 17 to 20 minutes, until golden brown. Remove from the oven and allow to cool for 5 minutes before serving.

## Diva Wisdom

Clotted cream, which is the traditional English accompaniment for scones, can be hard to find in your grocery store. By whipping 1 cup heavy cream until it is very stiff (your spatula should stand up in it), you can make a good substitute for the traditional clotted cream served in England.

### Diva Variation

Substitute dried cranberries, cherries, or raspberries for the blueberries.

# Goat Cheese, Prosciutto, and Artichoke Heart Strata

*Serves 10*

*This simple strata takes my favorite Mediterranean flavors—goat cheese, salty prosciutto, and artichokes—and turns them into a great breakfast main course. The best part is that it has to be prepared ahead of time, giving you more time to enjoy the day.*

One 1-pound loaf sturdy white bread, torn into 1/2-inch pieces

6 ounces prosciutto, thinly sliced

8 ounces goat cheese, crumbled

1 1/2 cups grated Parmesan cheese

4 scallions (white and tender green parts), chopped

1/4 cup firmly packed fresh basil leaves, finely sliced

One 14.5-ounce can artichoke hearts, drained and coarsely chopped

8 large eggs

2 1/2 cups whole milk

1 tablespoon Dijon mustard

1 teaspoon salt

1/2 teaspoon freshly ground black pepper

1/4 cup (1/2 stick) unsalted butter, melted

**1.** Coat the inside of a 13 x 9-inch baking dish with nonstick cooking spray.

**2.** Lay about half the bread on the bottom of the baking dish. Sprinkle half the prosciutto evenly over the bread; top with half the goat cheese, Parmesan cheese, scallions, basil, and all of the artichoke hearts. Top with a second layer of bread and the remaining prosciutto, goat cheese, Parmesan, scallions, and basil. Sprinkle any remaining bread on top.

**3.** In a large mixing bowl, whisk together the eggs, milk, mustard, salt, and pepper. Pour the mixture over the bread and press down on the strata with a spatula. Drizzle the butter over the strata, cover, and refrigerate at least 6 hours, or overnight.

**4.** Preheat the oven to 350°F. Allow the casserole to come to room temperature and then bake uncovered for 45 minutes, until the center is set and the strata is golden brown. Serve warm or at room temperature.

## Diva Variation

For a fancier presentation, you can make this strata in individual ramekins. Follow the layering instructions for the ingredients, dividing them evenly among ten 4-ounce ramekins. Bake the ramekins for 20 to 25 minutes.

# Fresh Fruit Parfaits with Orange Mascarpone Crème

*Serves 8*

*Multicolored fruit layered in parfait glasses is a jewel-like addition to this breakfast in bed. You can layer the fruit with your mother's favorite flavor of yogurt instead of with the orange mascarpone that I've included in the recipe, if you wish. Either way, it's a delicious beginning to Mom's perfect day. The fruits here are only suggestions; you should feel free to substitute any fruit that your family likes, or double up on a few.*

1 cup heavy cream

2 cups mascarpone cheese

2 tablespoons Grand Marnier or 2 teaspoons orange extract

1/4 cup sugar (or more to taste)

1 cup sliced strawberries

1/2 cup fresh blueberries

1/2 cup fresh raspberries

2 bananas, peeled, sliced, and sprinkled with lemon juice to prevent discoloration

1 cup diced cantaloupe or 2 ripe peaches, peeled and diced

1 kiwi fruit, peeled and diced

**1.** In a large mixing bowl, whip the cream until stiff. Stir in the mascarpone, Grand Marnier, and sugar until blended. Taste the crème and add more sugar or flavoring if desired. **Diva Do-Ahead:** At this point, you can refrigerate the crème in an airtight container for up to 3 days or freeze it for up to 1 month. Defrost in the refrigerator and rewhip the crème with a whisk before proceeding.

**2.** In a large bowl, combine all the fruits. Spoon some of the fruit into parfait glasses and top with some of the crème (the amounts will depend upon your glasses). Repeat the layering until your glasses are filled, ending with a dollop of the crème. **Diva Do-Ahead:** You can cover and refrigerate for up to 12 hours before serving.

## Diva Wisdom

Mascarpone is an Italian cream cheese, which is sweeter and creamier than regular cream cheese. You can substitute whipped cream cheese, but you will need to add a bit more sugar to approximate the crème.

*Diva Variation*

To serve this dish on a buffet table in a trifle bowl, layer the fruit and crème in the bowl, ending with the crème. Cover with plastic wrap and refrigerate for up to 12 hours before serving.

Diva Tip

If you don't own parfait glasses, you can use brandy snifters, balloon wineglasses, or 6-ounce old-fashioned glasses.

# Movable Feast
# A Memorial Day Picnic

The traditional kickoff to summer, Memorial Day is the day set aside for remembering our war dead. Many times when I was a child, my parents brought my siblings and me to Arlington National Cemetery in Washington, D.C., to see the changing of the guard at the Tomb of the Unknown Soldier. Afterward we would take a ride west toward Manassas, Virginia, the site of the Battles of Bull Run during the Civil War. We'd bring a picnic hamper filled with goodies and spend the day eating and playing in the countryside.

This picnic, for eight to ten people, is a bit different from my mom's, but it is sure to please because all the items can be made ahead of time, then taken along to the picnic area. If you decide that you want to serve this meal at home, it's perfect for a big lunch or an early evening supper on the patio or deck.

Taking food along for the ride does require some planning, and I recommend a rolling cooler to keep your food cold. If you don't have a rolling cooler, you can build you own cooler with a cardboard or plastic file box with a top. Just before leaving for your picnic, line the box with a large plastic garbage bag, making sure to pull the sides of the bag down over the outside of the box. Fill zipper-top plastic bags with ice and lay them on the bottom. Next, arrange your food in the box and place another bag of ice on top. Place several kitchen towels on top, then cover. Your food should keep very nicely for about six hours. The bagged ice can be used for the drinks at the picnic. When you are ready to leave, toss all your trash into the plastic garbage bag and dispose of it in the proper receptacle, then arrange your serving dishes in the box and transport them home. A nice picnic basket (or another box) can hold all the flatware, serving utensils (don't forget these!), napkins and wet wipes, tablecloth or blanket, and food that doesn't need to be kept cold.

To keep your drinks cold, a cooler is ideal, but the "icebox" trick works well, too. If your drinks will freeze, you can tote them frozen to the picnic site. Not only will they keep your other items cold, but you won't have to carry as much ice with you. I don't recommend adding ice to your drinks before transporting them, because the ice will water them down.

When planning an outdoor picnic, always have a backup plan in case of inclement weather. Eating outdoors comes with its own set of circumstances, some of them unforeseen, such as wind that can blow the tablecloth and paper products away, insects (pack some repellent), and cold temperatures. If it's cold, replan your day and serve your picnic at home, or set up a tent to protect your party from the elements, or, if all else fails, reschedule. All the food will keep for a day if you absolutely want to eat outside.

For this picnic I'm recommending a delicious watermelon lemonade, but you should also have water, soft drinks, and wine and/or beer for your guests if the place where you are picnicking permits it. A nice crisp citrusy white or a rosé works well with this menu. Remember to have some juice boxes or something fun for the kids to drink. Chances are they will be playing more than eating, so they'll need something safe that they can take off with!

# Do-Ahead Countdown

## * 6 weeks ahead

Download shopping list and do-ahead calendar and fill them out

Shop for nonperishables

Grill and freeze chicken for Layered Picnic Chicken Caesar Salad

Make and freeze Mocha–Cream Cheese Brownies

Make and freeze Lime Pound Cake with Fresh Lime Glaze

## * 5 days ahead

Make base for Watermelon Lemonade

## * 2 days ahead

Make Creamy Caesar Dressing

Slice citrus fruits and mozzarella cheese for Orange, Red Grapefruit, and Mozzarella Salad

## * 1 day ahead

Add watermelon puree to the lemonade

Make White Gazpacho

Make Tuna Niçoise Sandwich

Make Shrimply Deviled Eggs

Remove chicken from freezer, defrost, and make Layered Picnic Chicken Caesar Salad

Remove brownies and pound cake from freezer and defrost in refrigerator

## * Day of

Make Avocado-Corn Relish

Slice Tuna Niçoise Sandwich

Assemble Orange, Red Grapefruit, and Mozzarella Salad

Cut Mocha–Cream Cheese Brownies into squares

Pack your picnic basket

## Picnic Essentials

* Blanket
* Sunscreen
* Insect repellent
* Radio/CD player and mood music
* Napkins
* Plates: soup bowls or mugs, dinner-size plates, dessert plates
* Flatware: forks, knives, spoons
* Serving utensils, including a ladle for the gazpacho and tongs or 2 large spoons for serving the salad

* Cups and wineglasses
* Corkscrew
* Damp wipes or cloths for washing up or a roll of paper towels and a bottle of water
* Garbage bag

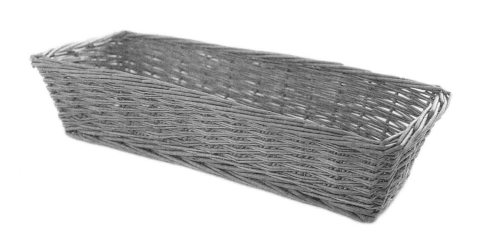

# Watermelon Lemonade

*Serves 10 to 12*

*There is nothing more refreshing on a hot day than a pitcher of fresh lemonade. I know most of us grew up with either the powdered stuff or the frozen concentrate, but fresh lemonade knocks the others out of the ballpark when it comes to taste, and it's simple to put together. Superfine sugar dissolves in a wink, so it's my choice when making homemade lemonade. And I recommend Minute Maid's frozen lemon juice, not the plastic lemon or the unrefrigerated lemon juice in the juice section of the grocery store. You can also make limeade by substituting limes for lemons in the recipe.*

1²/3 cups freshly squeezed lemon juice (from about 9 lemons, or more to taste)

1¹/2 cups superfine sugar (or more to taste)

4¹/2 cups water

2 cups watermelon puree (puree seedless watermelon chunks in a blender or food processor)

2 lemons, sliced and seeded

Ice cubes

**1.** In a large pitcher, combine the lemon juice and sugar, stirring to dissolve the sugar. Slowly pour in the water and continue to stir until the mixture is blended. Taste the lemonade, adding more sugar or lemon juice if desired. Refrigerate the lemonade for at least 4 hours. **Diva Do-Ahead:** At this point, you can refrigerate for up to 5 days or freeze for up to 6 weeks.

**2.** When ready to serve, add the watermelon puree and stir. Float the sliced lemons in the lemonade and serve over ice.

## Diva Lemonade Variations

**Arnold Palmer Lemonade:** 1 part lemonade and 1 part iced tea

**Raspberry or Strawberry Lemonade:** Add 1¹/2 cups berry puree to the lemonade, instead of the watermelon, the day before serving. (Seed the puree by pushing it through a sieve.)

**Mint Lemonade:** Crush 1 cup of mint leaves and steep in 2 cups boiling water with 1¹/2 cups superfine sugar. Strain out the leaves and reserve the syrup. Follow the Watermelon Lemonade recipe, omitting the sugar and the watermelon puree and using only 2¹/2 cups of water. Garnish each drink with mint leaves.

**Pomegranate Lemonade:** Add 1 to 1¹/2 cups pomegranate juice to lemonade the day before serving.

## Diva Tip

To avoid watering down the lemonade, make a batch of lemonade or watermelon-puree ice cubes to toss into the pitcher, or fill an ice bucket with cubes for serving.

# White Gazpacho with Avocado-Corn Relish

*Serves 8*

*This cooling soup can be transported in thermal containers to keep it cold, or packed in ice and carried to your picnic. A great starter for any meal, it's cool, creamy, and filled with crispy veggies, then topped off with a spicy garnish to give it a little something extra. For a unique serving container, cut the stems off green and yellow bell peppers and remove the core and seeds. Then trim the bottoms of the peppers so that they stand flat on the countertop (but don't cut through the bottoms). Fill the peppers with the gazpacho and serve garnished with the relish.*

3 cups chicken broth

2 European cucumbers, peeled and diced

3 tablespoons white vinegar

1 large clove garlic, mashed

3 cups regular or low-fat sour cream or plain yogurt

2 plum tomatoes, diced

4 scallions, chopped

1 medium-size green bell pepper, cored, seeded, and diced

1 medium-size yellow bell pepper, cored, seeded, and diced

1/2 cup chopped fresh Italian parsley

2 Hass avocados, peeled, pitted, and diced

2 cups white corn, cut from the cob or frozen and defrosted

2 teaspoons freshly squeezed lime juice

2 tablespoons chopped fresh cilantro

1/4 teaspoon chipotle chile powder

1 cup sliced almonds, toasted (see page 114)

**1.** In a blender or food processor, process 1 cup of the chicken broth, half of the cucumbers, the vinegar, and garlic. Pour into a large serving bowl. Whisk in the rest of the broth and the sour cream.

**2.** Add the remaining diced cucumber, the tomatoes, scallions, green and yellow peppers, and parsley, stirring until blended. Cover and refrigerate for at least 4 hours. **Diva Do-Ahead:** At this point, you can refrigerate for up to 24 hours.

**3.** To make the relish, in a small bowl, combine the avocados, corn, lime juice, cilantro, and chile powder. Cover and refrigerate for at least 1 hour. **Diva Do-Ahead:** At this point, you can refrigerate for up to 8 hours. At serving time, ladle the gazpacho into individual bowls and top with the relish and sliced almonds.

# Tuna Niçoise Sandwich

*Serves 8 to 10*

*This savory jumble of tuna, artichoke hearts, capers, red onion, and olives is packed into a loaf of hearty Italian bread. You can refrigerate it for up to 24 hours before serving, making it the perfect take-along entrée for your movable feast.*

Three 7.5-ounce cans Italian tuna packed in olive oil, drained

One 6-ounce jar marinated artichoke hearts, drained (marinade reserved) and coarsely chopped

1/2 cup finely chopped red onion

1/2 cup capers, drained and chopped

1/4 cup pitted Kalamata olives, chopped

1/4 cup pimiento-stuffed green olives, chopped

1/4 cup chopped fresh Italian parsley

2 tablespoons red wine vinegar

1 loaf soft-crusted Italian bread, split lengthwise

Decorative toothpicks

**1.** In a large mixing bowl, stir together the tuna, artichoke hearts, onion, capers, olives, parsley, and vinegar, mixing until thoroughly combined. Taste the tuna and add some of the reserved artichoke marinade, a few tablespoons at a time, until the mixture is nicely seasoned.

**2.** Remove and discard some of the soft inside of the bottom of the bread with a knife or pull with your hands and fill in the shell with the tuna salad. Place the top on the bread and wrap in aluminum foil or plastic wrap. Refrigerate for at least 4 hours to allow the flavors to blend and soak into the bread. **Diva Do-Ahead:** At this point, you can refrigerate for up to 24 hours.

**3.** One hour before serving, remove from the refrigerator and allow to come to room temperature. Slice into 2-inch sections, secure each sandwich with a long frilled toothpick, and arrange on a platter.

## Diva Note

Italian tuna, which is packed in olive oil, has a completely different flavor from water-packed domestic tuna. It results in a much more interesting tuna salad than that bland scoop you usually get between two slices of white bread. If you cannot find Italian tuna in the tuna section, look in the Italian foods aisle (where you find marinated artichoke hearts, jarred olives, and clam sauce, for instance).

# Shrimply Deviled Eggs

*Serves 10 to 12*

*Store these in a cooler and set on field greens so they don't slide. They are picture perfect for a picnic.*

12 large hard-cooked eggs

1/2 to 3/4 cup mayonnaise, as needed

2 teaspoons yellow mustard or another mustard of your choice

1 teaspoon salt

1/4 teaspoon Tabasco sauce

1/2 cup finely chopped cooked shrimp

2 tablespoons chopped fresh dill

**1.** When the eggs are cool enough to handle, peel them under cold running water to remove the shells. Cut the eggs in half lengthwise, carefully remove the yolks, and put the yolks in a medium-size bowl. Set the whites aside.

**2.** Mash the yolks, then add 1/2 cup of the mayonnaise, the mustard, salt, Tabasco, shrimp, and dill and stir to blend. Taste and adjust the seasonings if necessary; add more of the mayonnaise if needed to get the consistency and flavor you want.

**3.** Fill each egg white with about 1 tablespoon of the mixture. **Diva Do-Ahead:** At this point, you can cover and refrigerate overnight. Serve cold.

# Layered Picnic Chicken Caesar Salad

*Serves 10*

*Layered salads got a bad rap from the days when they appeared at every potluck dinner on the planet. But this layered salad is delicious and makes a stunning and easily transportable entrée for your feast.*

Three 10-ounce bags romaine lettuce leaves

Grilled Lemon Chicken Breasts (page 150), thinly sliced

2 1/3 cups Creamy Caesar Dressing (page 151)

1 1/2 cups finely shredded Parmesan cheese

2 cups garlic croutons, homemade or store-bought

Layer some of the lettuce in the bottom of a large salad bowl. Cover the lettuce with some of the chicken in an even layer. Spread a thin layer of dressing over the chicken breasts, sprinkle with some of the cheese, and continue to layer these ingredients, ending with dressing and Parmesan, until you use them up. Sprinkle with croutons, cover with plastic wrap, and refrigerate for 4 hours. **Diva Do-Ahead:** At this point, you can refrigerate for up to 24 hours. Serve cold or at room temperature.

# Grilled Lemon Chicken Breasts

*Serves 6*

*This simple grilled chicken is a great do-ahead basic that you can serve on its own or in a myriad of different ways: on a bed of sliced tomatoes and cucumbers dressed with good-quality extra-virgin olive oil and fresh lemon juice; in sandwiches on crusty rolls, slathered with your favorite spread and topped with lettuce and sliced tomato; or sliced on the diagonal and served over Caesar salad or other dressed greens. It's also terrific cut up and added to pasta salad.*

1/2 cup extra-virgin olive oil

1/3 cup freshly squeezed lemon juice

1 tablespoon dried rosemary

1 teaspoon salt

1/2 teaspoon freshly ground black pepper

2 cloves garlic, minced

6 skinless, boneless chicken breast halves, tenders removed (reserve for another purpose)

**1.** In a zipper-top plastic bag, combine the oil, lemon juice, rosemary, salt, pepper, and garlic, shaking to blend. Add the chicken, turning to coat it, and seal. Refrigerate for at least 2 hours. **Diva Do-Ahead:** At this point, you can refrigerate for up to 2 days.

**2.** Build a hot charcoal fire or preheat a gas grill, or preheat the broiler for 10 minutes. Remove the chicken from the marinade and grill, or place on a baking sheet lined with aluminum foil and broil until cooked through, 3 to 5 minutes per side. **Diva Do-Ahead:** At this point, you can let cool, store in an airtight container, and refrigerate for up to 8 hours or freeze for up to 6 weeks.

## Diva Variation
Substitute dried oregano or marjoram for the rosemary.

# Creamy Caesar Dressing

*Makes about 2¹/3 cups*

*This creamy dressing is great for sturdy greens like romaine, or you can use it as a dip for veggies or a spread for sandwiches. Unlike traditional Caesar dressing, this one omits the raw egg so it keeps well in the refrigerator for up to one week.*

1¹/2 cups regular or low-fat
  mayonnaise
¹/2 cup grated Parmesan
  cheese
¹/4 cup regular or low-fat sour
  cream
2 tablespoons freshly squeezed
  lemon juice
2 teaspoons anchovy paste
1 tablespoon Worcestershire
  sauce
2 cloves garlic, minced
Salt and freshly ground black
  pepper to taste

In a mixing bowl, whisk together all the ingredients until blended. Taste for salt and pepper and adjust as needed. Cover and refrigerate the dressing for at least 4 hours. **Diva Do-Ahead:** At this point, you can refrigerate for up to 2 weeks. Rewhisk to blend before serving.

# Orange, Red Grapefruit, and Mozzarella Salad

*Serves 10*

*My favorite salad from Italy marinates oranges with extra-virgin olive oil, red wine vinegar, and oregano. I've taken that idea, substituted grapefruit for the vinegar and aromatic basil for the oregano, and added creamy fresh mozzarella cheese. The colors and flavors all balance the rest of your menu nicely.*

3 large navel oranges

2 red grapefruits

1 pound fresh mozzarella cheese, sliced 1/4 inch thick

1/2 cup extra-virgin olive oil

2 tablespoons finely chopped fresh basil

Freshly ground black pepper to taste

**1.** Slice off the bottoms and tops of the oranges and grapefruits. Stand each fruit on a flat end and, using a boning knife or thin flexible knife, cut down the sides, removing the peel and white pith.

**2.** Slice each orange into 1/2-inch slices. Slice each grapefruit into 1/2-inch slices, then cut each grapefruit slice into quarters. **Diva Do-Ahead:** At this point, you can store the cut fruit in zipper-top plastic bags in the refrigerator crisper for up to 3 days.

**3.** Four hours before serving, arrange the fruit in a 13 x 9-inch casserole dish (disposable aluminum pans work fine here), alternating pieces of fruit with the mozzarella slices. Drizzle with the oil and basil, cover, and let sit at room temperature. Just before serving, grind black pepper over the top of the salad.

# Mocha–Cream Cheese Brownies

*Makes twenty-four 2-inch squares*

*Chocolate and coffee are a great match, and when they are put together in a decadent brownie, I'm not sure there is anything better. The brownies can be baked and frozen, then defrosted the day before your picnic. Brownies and other bars are a great choice for a picnic because you can pick them up and eat them while talking, walking, or watching the kids.*

### Filling

One 8-ounce package cream
cheese, softened
1/3 cup sugar
1 large egg
1 teaspoon instant espresso
powder

### Brownie Batter

2 cups sugar
1 cup (2 sticks) unsalted
butter, softened and cut into
chunks
4 large eggs
1 tablespoon Kahlúa or crème
de cacao
1 cup Dutch-processed cocoa
powder
1 cup all-purpose flour

### Frosting

1 cup sugar
5 tablespoons unsalted butter
1/3 cup whole milk
One 6-ounce package semi-
sweet chocolate chips
1 teaspoon instant espresso
powder
2/3 cup chocolate-covered
espresso beans

**1.** To make the filling, put all the ingredients in a food processor and process until smooth. Remove from the work bowl and set aside.

**2.** Preheat the oven to 350°F. Coat a 13 x 9-inch baking pan with nonstick cooking spray.

**3.** To make the batter, combine the sugar, butter, eggs, and Kahlúa in the food processor and process until smooth. Add the cocoa powder and pulse 4 or 5 times. Add the flour and pulse until it disappears into the mixture.

**4.** Spread half the chocolate batter over the bottom of the prepared pan. Dot with the cream cheese filling, then top with the remaining chocolate batter. Swirl the batter and filling with a spatula to marble. Bake until a skewer inserted in the center comes out with some crumbs adhering to it, 35 to 40 minutes. Remove the pan to a cooling rack.

**5.** To make the frosting, combine the sugar, butter, and milk in a small saucepan. Bring to a boil and continue boiling for 1 minute, stirring constantly. Remove from the heat and stir in chocolate chips and espresso powder until smooth. Pour the frosting over the warm brownies. While the brownies are still warm, cut them and sprinkle with the espresso beans. Then allow them to cool completely on a rack, still in the pan. **Diva Do-Ahead**: At this point, you can cover and refrigerate for up to 2 days or freeze for up to 2 months. Defrost in the refrigerator and bring to room temperature before serving for the best flavor and texture.

# Lime Pound Cake with Fresh Lime Glaze and Strawberries

*Makes two 8-inch loaves or one 12-cup bundt or tube cake*

*This dense, citrusy cake is simple to put together, and you can freeze it for up to two months. Infused with lime juice and a lime syrup, the cake has rich flavor, and you'll picture yourself in a tropical paradise with each bite. Feel free to use Key limes instead of regular limes if you can find them. I love this pound cake with sliced strawberries, but it's just as delicious plain. You'll want to serve it on plates with forks at your picnic, as it's rather sticky.*

## Cake

2 cups granulated sugar

1 cup (2 sticks) unsalted butter, at room temperature

4 large eggs

Zest of 2 limes or $1/2$ teaspoon lime oil

3 cups all-purpose flour

1 teaspoon salt

$1/2$ teaspoon baking powder

$1/2$ teaspoon baking soda

$3/4$ cup buttermilk (or $3/4$ cup whole milk with 1 teaspoon lemon juice added)

2 tablespoons freshly squeezed lime juice

2 tablespoons freshly squeezed lemon juice

## Syrup

$1/2$ cup granulated sugar

$1/2$ cup freshly squeezed lime juice

## Glaze

$2^1/2$ cups sifted confectioners' sugar

$1/4$ cup freshly squeezed lime juice

4 cups sliced strawberries for garnish (optional)

**1.** Preheat the oven to 350°F. Coat the inside of two 8-inch loaf pans or a 12-cup bundt pan with nonstick cooking spray.

**2.** Cream the sugar and butter together in the bowl of an electric mixer until light and fluffy. Add the eggs one at a time, then the zest. Add the flour, salt, baking powder, and baking soda to the bowl.

**3.** In a measuring cup, combine the buttermilk, lime juice, and lemon juice, and with the mixer on low, begin to add the buttermilk mixture to the bowl, beating until the batter begins to come together and is smooth. Stop the mixer a few times to scrape down the sides.

**4.** Divide the batter between the two loaf pans and bake for 1 hour, until a cake tester comes out clean. If using a bundt pan, bake for 1 hour and 15 minutes, until a cake tester comes out clean.

**5.** Cool the cakes for 15 minutes on a rack, then remove from the pans.

**6.** To make the syrup, combine the sugar and juice in a small saucepan and cook over low heat until the sugar dissolves.

**7.** Using a long skewer, poke holes through the cakes, and spoon the syrup over, allowing it to soak in. Allow the cakes to cool completely.

**8.** To make the glaze, whisk together the sugar and lime juice with a wire whisk. Pour over the top of the cakes and allow the glaze to drizzle down the sides. **Diva Do-Ahead:** Allow the glaze to set, then wrap the cakes in plastic wrap and store in the refrigerator for up to 4 days or freeze for 2 months. Serve at room temperature with sliced strawberries, if desired.

## Diva Note

Citrus oils are terrific for giving your baked goods an intense flavor, but a little goes a long way. I generally use half the amount of oil when substituting oil for an extract.

Fajita!
# A Father's Day Party

Celebrate Dad with this lively fajita fiesta featuring grilled chicken and beef to stuff into tortillas. This dinner, which is geared for eight to ten celebrants, is so much fun: Start with a make-your-own-drink bar, with guacamole and Chipotle-Corn Salsa with chips for munching. Follow it with a buffet of two different types of fajitas accompanied by a condiment bar, along with interesting Southwestern-inspired side dishes. The dessert is one of my favorites: chocolate cupcakes with a cinnamon frosting, which taste very much like Mexican hot chocolate.

For this casual party, I recommend bold colors, maybe the red, green, and white of the Mexican flag, or other bold primary colors. A serape could serve as your tablecloth, or if you can't find one, a brightly colored tablecloth in a primary color will work well. Small sombreros could serve as place-card holders, and vases filled with cilantro and bright flowers, like sunflowers or Gerbera daisies, will make the table look very festive. Strew red and green chiles down the center of the table as well, to give it a Southwestern feel. If you have a big sombrero, make that your centerpiece: line the crown with plastic to prevent leaks, and arrange small groupings of flowers, chiles, and cilantro around the brim.

# Do-Ahead Countdown

## * 6 weeks ahead

Download shopping list and do-ahead calendar and fill them out

Shop for nonperishables

Make and freeze Fiesta Chocolate Cupcakes and the Cinnamon Buttercream Frosting separately

## * 1 month ahead

Make (but reserve cilantro) and freeze Southwestern Rice

## * 3 days ahead

Make Fresh Lime Margaritas

Make Chipotle-Corn Salsa

## * 2 days ahead

Roast vegetables for America's-Finest-City Guacamole

Marinate chicken for Margaritaville Grilled Chicken and steaks for Grilled Carne Asada

Make Confetti Peppers and Onions

Make (but don't bake) Refried Bean Bake

Remove cupcakes, frosting, and rice from freezer and defrost in refrigerator

## * 1 day ahead

Set the table

Grill (but don't slice) steaks

Cook (but don't slice) Margaritaville Grilled Chicken

Make and refrigerate Cilantro-Onion Relish

## * Day of

Make America's-Finest-City Guacamole

Slice steaks and chicken for fajitas

Bake Refried Bean Bake

Reheat Southwestern Rice with cilantro

Frost cupcakes

# Fresh Lime Margaritas

*Serves 12*

*My family has been eating at Alfonso's of La Jolla, a great Mexican restaurant, for more than 25 years, and in all that time Alfonso has never changed his margaritas. He still makes them with fresh lime and lemon juice. We think this recipe nails Alfonso's secret, so if you can't get to San Diego, try ours. We know you'll love them!*

1 cup freshly squeezed lime juice (from 4 to 5 limes)

6 tablespoons freshly squeezed lemon juice

2 cups triple sec

2 cups white or silver tequila

3 cups ice cubes

**1.** In a large pitcher, stir together the lime juice, lemon juice, triple sec, and tequila.

**2.** Put $1^1/_2$ cups of the ice in a blender and add half of the tequila mixture. Blend until slushy and transfer to a zipper-top plastic bag. Repeat with the remaining ice and tequila mixture. Refrigerate for at least 2 hours. **Diva Do-Ahead:** At this point, you can refrigerate for up to 3 days.

**3.** Pour the margarita mix into a serving pitcher and serve cold.

## Diva Variations

**Margaritas on the Rocks:** Rub a cut lime over the rim of a double rocks glass and dip the rim lightly in coarse kosher salt. Fill with ice and pour tequila mixture from step 1 to the top.

**Virgin Margaritas:** Substitute 2 cups fresh orange juice for the triple sec and 2 cups club soda for the tequila.

# No Shandies? What a Gaff!

Beer is an essential at any barbecue, so why not concoct a special beer drink to help Dad celebrate? A shandy or shandygaff is a mixture of beer and ginger ale, ginger beer, or lemonade. Legend has it that this drink was born when an English pub freshened up some stale beer with a sweet lemon syrup. A thirst-quenching drink to sip on the deck while the barbecue is in full swing, it contains less alcohol than beer. I recommend making ice cubes from lemonade to keep from watering down the shandies.

The formula is simple: 1 part beer, often lager or ale, mixed with 1 part ginger ale, ginger beer, or lemonade, served over crushed or cubed ice if desired. I use 5 ounces of each when making drinks for guests. Serve the shandies in tall pilsner glasses or 12-ounce highball glasses, garnished with a slice of citrus fruit, if you wish.

For a different special beer drink, you could also make something called a snakebite, which is an equal mix of beer (typically lager) and hard cider.

If your guests prefer their beer straight, make sure to buy Mexican beer to go along with the fiesta menu—Dos Equis, Corona, Pacifico, or any other Mexican beer will work. Place a lime wedge in the glass, or on the neck of the bottle, which is the traditional way to serve beer in Mexico.

# America's-Finest-City Guacamole

*Makes about 2 1/2 cups*

*Super Bowl XXXVII was played in San Diego, home to a lot of avocado groves. The growers shared their favorite guacamole recipes with the local newspaper. I've tweaked their recipes and come up with this colorful and spicy variation. You can serve it with tortilla chips or on the condiment bar as a fajita topping.*

1 cup frozen corn kernels, defrosted

1/2 cup coarsely chopped onion

1 jalapeño chile, halved and seeded

2 cloves garlic, unpeeled

2 tablespoons olive oil

1 teaspoon salt

1/2 teaspoon freshly ground black pepper

2 large ripe Hass avocados, peeled and pitted

2 tablespoons freshly squeezed lime juice

2 tablespoons bottled tomatillo salsa (I recommend Frontera brand)

1/4 cup chopped fresh cilantro

6 shakes hot sauce

**1.** Preheat the oven to 400°F. Line a baking sheet with parchment paper, aluminum foil, or a silicone baking liner.

**2.** In a small bowl, toss together the corn, onion, jalapeño, garlic, olive oil, salt, and pepper. Spread the mixture on the prepared baking sheet and roast until the vegetables are lightly browned, 15 to 20 minutes. Remove the mixture from the oven and, when cool enough to handle, peel and chop the jalapeño and squeeze the garlic from its skin.
**Diva Do-Ahead:** At this point, you can cover the mixture and refrigerate for up to 2 days.

**3.** In a medium-size bowl, mash the avocados with the lime juice. Stir in the roasted mixture, then add the salsa, cilantro, and hot sauce, stirring until blended. Taste for seasoning, transfer to a serving bowl, and press plastic wrap onto the surface of the guacamole to keep it from browning.
**Diva Do-Ahead:** At this point, you can refrigerate for up to 12 hours. Serve at room temperature.

## Diva Tip

My friend Phyllis Carey (the Diva of Chicken) sprays water on the cut avocados to keep them from discoloring—it works!

# Chipotle-Corn Salsa

*Serves 8 to 10*

*This crunchy, smoky dip is delicious with tortilla chips, but it's equally good as a relish to serve on the side of grilled pork, seafood, poultry, or beef. Because you may have most of the ingredients in your pantry, this dip is great for spur-of-the-moment get-togethers, though it benefits from allowing the flavors to meld for a few hours before serving.*

2 cups corn kernels, cut from the cob or frozen and defrosted

$1/2$ cup finely chopped red bell pepper

$1/2$ cup finely chopped jicama

4 scallions (white and some tender green parts), chopped

2 chipotle chiles in adobo sauce, finely minced

1 clove garlic, minced

3 tablespoons vegetable oil

2 tablespoons freshly squeezed lime juice

2 tablespoons chopped fresh cilantro

Salt and freshly ground black pepper to taste

In a small mixing bowl, stir together all the ingredients until blended. Taste and adjust seasonings as needed. **Diva Do-Ahead:** At this point, you can cover and refrigerate for up to 3 days. Serve at room temperature.

## Diva Tip

Chipotles in adobo are smoked jalapeño chiles in a sauce. They can be found in cans in the Southwestern section of your supermarket. There are about 6 chiles in a can, and if you are not going to use them all at once you can freeze them for future use. Line a baking sheet or plate with plastic wrap and separate the chiles on the plastic, topping each with a little of the adobo sauce. Freeze the chiles until firm, then store them in a zipper-top plastic bag for up to 6 months. Once you remove them from the freezer, they should defrost in about 30 minutes.

# Grilled Carne Asada

*Serves 8 to 10*

*Dad will be delighted to see Mom and the kids take over the grill for a change! Because the steak needs to be marinated, you can actually grill it ahead of the party, then slice it and serve it at room temperature. Most carne asada in Mexico is made from skirt or hanger steaks, which can be difficult to find in American supermarkets, so the lean flank steak is an easy and delicious substitution.*

1/2 cup freshly squeezed lime juice

1/2 cup spicy tomato juice (such as Bloody Mary mix or Spicy Hot V8 juice)

1/4 cup gold tequila

1/4 cup vegetable oil

1 teaspoon ground cumin

1/2 teaspoon ancho chile powder

1/2 teaspoon dried oregano

Two 1-pound flank steaks

**1.** In a small mixing bowl, whisk together the lime juice, tomato juice, tequila, oil, cumin, chile powder, and oregano until blended.

**2.** Pour the mixture into a 2-gallon zipper-top plastic bag and add the flank steaks to the bag. Seal the bag and turn the steaks in the marinade to coat them. Refrigerate the steaks for at least 8 hours. **Diva Do-Ahead:** At this point, you can refrigerate up to 2 days.

**3.** Prepare a hot charcoal fire or preheat a gas grill or broiler for 10 minutes. Remove the steaks from the marinade and discard the marinade. Grill or broil the steaks on a baking sheet lined with aluminum foil for 4 minutes per side, or until the internal temperature registers 135°F on an instant-read thermometer. **Diva Do-Ahead:** At this point, you can cool the meat to room temperature and refrigerate it for up to 24 hours. One hour before serving, remove from the refrigerator and slice. Allow the meat to rest for 5 minutes before slicing across the grain on an angle into thin strips. Serve at room temperature.

# Cilantro-Onion Relish

*Makes about 2 cups*

**This tangy relish isn't much more than onion and cilantro chopped together, but it's a terrific condiment for fajitas or as a steak or chicken topping.**

1 cup packed fresh cilantro,
  finely chopped
1/2 cup finely chopped sweet
  yellow onion
2 tablespoons finely chopped
  fresh Italian parsley
1 teaspoon salt
1/2 teaspoon freshly ground
  black pepper

In a small bowl, combine all the ingredients. Cover and refrigerate for at least 2 hours to allow the flavors to blend. **Diva Do-Ahead:** At this point, you can refrigerate for up to 24 hours.

## Diva Variation

Stir the relish into 2 cups sour cream to make a delicious sauce for chicken, shrimp, salmon, or beef, or a dip for corn chips.

## Condiments for Fajitas

A big part of this meal will be a condiment bar that should follow the tortillas and meats on the buffet table. Here are a few of my favorite condiments to put out for these fajitas:

* 3 cups salsa
* 3 cups sour cream
* 3 to 4 cups shredded mild cheddar cheese, pepper Jack, Monterey Jack, or *queso fresco*

* Lime wedges (from about 4 limes) for squeezing over the meat
* America's-Finest-City Guacamole (page 162)
* Confetti Peppers and Onions (page 167)
* Cilantro-Onion Relish (above)

# Margaritaville Grilled Chicken

*Serves 8 to 10*

*Nicely spiced, these chicken breasts are simple to marinate and then throw onto the grill for your fajita party. You should slice them into strips after you've grilled them to make them easy to fit into the tortillas for wrapping. Or, if you wish, you can serve them whole.*

1/2 cup fresh orange juice

1/4 cup freshly squeezed lime juice

1/4 cup gold tequila

1/4 cup olive oil

1/2 teaspoon ground cumin

1 chipotle chile in adobo sauce

1/4 cup packed fresh cilantro, plus extra for garnish

10 skinless, boneless chicken breast halves, tenders removed (reserve for another purpose)

**1.** In a food processor or blender, combine the orange juice, lime juice, tequila, oil, cumin, chipotle, and cilantro, and process until smooth.

**2.** Pour the mixture into a 2-gallon zipper-top plastic bag and add the chicken. Seal the bag and turn the chicken in the marinade to coat. Refrigerate for at least 4 hours. **Diva Do-Ahead:** At this point, you can refrigerate overnight. Bring to room temperature before continuing.

**3.** Prepare a hot charcoal fire or preheat a gas grill or the broiler for 10 minutes. Remove the chicken from the marinade, pat dry, and discard the marinade. Grill or broil the chicken on a baking sheet lined with aluminum foil until cooked through and golden brown, about 3 minutes per side. **Diva Do-Ahead:** At this point, you can let cool, cover, and refrigerate for up to 2 days.

**4.** Slice into strips and serve hot, warm, cold, or at room temperature, garnished with chopped cilantro.

## Warming Tortillas for the Crowd

Keeping tortillas warm is sometimes a headache, but if you have a slow cooker, you can wrap the tortillas in aluminum foil and keep them on low; they won't dry out, as they sometimes do in the oven. Otherwise, preheat the oven to 350°F. Wrap the tortillas in aluminum foil and bake on a baking sheet for 10 minutes. Keep them wrapped in foil until ready to use.

# Confetti Peppers and Onions

*Serves 8 to 10*

*These beautifully colored peppers and onions are sautéed until their sugars caramelize, making a delicious topping not only for fajitas, but also for grilled steak, sausages, and chicken. The added spike of tequila gives this dish a wonderfully different flavor, and, although it's optional, works well with the theme. You will need a large and deep sauté pan to accommodate the vegetables until they cook down. Or you may use two smaller sauté pans and divide the batch.*

3 tablespoons olive oil

2 large sweet yellow onions, thinly sliced into half-moons

1 large red onion, thinly sliced into half-moons

2 large red bell peppers, cored, seeded, and cut into thin strips

2 large yellow bell peppers, cored, seeded, and cut into thin strips

1 large green bell pepper, cored, seeded, and cut into thin strips

1$^1$/$_2$ teaspoons sugar

1 teaspoon salt

$^1$/$_2$ teaspoon freshly ground black pepper

1 to 2 tablespoons tequila (optional)

**1.** Heat the oil in a large, deep sauté pan over high heat and add the yellow and red onions, sautéing for about 3 minutes, until they begin to soften.

**2.** Add the bell peppers and continue to sauté for another 5 minutes, until they begin to soften. Add the sugar, salt, and pepper and continue to sauté until the onions begin to turn golden and the mixture is softened. Add the tequila, if using, and sauté another 2 minutes. Taste for seasoning, and add more salt or pepper as necessary. **Diva Do-Ahead:** At this point, you can cool the peppers and onions to room temperature and store in an airtight container in the refrigerator for up to 2 days. Reheat before serving or place in a slow cooker on low to keep warm during the party.

## How Many Tortillas Are Enough?

How many tortillas you need will depend upon the size of the tortilla—for 12-inch tortillas, figure 1 or 2 per person. For 6-inch tortillas, figure 2 or 3 per person. Your choices for tortillas are endless: flour, yellow corn, white corn, spinach, tomato, low-fat, nonfat. For a large gathering, I usually put out an even mix of flour and corn tortillas in the 6-inch size, which is actually much more manageable for eating than the 12-inch size.

# Refried Bean Bake

*Serves 8 to 10*

*This creamy bean casserole, spiked with ground ancho chiles and crowned with melting cheese, is a wonderful side dish not only for this fajita fiesta, but for any barbecue meal. It comes together in less than five minutes, which is a real selling point for me!*

2 tablespoons vegetable oil

1/2 cup chopped sweet yellow onion

1/2 cup chopped green bell pepper

2 teaspoons ancho chile powder

Four 16-ounce cans refried beans

1 cup sour cream

3/4 cup finely shredded mild cheddar cheese

3/4 cup finely shredded Monterey Jack cheese (for more spice, use pepper Jack cheese)

**1.** Coat the inside of a 13 x 9-inch baking dish with nonstick cooking spray. Preheat the oven to 350°F.

**2.** In a medium-size sauté pan, heat the oil over medium-high heat and sauté the onion, pepper, and chile powder for 3 to 4 minutes, until the vegetables just soften. Remove from the heat and transfer to a large mixing bowl to cool slightly.

**3.** Add the refried beans to the cooled vegetables and stir to blend. Add the sour cream and stir until the mixture is blended. Transfer to the prepared baking dish and sprinkle with both cheeses. **Diva Do-Ahead:** At this point, you can cover and refrigerate the casserole for up to 2 days.

**4.** Bake the beans for 20 to 25 minutes, or until the cheese is melted and the casserole is bubbling. Serve hot.

## Slow Cooker Savvy

Coat the inside of a 4- to 6-quart slow cooker insert with nonstick cooking spray. Prepare the casserole up through the sour cream and transfer the mixture to the slow cooker insert. Top with the cheese and cook on low for 4 to 6 hours.

# Southwestern Rice

*Serves 8 to 10*

*This simple rice dish has a lot of flavor and personality, with its spicy bits of sausage, bright red color, and crunchy vegetables. It can be made a couple of days ahead of time and then reheated in the microwave or slow cooker or on the stovetop.*

1 tablespoon vegetable oil

1/2 pound chorizo, finely diced

1/2 cup chopped onion

1/2 cup chopped green bell pepper

2 cloves garlic, minced

1/2 teaspoon ground cumin

1 1/2 cups long-grain rice

2 cups chicken broth

1 cup Bloody Mary mix, spicy tomato juice, or regular tomato juice

1/2 cup chopped fresh cilantro

**1.** In a large saucepan, heat the oil and add the chorizo, rendering the fat in the sausage. Remove all but 1 tablespoon of fat from the bottom of the pan.

**2.** Add the onion, green pepper, garlic, and cumin, sautéing until the onion is softened, about 3 minutes. Add the rice and stir to coat.

**3.** Carefully pour in the chicken broth and Bloody Mary mix. Bring the mixture to a boil, reduce the heat to a simmer, and cook, covered, for 17 minutes, or until the liquid in the pan has evaporated and the rice is fluffy. **Diva Do-Ahead:** At this point, bring the rice to room temperature, transfer to a large zipper-top plastic bag, and refrigerate for up to 2 days or freeze for up to 1 month. Before serving defrost, if necessary, then reheat in the microwave on 50 percent power for 5 to 7 minutes until heated through. **Stir in the cilantro and serve.**

## Slow Cooker Savvy

To reheat in the slow cooker, add 1/4 cup chicken broth to the slow cooker along with the cold rice and heat on low for 2 hours, stirring a few times during the heating cycle.

# Fiesta Chocolate Cupcakes with Cinnamon Buttercream Frosting

*Makes 24 cupcakes*

*Just the right size to end the fajita buffet, these little bites will become a favorite with any dad and his clan. Cupcakes are all the rage these days, and these deep chocolate cupcakes taste like a cup of Mexican hot chocolate.*

## Cupcakes

2 cups granulated sugar

1 cup whole milk

1/2 cup vegetable oil

2 large eggs

2 teaspoons pure vanilla extract or vanilla bean paste (see page 171)

1 3/4 cups all-purpose flour

3/4 cup Dutch-processed cocoa powder

1 1/2 teaspoons baking powder

1 1/2 teaspoons baking soda

1 teaspoon salt

1/2 teaspoon ground cinnamon

1 cup boiling water

## Frosting

4 1/2 cups confectioners' sugar

1 cup (2 sticks) unsalted butter, at room temperature

1 tablespoon pure vanilla extract

1 1/2 teaspoons ground cinnamon

2 tablespoons milk

1/4 cup sour cream

**1.** Preheat the oven to 350°F. Line all the wells in two 12-cup muffin tins with liners or coat with nonstick cooking spray. In the large bowl of an electric mixer, mix together the granulated sugar, milk, oil, eggs, and vanilla extract until blended.

**2.** Combine the flour, cocoa powder, baking powder, baking soda, salt, and cinnamon in a medium-size mixing bowl. Gradually add to the sugar mixture, blending until the mixture begins to come together. Very slowly, add the boiling water to the bowl and blend until the mixture is smooth.

**3.** Ladle or scoop the batter into the muffin tins, filling each cup three-quarters full. Bake the cupcakes for 15 to 18 minutes, until a skewer inserted into the center of each one comes out clean.

## Chocolate Shavings and Curls

A simple garnish for any chocolate dessert is shaved chocolate. I recommend using a microplane grater, which is a handy gadget that will grate not only chocolate, but citrus zest, fresh ginger, whole nutmeg, cinnamon sticks, and a host of other ingredients.

For chocolate curls, you will need a swivel peeler and a block of chocolate. Make long swipes down the block with the peeler to get long curls.

**4.** Cool the cupcakes completely in their pans on wire racks. **Diva Do-Ahead:** At this point, you can cover the cupcakes and keep them at room temperature for up to 2 days or freeze them for up to 6 weeks. Defrost before proceeding.

**5.** To make the frosting, in the bowl of an electric mixer, stir the confectioners' sugar to aerate it. Add the butter, vanilla extract, cinnamon, and 1 tablespoon of the milk. Beat on high speed until the frosting is spreadable. Add the sour cream and beat again. If the frosting is stiff, add a few more drops of milk, beating after each addition. **Diva Do-Ahead:** At this point, you can cover the frosting and refrigerate for up to 5 days or freeze for up to 6 weeks. Bring to room temperature before proceeding. Frost the cooled cupcakes.

*The Diva Says*

Vanilla bean-paste, vanilla extract— what's a Diva to do? For cooked or baked items I recommend vanilla bean paste because it contains less alcohol, which burns off during cooking, leaving less vanilla flavor. For uncooked items, frostings, whipped creams, extract is fine. Use paste in the same amount as the extract.

The Grand Old Flag

# An All-American Fourth of July Barbecue

July 4, 1776, was the day that the Declaration of Independence was adopted by the Continental Congress to declare the United States free from British rule. A quotation in 1777 in the *Virginia Gazette* sums up the feeling about this important occasion: "Thus may the 4th of July, that glorious and ever memorable day, be celebrated through America, by the sons of freedom from age to age till time shall be no more."

Modern celebrations of Independence Day usually include a barbecue, followed by the traditional trek to watch fireworks. In July, summer fruits and vegetables are at their peak, so take advantage of their abundance to make this terrific fresh dinner for eight to ten people.

For starters, the red limonata is a great refresher for the adults. For nonalcoholic beverages, try adding a bit of green food coloring to lemonade to get a light blue drink, or add grenadine for red lemonade. Blue cheese and roasted pecans make a tasty dip for crudités, and some spiced crackers provide an addictive snack for young and old alike.

Burgers and hot dogs are typically the entrées of choice for this holiday. Spice up your burgers with zesty compound butters to keep them moist during grilling and give them a dynamic flavor. Instead of hot dogs, grill your favorite sausages, topping them with sautéed onions and peppers. (But feel free to toss some hot dogs on the grill for the kids.) Corn on the cob is traditional, and you can pair yours with the same compound butters used for stuffing the burgers. A savory new twist on traditional baked beans, a layered salad with bright sun-dried tomato vinaigrette, and a potato salad flavored with scallions and bacon round out the holiday side dishes. To top off the barbecue, for dessert there's a choice between cake decorated with a flag design in berries and whipped cream and a patriotic ice cream cake, as well as macadamia nut ice cream sandwiches.

Decorations for this barbecue must include the colors of the flag! Choose one color as the primary décor and accent with the other two, or use them all in punches of color, in the tablecloth, napkins, plates, cutlery, and glassware. For this casual dinner, which you may well serve in the backyard, I think paper and heavy plastic work very well for all the tableware, but you can certainly use your everyday dishes and stainless if you wish.

Flowers such as red and white carnations or pots of red geraniums, plus citronella candles for outdoor dining, are a good bet for table decorations, as are red, white, and silver Mylar streamers. Roll flatware with red, white, and blue ribbons and attach an American flag sticker to secure the napkin around the flatware, or use small star-shaped cookie cutters as napkin rings.

## 3...2...1...

## Do-Ahead Countdown

Choose between the Old Glory Cake and Red, White, and Blue Ice Cream Cake. Then:

### ✴ 2 months ahead

Download shopping list and do-ahead calendar and fill them out

Shop for nonperishables

Bake and freeze cookies for Macadamia Nut Ice Cream Sandwiches

Bake and freeze cake for Old Glory Cake (if serving)

### ✴ 1 month ahead

Make and freeze Crazy Crackers

Make and freeze compound butters and patties for Grilled Stuffed Burgers

Make and freeze Macademia Nut Ice Cream Sandwiches

Make and freeze Red, White, and Blue Ice Cream Cake (if serving)

### ✴ 1 week ahead

Make base for Limonata alla Lambrusco

### ✴ 5 days ahead

Make Sautéed Peppers

### ✴ 4 days ahead

Make Sun-Dried Tomato Vinaigrette

### ✴ 3 days ahead

Remove Crazy Crackers, burgers, compound butters, and cake from freezer and defrost in refrigerator

Make Roasted Pecan–Blue Cheese Dip

Poach sausages

Make Smoky Maple Baked Beans

### ✴ 1 day ahead

Prepare and assemble crudités

Assemble Greens and Veggies

Make Red Bliss Potato Salad with Bacon and Scallion Dressing

Assemble Old Glory Cake if serving

### ✴ Day of

Set the table

Grill sausages

Boil corn for Perfect Corn on the Cob

Toss Greens and Veggies with Sun-Dried Tomato Vinaigrette

Finish Red, White, and Blue Ice Cream Cake (if serving)

# Limonata alla Lambrusco

*Serves 12*

*A terrific apéritif, this combination of lemon juice, white wine, and sparkling red wine will make a splash at any summertime get-together. Its reddish color makes it perfect for a Fourth of July celebration. Lambrusco is what the Italians call a particular soft (not too overpowering) sparkling red wine; it's inexpensive and pairs well with the lemonade. You can certainly continue to serve plain Lambrusco throughout the meal if you wish; it will go well with the burgers and sausages. Or you may want to switch to beer; see page 161 for some tips on beer drinks.*

One 750-milliliter bottle chilled white wine, such as Sauvignon Blanc or Pinot Grigio

2 cups superfine sugar

1½ cups freshly squeezed lemon juice (from about 3 lemons)

Two 750-milliliter bottles chilled Lambrusco

Ice cubes

**1.** In a large pitcher, combine the white wine, sugar, and lemon juice, stirring until the sugar is dissolved. **Diva Do-Ahead:** At this point, you can cover and refrigerate for up to 1 week.

**2.** When ready to serve, divide the white wine mixture between 2 large pitchers, and add a bottle of Lambrusco to each pitcher, stirring to combine.

**3.** Fill double rocks glasses with ice cubes and pour the limonata over the ice. Serve immediately.

The Diva Says

Because the Lambrusco is bubbly, add it at the last minute so that it maintains its fizz.

# Roasted Pecan–Blue Cheese Dip with Crudités

*Makes about 2¹/₂ cups*

*My favorite nut and my favorite cheese—I'm in heaven! This dip is terrific with fresh vegetables or crackers. I've even served it on a cheese and fruit tray in small ramekins, accompanied by apple wedges. It is also delicious spread on endive leaves and garnished with more toasted chopped pecans. You can toast extra pecans and freeze them, then defrost and prepare the dip.*

One 8-ounce package cream
  cheese, softened
1 cup crumbled blue cheese
¹/₂ cup mayonnaise
2 teaspoons Worcestershire
  sauce
¹/₄ teaspoon hot sauce
1 cup chopped toasted pecans
  (see page 114)
Crudités of your choice
  (see pages 23–25)

**1.** In a food processor or medium-size bowl using an electric mixer, combine the cream cheese, blue cheese, mayonnaise, Worcestershire, and hot sauce until smooth. Cover and refrigerate for at least 2 hours. **Diva Do-Ahead:** At this point, you can refrigerate for up to 3 days or freeze for up to 6 weeks.

**2.** When ready to serve, stir in ³/₄ cup of the pecans. Place dip in a serving bowl and garnish with the remaining pecans. Serve with crudités.

# Crazy Crackers

*Makes about 8 cups*

*These little crackers are one of the most popular snacks at my picnic and tailgate cooking classes. Crispy, salty, and buttery, they are addictive! Try them for a quick snack or keep them in the freezer for unexpected company.*

Two 10-ounce boxes Sunshine brand oyster crackers

1 cup Orville Redenbacher's Butter Flavor Popping and Topping Oil

1 envelope Hidden Valley Ranch salad dressing mix

2 tablespoons dried dill

1 tablespoon lemon pepper seasoning

1 teaspoon Lawry's garlic salt

1/2 teaspoon cayenne pepper

Empty the crackers into a large bowl. Pour the oil over the crackers and sprinkle with the remaining ingredients. Stir with a large spoon, being careful not to break up the crackers. When evenly coated, continue to toss until the crackers appear to be dry, about 5 minutes. **Diva Do-Ahead:** At this point, you can transfer to zipper-top plastic bags and store at room temperature for 1 week or freeze for up to 6 months.

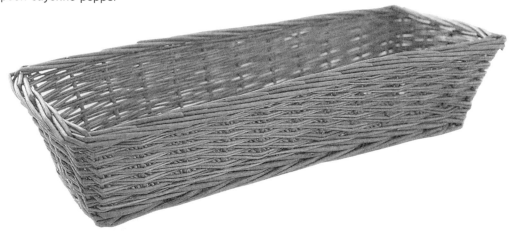

# Grilled Stuffed Burgers

*Makes 8 burgers*

*I've had all kinds of burgers stuffed with vegetables, with cheese, and with a myriad of other foods, but my favorite way to stuff a burger is with a compound butter. The butter melts during the cooking process, keeping the burgers moist and infusing the meat with a delightful flavor. You can ask your guests which "flavor" burger they want and then stuff in the appropriate compound butter, or just make up the burgers ahead of time with your theme flavor. A small dollop of the butter served over the finished burger will be the icing on the patty!*

3 pounds ground round

2 teaspoons salt

1 teaspoon freshly ground black pepper

4 tablespoons compound butter of your choice (see pages 181–184), plus more for garnish

**1.** In a large mixing bowl, break the meat apart and sprinkle with the salt and pepper. Blend until combined. Using both hands, form the meat into 8 equal portions. Shape each portion into a ball, break the ball in half, and place $1/2$ tablespoon of compound butter in the center of the ball, enclosing it in the meat and flattening the ball into a $3/4$-inch-thick patty. Continue to shape the remaining meat in the same way, stacking the patties separated by waxed paper or plastic wrap. **Diva Do-Ahead:** At this point, you can refrigerate the patties for up to 12 hours, or freeze for up to 1 month. Defrost before proceeding.

**2.** Prepare a hot fire in a charcoal grill or preheat a gas grill for 10 minutes. Grill the patties for about 4 minutes per side, turning once during the cooking time for medium-rare burgers. If you like your burgers a bit more well done, move them to a cooler part of the grill once they reach the medium-rare stage, and cook for another 2 minutes. Serve the burgers garnished with a pat of compound butter.

## Diva Wisdom

Never press down on burgers while they are grilling. This will drain all the juices away and give you a dry burger, as well as fire flare-ups.

# Burger Condiments

Every burger needs its garnish, so make sure to have a condiment bar set up for your burgers. It can be as simple as ketchup, mustard, and relish, but I find it interesting and much more fun to have lots of choices.

Here are a few of my family's favorites:

* Ketchup
* Mustard (whole-grain, ballpark style, and Dijon)
* Mayonnaise
* Teriyaki sauce
* Green and red relish
* Sliced dill pickles
* Lettuce
* Sliced tomatoes
* Sliced red onion or sautéed sweet yellow onions
* Sautéed or roasted sliced mushrooms
* Chunky salsa
* Pineapple slices
* Sliced cheeses (cheddar, American, Swiss)
* Crumbled cheeses (blue, feta, goat)
* Cooked bacon strips or crumbles

## COMPOUND BUTTERS

### Béarnaise Butter

Makes 1 cup

*The flavors of France will enhance any burger, but you can also use this butter over cooked vegetables, grilled meats, seafood, or poultry.*

**1 cup (2 sticks) unsalted butter, softened**
**2 cloves garlic, minced**
**2 tablespoons Dijon mustard**
**2 tablespoons Worcestershire sauce**
**2 teaspoons dried tarragon**

In a medium-size bowl, cream the butter together with the other ingredients. Place a large piece of plastic wrap on the counter and transfer the butter to the plastic wrap, rolling it and forming a 1-inch-thick log. Twist the ends of the plastic wrap to seal. **Diva Do-Ahead:** At this point, you can refrigerate for up to 5 days or freeze for up to 1 month.

### Blue Cheese Butter

Makes about 1²/₃ cups

*Tangy blue cheese, butter, and a few other flavors combine to make this dynamite burger stuffer, which is also a great topper for grilled steak, chicken, steamed potatoes, or grilled bread. I love the flavor of Maytag blue cheese, but you can substitute your favorite blue-veined cheese, such as Stilton, Gorgonzola, or Point Reyes.*

**1 cup (2 sticks) unsalted butter, softened**
**²/₃ cup crumbled blue cheese**
**2 teaspoons Worcestershire sauce**
**¹/₂ teaspoon freshly ground black pepper**
**4 shakes hot sauce**

In a medium-size bowl, cream together the butter, blue cheese, Worcestershire, pepper, and hot sauce. Place a large piece of plastic wrap on the counter and transfer the butter to the plastic wrap, rolling it and forming a 1-inch-thick log. Twist the ends of the plastic wrap to seal. **Diva Do-Ahead:** At this point, you can refrigerate for up to 5 days or freeze for up to 1 month.

## Chipotle-Lime-Cilantro Butter

Makes about 1 1/3 cups

*Smoky rather than hot, this compound butter gets a real zip from chipotles and a bit of cheese.*

**1 chipotle chile in adobo sauce, minced, with about a teaspoon of adobo sauce**
**2 tablespoons freshly squeezed lime juice**
**1 cup (2 sticks) unsalted butter, softened**
**1/3 cup finely shredded Monterey Jack cheese**
**1/4 cup chopped fresh cilantro**

In a medium-size bowl, cream together the butter, chipotle in adobo sauce, lime juice, cheese, and cilantro until blended. Place a large piece of plastic wrap on the counter and transfer the butter to the plastic wrap, rolling it and forming a 1-inch-thick log. Twist the ends of the plastic wrap to seal. **Diva Do-Ahead:** At this point, you can refrigerate for up to 5 days or freeze for up to 1 month.

## Sun-Dried Tomato Butter

Makes about 1 1/3 cups

*This bit of Italy will give your burgers, steaks, chicken, seafood, or breads a beautiful hint of red. I like to make this compound butter in the food processor so that I can chop all the ingredients in one step. If you don't have a food processor, chop the tomatoes,* garlic, basil, and parsley by hand and mix them into the butter.

**1 cup (2 sticks) unsalted butter, softened**
**1/4 cup grated pecorino Romano cheese**
**6 oil-packed sun-dried tomatoes, halved**
**1/4 cup packed fresh Italian parsley leaves**
**6 fresh basil leaves**
**2 cloves garlic**

Place all the ingredients in the work bowl of a food processor and process until smooth. Place a large piece of plastic wrap on the counter and transfer the butter to the plastic wrap, rolling it and forming a 1-inch-thick log. Twist the ends of the plastic wrap to seal. **Diva Do-Ahead:** At this point, you can refrigerate for up to 5 days or freeze for up to 1 month.

## Basil-Pesto Butter

Makes 1 cup

*This simple butter is also terrific on seafood and chicken. I love to stir it into orzo pasta for a quick side dish and slather it on bread for a peppy counterpart to the main course.*

**1/2 cup (1 stick) unsalted butter, softened**
**1/2 cup basil pesto, homemade (see page 36) or store-bought**

In a small bowl, stir together the butter and pesto until blended. Place a large piece of plastic wrap on the counter and transfer the butter to the plastic wrap, rolling it and forming a 1-inch-thick log. Twist the ends of the plastic wrap to seal. **Diva Do-Ahead:** At this point, you can refrigerate for up to 5 days or freeze for up to 1 month.

## Diva Tip

Try using cilantro pesto or sun-dried tomato pesto for a different flavor combination.

# Roasted Garlic Butter

Makes about 1 1/3 cups

*This robust butter is also delicious spread on steaks, chicken, and breads, and it's super melted, then tossed with pasta. It is the only compound butter here that does not freeze well, because the mellow flavor of the roasted garlic will fade. Store it in the refrigerator, where it will keep for up to a week.*

**1 cup (2 sticks) unsalted butter, softened**
**10 cloves garlic, roasted (see The Diva Says) and squeezed from their skins**
**1/4 cup chopped fresh Italian parsley**

In a medium-size bowl, mash the butter into the garlic until the mixture is smooth. Add the parsley and continue to blend until well combined. Transfer to an airtight container or place a large piece of plastic wrap on the counter and transfer the butter to the plastic wrap, rolling it and forming a 1-inch-thick log. Twist the ends of the plastic wrap to seal. **Diva Do-Ahead:** At this point, you can refrigerate for up to 1 week.

# Romano-Oregano Butter

Makes about 1 2/3 cups

*Strong Romano cheese, spicy red pepper flakes, and pungent oregano combine to make this butter a perfect complement to chicken, vegetables, and pastas, as well as burgers. I love to spread this butter on bread and grill it until golden brown.*

**1 cup (2 sticks) unsalted butter, softened**
**2/3 cup grated pecorino Romano cheese**
**2 teaspoons dried oregano**
**1/4 teaspoon red pepper flakes**

In a medium-size bowl, cream together all the ingredients until blended. Place a large piece of plastic wrap on the counter and transfer the butter to the plastic wrap, rolling it and forming a 1-inch-thick log. Twist the ends of the plastic wrap to seal. **Diva Do-Ahead:** At this point, you can refrigerate for up to 5 days or freeze for up to 1 month.

The Diva Says

To roast a head of garlic, preheat the oven to 400°F. Remove the wispy, papery outsides of the garlic and cut off the top of the head to expose the cloves. Place on a piece of aluminum foil large enough to wrap around the garlic. Drizzle the garlic with olive oil, sprinkle with salt and pepper, and wrap in the foil. Bake until the garlic is soft, about 30 minutes. Let cool for 15 minutes, then press the garlic out of the skin by gently squeezing. Roasted garlic can be stored in olive oil in the refrigerator for up to 1 week.

## Porcini-Sage Butter

Makes about 1½ cups

*Earthy porcini mushrooms will flavor your burgers, as well as chicken, steaks, potatoes, rice, and pasta.*

**1 cup (2 sticks) unsalted butter**
**½ cup dried porcini mushrooms**
**2 teaspoons dried sage**
**½ teaspoon salt**
**4 shakes hot sauce**

Place all the ingredients in the work bowl of a food processor and process until smooth. Place a large piece of plastic wrap on the counter and transfer the butter to the plastic wrap, rolling it and forming a 1-inch-thick log. Twist the ends of the plastic wrap to seal. **Diva Do-Ahead:** At this point, you can refrigerate for up to 5 days or freeze for up to 1 month.

## Teriyaki-Sesame Butter

Makes about 1½ cups

*A great way to infuse your burgers with some Asian flavor, this butter is also delicious over asparagus or stirred into cooked rice. This butter doesn't freeze rock-solid, so it will be a little soft even when you remove it from the freezer.*

**1 cup (2 sticks) unsalted butter**
**¼ cup teriyaki sauce**
**¼ cup sesame seeds**
**2 scallions (white and some tender green parts), finely chopped**

In a small bowl, stir together all the ingredients. Place a large piece of plastic wrap on the counter and transfer the butter to the plastic wrap, rolling it and forming a 1-inch-thick log. Twist the ends of the plastic wrap to seal. **Diva Do-Ahead:** At this point, you can refrigerate for up to 5 days or freeze for up to 1 month.

## Mediterranean Butter

Makes about 1½ cups

*Kalamata olives, garlic, oregano, and lemon zest give this butter a taste of the Greek islands. The food processor does a great job of pureeing, but you can mince all the ingredients together by hand for a chunkier butter.*

**1 cup (2 sticks) unsalted butter**
**½ cup Kalamata olives, pitted**
**3 cloves garlic**
**2 teaspoons dried oregano**
**2 teaspoons lemon zest**
**Pinch red pepper flakes**

Place all the ingredients in the work bowl of a food processor and process until smooth. Place a large piece of plastic wrap on the counter and transfer the butter to the plastic wrap, rolling it and forming a 1-inch-thick log. Twist the ends of the plastic wrap to seal. **Diva Do-Ahead:** At this point, you can refrigerate for up to 5 days or freeze for up to 1 month.

# Grilled Sausages and Sautéed Peppers

*Serves 8*

*The combination of sausage and sautéed peppers brings back memories of childhood picnics with my grandparents and their Italian friends. My grandfather made his own Italian fennel-seasoned sweet sausage, which he grilled over charcoal. Grandma would then stuff them into her homemade bread, along with a good serving of her sautéed sweet peppers, onions, and a bit of tomato. Each bite was punctuated by the squirt of sausage, then the sweetness of peppers, and finally the crusty bread. The sausages can be poached ahead of time and then grilled right before serving, and the peppers can be prepared up to five days in advance, and reheated or served at room temperature. These sausages are delicious on ciabatta or another type of thin crusty roll.*

16 sweet Italian sausages

2 cups beer or water

2 tablespoons olive oil

2 large onions, thinly sliced into half-moons

3 large red bell peppers, cored, seeded, and thinly sliced

6 small Italian frying peppers, cored, seeded, and thinly sliced

2 tablespoons sugar

1 teaspoon salt

1/2 teaspoon freshly ground black pepper

1/4 cup tomato puree

2 tablespoons balsamic vinegar

**1.** Arrange the sausages in a skillet large enough to accommodate them in one layer or use 2 skillets. Add the beer to the skillet and enough water, if necessary, to come up halfway around the sausages. Bring to a boil and simmer the sausages for about 5 minutes. Prick the sausages with the tip of a sharp knife to allow some of the fat to escape. They should be cooked about halfway. **Diva Do-Ahead:** At this point, you can allow them to cool and refrigerate in an airtight container for up to 3 days.

**2.** Prepare a hot fire in a charcoal grill or preheat a gas grill for 10 minutes. Grill the sausages until they are browned and cooked through, about 5 minutes per side. Transfer the sausages to a platter and keep warm.

**3.** In a large skillet, heat the olive oil and add the onions, sautéing for about 4 minutes, until the onions begin to soften and become translucent. Add the bell peppers, frying peppers, sugar, salt, and pepper, and sauté another 7 to 8 minutes, until the peppers begins to soften and brown.

*continued on next page*

## Grilled Sausages and Sautéed Peppers *continued*

**4.** Add the tomato puree and cook another 4 to 5 minutes, until the mixture is thickened. Stir in the vinegar and cook another minute. Taste for seasoning and add additional salt and pepper if desired. **Diva Do-Ahead:** At this point, you can cover and refrigerate the peppers for up to 5 days. Reheat on the stovetop or allow to come to room temperature before serving. Serve the grilled sausages in rolls topped with some of the pepper mixture.

### Diva Variations

Your favorite sausages can be substituted: bratwurst, knockwurst, kielbasa, andouille (heat meter warning!), hot or spicy Italian sausages, chicken or turkey varieties, linguiça, chorizo, etc. Some sausages are already cooked, such as kielbasa or smoked sausages; in that case, you can forgo the poaching in step 1.

## Diva Grill Tip

If you like, you can grill slices of onions and peppers and use those with the sausages, rather than sautéing them. I recommend using varicolored bell peppers, as the Italian frying peppers don't stand up to the grill very well.

# Perfect Corn on the Cob

*Serves 8 to 10*

*Corn on the cob is the quintessential summertime treat—white, yellow, and bicolored corn picked fresh and then steamed, boiled, or grilled is a mouthwatering addition to any Independence Day feast. Up the ante a bit with a selection of compound butters that will give this corn a tasty new twist. Because you'll be grilling the main course, I think boiling the corn indoors is a great option, giving the grillmaster room to work. You will need two large pots of boiling water on the stovetop, and you can keep the corn in the hot water for up to 30 minutes before serving.*

8 quarts water

¼ cup sugar

16 ears corn, husks and silks removed and ends trimmed if necessary

Compound butter of your choice (see pages 181–184)

Divide the water and sugar between two large stockpots. Add 8 ears corn to each pot and bring the water to a boil. Once the corn has come to a boil, turn off the heat and allow the corn to sit in the water for 10 minutes. **Diva-Do-Ahead:** The corn can sit in the water for 30 minutes total before serving. Remove from the water and serve hot with your choice of compound butter.

# Smoky Maple Baked Beans

*Serves 8 to 10*

*These baked beans in a smoky maple syrup barbecue sauce are chock full of delicious bits of pork sausage, sautéed onion, and bacon, making them a delicious side dish for your Fourth of July barbecue party or a great take-along to a picnic or potluck. The beans actually improve if they are made a day or two ahead of time, and you can keep them warm in the slow cooker for serving. And vegetarians can omit the bacon and sausage.*

6 slices bacon, chopped

3/4 pound bulk pork sausage (I like Jimmy Dean)

1 large sweet onion, chopped

1 1/2 cups ketchup

1/2 cup firmly packed dark brown sugar

1/4 cup light molasses

1/4 cup pure maple syrup

2 tablespoons Worcestershire sauce

2 tablespoons yellow mustard

2 tablespoons apple cider vinegar

1/2 teaspoon chipotle chile powder, or more to taste (optional)

Five 16-ounce cans plain baked beans

**1.** In a large Dutch oven, fry the bacon until it is almost crisp. Remove from the pot and set aside. Add the sausage and onion and sauté, breaking up the sausage into small pieces until it is no longer pink and the onion is translucent. Remove all the fat from the pot.

**2.** Add the reserved bacon, the ketchup, brown sugar, molasses, maple syrup, Worcestershire, mustard, vinegar, and the chile powder, if using, to the pot and bring to a boil, stirring until the mixture is incorporated.

**3.** Add the beans to the pot, stirring to combine, and simmer for 1 hour. **Diva Do-Ahead:** At this point, you can cool the beans to room temperature, cover, and refrigerate for up to 3 days. Reheat on the stovetop or bake uncovered in a Dutch oven in a 350°F oven for 1 hour. Serve hot.

## Diva Tip

To remove large amounts of fat or water from a pan, use a bulb baster. But don't discard the fat in the sink, as it will solidify and clog your pipes. Learn from the Diva's mistakes!

## Slow Cooker Savvy

Prepare the recipe through step 2, pour the sauce mixture into a 5- to 6-quart slow cooker, add the beans, and cook on low for 6 hours.

# Greens and Veggies with Sun-Dried Tomato Vinaigrette

*Serves 10*

*This beautiful salad, with crisp lettuce and other colorful veggies, is tossed with a zesty sun-dried tomato vinaigrette (which is also scrumptious tossed into pasta or potato salads). The dressing is best made at least eight hours ahead of time to allow the flavors to develop, and it can be refrigerated for up to four days. The veggies and greens can be layered in the salad bowl and refrigerated overnight. Or you can cut up all the vegetables and store them overnight in zipper-top plastic bags before assembling the salad.*

1/2 cup extra-virgin olive oil

1/4 cup red wine vinegar

1/2 cup finely chopped red onion

1/2 cup oil-packed sun-dried tomatoes, drained and cut into matchsticks

2 cloves garlic, minced

1 teaspoon salt

1/2 teaspoon freshly ground black pepper

One 10-ounce bag romaine lettuce, chopped

4 slices red onion, separated into rings

1 European cucumber, cut into 1/4-inch slices

1 cup cherry or pear tomatoes

1 cup cheese tortellini, cooked and cooled

One 10-ounce bag baby spinach

One 6-ounce jar marinated artichoke hearts, drained and halved

1/2 cup coarsely shredded aged provolone cheese or Parmesan cheese

1/4 cup chopped fresh basil

**1.** In a small mixing bowl, whisk together the oil and vinegar, then stir in the onion, tomatoes, garlic, salt, and pepper. Refrigerate for at least 8 hours. **Diva Do-Ahead:** At this point, you can refrigerate for up to 4 days. Remove from the refrigerator about an hour before serving, to allow the oil to come to room temperature.

**2.** In a large salad bowl, layer the remaining ingredients in the order listed, sprinkling the basil over the top. **Diva Do-Ahead:** At this point, you can cover and refrigerate for up to 24 hours.

**3.** When ready to serve, pour the dressing over the salad and serve at room temperature.

# Red Bliss Potato Salad with Bacon and Scallion Dressing

*Serves 8 to 10*

*Red bliss is a type of red potato, but the real "bliss" here is in the sublime taste of this delicious summer side dish. If you can't find red bliss, then new potatoes, white creamers, or Yukon Golds will also work well. I like to make the salad the day before serving it so that the potatoes absorb the flavors from the dressing.*

4 pounds medium-size red potatoes

2 teaspoons salt

4 ribs celery, finely chopped

4 scallions (white and tender green parts), finely chopped

1¹/2 tablespoons white vinegar

1 tablespoon olive oil

1/2 teaspoon freshly ground black pepper

1¹/2 cups mayonnaise

1/4 cup sour cream

2 teaspoons lemon zest

2 to 3 tablespoons whole milk

12 strips bacon, cooked and crumbled

1 teaspoon sweet paprika, for garnish

**1.** Place the potatoes in a 5-quart saucepan and cover with water. Add 1 teaspoon of the salt and bring to a boil. Simmer the potatoes for 20 to 25 minutes, or until a sharp knife inserted into the potatoes goes in easily.

**2.** Drain the potatoes and cool completely, or they will crumble and fall apart. **Diva Do-Ahead:** At this point, you can refrigerate for up to 24 hours.

**3.** Peel the potatoes if you prefer, or leave the skins on. Cut them into bite-size pieces and place in a large mixing bowl. Sprinkle the potatoes with remaining 1 teaspoon salt and add the celery and scallions to the bowl, tossing to mix. Add the vinegar, oil, and pepper to the potatoes and toss to coat.

**4.** In a small bowl, whisk together the mayonnaise, sour cream, and lemon zest, stirring in 2 tablespoons of the milk to thin the dressing, or more if necessary. Add some of the mayonnaise mixture to the potatoes, tossing to coat. Taste the potatoes for seasoning, adding more salt and pepper if necessary. Cover and refrigerate the salad and leftover dressing for at least 4 hours. **Diva Do-Ahead:** At this point, you can refrigerate for up to 24 hours.

**5.** Thirty minutes before serving, stir the potatoes and add more dressing if necessary. Stir in the bacon and toss again. Serve the potato salad cold, garnished with the paprika.

# Macadamia Nut Ice Cream Sandwiches

*Makes about 12 sandwiches*

*There is something so liberating about eating with your hands, and eating ice cream in the summer after a barbecue is a highlight for me. These creamy, crunchy, nutty cookie sandwiches are a delicious way to end your Fourth of July barbecue, and the best part is that you can be make a them a month ahead of time.*

1 cup (2 sticks) unsalted butter, at room temperature

1 cup firmly packed light brown sugar

1/2 cup granulated sugar

2 large eggs

1 tablespoon pure vanilla extract or vanilla bean paste (see page 171)

2 1/4 cups all-purpose flour

2 cups chopped macadamia nuts

1 1/2 cups chocolate chips (white, milk, or semisweet)

1 teaspoon salt

1 teaspoon baking soda

3 pints coffee or vanilla ice cream

Shaved chocolate, toasted coconut, toasted macadamia nuts, chocolate-covered espresso beans, and/or red, white, and blue sprinkles for garnish

**1.** In the bowl of an electric mixer, beat together the butter, brown sugar, and granulated sugar until fluffy. Add the eggs and vanilla extract and beat until the mixture appears curdled, scraping down the sides of the bowl if necessary.

**2.** Add the flour, nuts, chocolate chips, salt, and baking soda, beating until the mixture is combined. **Diva Do-Ahead:** At this point, you can refrigerate the cookie dough in zipper-top plastic bags for 3 days or freeze for up to 2 months. Defrost before proceeding.

**3.** Preheat the oven to 375°F. Line baking sheets with parchment paper, aluminum foil, or silicone baking liners. Using a scoop, drop tablespoon-size pieces of dough onto the cookie sheets about 3 inches apart. You should end up with about 24 cookies. Wet your hands and press the cookies down, so that they are uniform in thickness. **Diva Do-Ahead:** At this point, you can cover and freeze the cookie sheets. When the cookies are frozen, remove them to zipper-top plastic bags and freeze for up to 2 months. Defrost before baking. Bake the cookies for 10 to 12 minutes, until browned around the edges and beginning to set in the middle. Remove the sheets

*continued on next page*

# Macadamia Nut Ice Cream Sandwiches *continued*

to a rack to cool for 10 minutes. Remove the cookies from the sheets using a spatula and cool completely on wire racks. **Diva Do-Ahead:** At this point, you can freeze the cookies in an airtight container for up to 2 months.

**4.** Soften the ice cream so that it is spreadable. Place one cookie, flat side up, on a piece of plastic wrap about 12 inches square. Place a generous scoop of ice cream onto the cookie and spread to cover the cookie in an even layer. Top with another cookie, flat side down. Roll the sides in a garnish of your choice, coating the entire outside edge. Bring up the sides of the plastic wrap and secure with a twist tie. Freeze the sandwiches for at least 4 hours, until firm. **Diva Do-Ahead:** At this point, you can freeze for up to 1 month.

# Old Glory Cake

*Serves 10 to 12*

*This delicious cake is decorated to resemble the Stars and Stripes, with strawberry stripes and blueberries as the background for whipped cream stars. The plain cake can be baked two months ahead and frozen, and the final dessert can be assembled the day before and refrigerated until serving time.*

2 cups cake flour

1³/4 cups sugar

1 teaspoon baking powder

¹/2 teaspoon baking soda

¹/2 teaspoon salt

³/4 cup (1¹/2 sticks) unsalted butter, softened and cut into ¹/2-inch bits

1 cup buttermilk

4 large eggs

2 teaspoons lemon extract

1 teaspoon lemon zest

### Assembly

2 cups heavy cream

2 cups mascarpone cheese

¹/3 cup sugar

3 pints medium-size strawberries, stems removed (see page 194)

1 pint blueberries, picked over for stems

**1.** Preheat the oven to 375°F. Coat the inside of a 13 x 9-inch baking dish with nonstick cooking spray.

**2.** In the bowl of an electric mixer, combine the flour, sugar, baking powder, baking soda, and salt, stirring to blend. With the machine running on low, add the butter a few pieces at a time, beating until the flour mixture is crumbly.

**3.** In a large measuring cup, stir together the buttermilk, eggs, lemon extract, and lemon zest. With the mixer running on low, gradually pour in the buttermilk mixture, beating until the mixture is smooth, scraping down the sides of the bowl if necessary.

**4.** Pour the batter into the prepared pan and bake for 35 to 40 minutes, until a skewer inserted into the middle comes out clean. Cool the cake on a wire rack for 10 minutes, then turn the cake out onto the rack to cool completely. **Diva Do-Ahead:** At this point, you can slip the cake into a 2-gallon zipper-top plastic bag and refrigerate for up to 3 days or freeze for up to 2 months. Defrost overnight in the refrigerator before assembling.

**5.** To assemble the cake, in the bowl of an electric mixer, whip the cream until it is very stiff. Add the mascarpone and sugar and whip again until combined. **Diva Do-Ahead:** At this point, you can refrigerate the frosting for up to 24 hours.

*continued on next page*

**6.** Slice one pint of strawberries into ¹/₂-inch-thick slices and set aside. Slice the rest of the strawberries in half.

**7.** Using a serrated knife, carefully slice the cake in half to create 2 layers. Spread some frosting over 1 layer about ¹/₂-inch thick. Top with the sliced strawberries. Cover with the top cake layer and spread the top and sides with the remaining frosting, reserving about ¹/₂ cup. Trace a box in the upper left corner of the cake measuring 4 inches down from the top and 5 inches in from the left. Scatter this rectangle with some of the blueberries, so that you can still see some of the white frosting through the blueberries. Lightly mark lines 1 inch apart horizontally on the rest of the cake and, beginning at the top of the cake, place rows of halved strawberries, cut side down, alternating with rows of plain frosting. Continue to make the red stripe rows alternating with frosted rows all the way down the cake. Depending upon the size of your berries, you should have about 4 red rows and 4 white rows.

**8.** Place the remaining frosting into a zipper-top plastic bag with a small hole snipped into the corner of a pastry bag fitted with a star tip. At 1-inch intervals, pipe small stars between the blueberries to resemble stars on the flag. Cover the cake with plastic wrap and refrigerate for at least 4 hours. **Diva Do-Ahead:** At this point, you can refrigerate for up to 24 hours. Serve cold, garnishing slices with any remaining blueberries.

## Diva Tip

Size *does* matter in this dessert. The larger the strawberries, the fewer stripes you will have. Here in San Diego, the local berry stands sell berries that are gargantuan—sometimes 2 inches in length! But they aren't what you want for this cake. Instead look for small to medium size (1 inch maximum), so that you'll have enough stripes to make the cake look interesting. By the way, there will always be someone in the crowd who will point out that your cake isn't "actually" a flag because you don't have the requisite number of stripes. No kidding!

# Red, White, and Blue Ice Cream Cake

*Serves 8 to 10*

*I'm a firm believer in having lots of tricks up your chef's coat sleeve, and this simple ice cream dessert was inspired by one I saw in a magazine. If you don't have the time or inclination to make the Old Glory Cake but still want a pretty theme dessert for your Fourth party, this recipe takes about 10 minutes to come together and you can freeze it for up to six weeks. You can use a number of different kinds of pans: a star-shaped mold, a small bundt pan, or a 9-inch loaf pan. A nice berry sauce tops it all off beautifully.*

One 1-pound frozen vanilla pound cake, defrosted

1 quart vanilla ice cream, slightly softened

1 pint raspberry sorbet, slightly softened

1 cup fresh blueberries, picked over for stems

Quick Blueberry Sauce (optional, see page 105)

**1.** Line the mold of your choice with plastic wrap that is twice the size of the container, smoothing out any wrinkles and letting the ends hang out over the sides of the mold. Slice the pound cake the long way into four $1/2$-inch-thick slices.

**2.** Scoop half of the vanilla ice cream over the bottom of the mold, and, using an offset spatula or butter knife, spread the ice cream into an even layer out to the edges of the mold.

**3.** Scoop half of the sorbet over the vanilla layer and spread into an even layer. Top with half of the pound cake pieces, cutting them if necessary to form an even layer of cake that completely covers the sorbet.

**4.** Scoop the remaining vanilla ice cream over the cake layer, top with the remaining sorbet, and top that with another layer of cake. Fold the plastic wrap over the mold and freeze for at least 4 hours. **Diva Do-Ahead:** At this point, you can freeze for up to 6 weeks. Remove from the freezer about 15 minutes before serving, unmold onto a plate, remove the plastic wrap, and press the blueberries into the vanilla layer. Slice and serve. If desired, swirl some blueberry sauce onto each dessert plate and arrange a slice of the ice cream cake on top of the sauce.

Sounding the
Shofar

# A Rosh Hashanah Dinner

Rosh Hashanah is the celebration of the first day of the month of Tishri, which occurs in late September or early October on the Hebrew calendar and means "the beginning" or "head" of the year. The holiday marks the start of a 10-day period called the High Holy Days, which ends with Yom Kippur, the Day of Atonement. Like Passover, Rosh Hashanah has its own rituals, blessings, and traditional foods. Sweet hopes for the new year is the theme for this dinner and is reflected in the menu, including the ritual of dipping apples into honey.

I've devised a simple but elegant Rosh Hashanah dinner for 8 to 10 diners. Not bound by the restriction of avoiding flour or leavening during this holiday, you can make a ritual bread, challah, that is served during many Jewish meals. But this time the challah will be shaped into a round, rather than the traditional long braided loaf, to symbolize the circle of life. Some cooks even include dried apricots, golden raisins, and citrus zest in their challah loaves in keeping with the sweet theme of the holiday. If you wish to

make this meal kosher, substitute margarine wherever butter is called for, and skip the caramel sauce (which contains cream). Begin the celebration with a mix of dried fruits and nuts that are coated with a sweet and spicy mixture to be served as a snack along with some spicy warm olives. A beautiful poached salmon with herbed mayonnaise is a delectable first course, served on field greens. A gorgeous roast turkey is painted with a pomegranate glaze, stuffed with a fruited rice dressing, and served with roasted root vegetables and sautéed spinach. And save room for dessert: individual phyllo strudels with apples, raisins, and nuts.

For table decorations, I suggest an autumn centerpiece, such as a large, shallow wooden bowl filled with fruits, nuts, and vegetables. Or you may place a low flower arrangement in the center of the table, using your favorite colors and flowers of the season. Candles in cut-out small sugar pumpkins or gourds, or hollowed-out large apples, would look especially nice on this table. (When you hollow out vegetables or fruits

for candleholders, spray the inside with nonstick
cooking spray and then line the bottom with
aluminum foil to protect your tables from
dripping wax.) I recommend that you tie the
napkins and wine stems with ribbons to match
your color scheme. Make sure to have
plates of apple slices and honey around
the table. Play traditional music quietly
in the background, or something a little
different but lovely, like George
Winston's *Autumn*.

# Do-Ahead Countdown

**\* 2 months ahead**

Download shopping list and do-ahead calendar and fill them out

Shop for nonperishables

Make and freeze Sweet and Nutty Nibbles

**\* 1 month ahead**

Make, shape, and freeze dough for Holiday Challah

Make and freeze Fruited Rice Stuffing

Make (but don't bake) and freeze Individual Apple Strudels in Phyllo

**\* 1 week ahead**

Make Caramel Sauce

**\* 3 days ahead**

Marinate olives

Make Herbed Mayonnaise

Remove Sweet and Nutty Nibbles, challah, and stuffing from freezer and defrost in refrigerator

**\* 2 days ahead**

Make Roasted Sweet Potatoes, Parsnips, Beets, and Carrots

Make Sautéed Spinach

**\* 1 day ahead**

Set the table

Bake challah

Poach salmon

**\* Day of**

Bake Warm Rosemary Olives

Stuff and cook Roast Turkey with Pomegranate Glaze

Reheat challah, roasted vegetables, and spinach

Bake apple strudels

# Sweet and Nutty Nibbles

*Makes about 4 cups*

*This sweet and nutty mix is terrific any time of year, but it really is a great way to begin your Rosh Hashanah celebration. In some traditions, nuts are not eaten at the Rosh Hashanah meal, but they seem the perfect light snack for your guests before the main event. The mixture keeps well in the freezer for up to six months, so you can have it on hand when unexpected guests arrive; just defrost on the counter for about 30 minutes before serving.*

2 tablespoons unsalted butter

2 tablespoons vegetable oil

1/4 cup sugar

1 1/2 teaspoons seasoned salt

1/2 teaspoon Lawry's garlic salt

1/4 teaspoon cayenne pepper

2 cups pecan or walnut halves, whole cashews, or whole almonds (or a combination of your favorites)

1/2 cup dried cranberries

1/2 cup golden raisins

**1.** Preheat the oven to 300°F. Line a baking sheet with parchment paper, aluminum foil, or a silicone baking liner.

**2.** Melt the butter and oil together in a large nonstick skillet over medium heat. Add 2 tablespoons of the sugar, the seasoned salt, garlic salt, and cayenne, and stir until the spices give off some aroma, 1 to 2 minutes. Add the nuts and fruit and toss until well coated. Transfer to the prepared baking sheet and bake for 12 to 15 minutes, turning once, until the nuts are fragrant.

**3.** Remove from the heat and transfer the mixture to a large mixing bowl. Sprinkle the remaining sugar over the nuts and toss until coated. **Diva Do-Ahead:** At this point, you can let cool, transfer to zipper-top plastic bags, and store at room temperature for up to 3 days, refrigerate for up to 1 week, or freeze for up to 6 months.

The Diva Says

If you would like to toss this mixture into salads, chop the nuts before cooking them in the butter and seasonings.

# Warm Rosemary Olives

*Makes about 2 cups*

*A quick blast in the oven makes these spicy olives a terrific tidbit before dinner. Marinate them for a few days before serving, then grate lemon zest over them just before baking to give them an extra jolt of flavor. Hot pepper flakes are optional, but I think they're a great addition. Whether you use pitted olives or not is up to you.*

3/4 cup Kalamata olives

3/4 cup large green Spanish olives

1/3 cup niçoise or small green picholine olives

3/4 cup olive oil

2 teaspoon chopped fresh rosemary

3 cloves garlic, halved

Pinch of red pepper flakes (optional)

2 lemons

**1.** Combine the olives, oil, rosemary, garlic, and red pepper flakes, if using, in a large mixing bowl, stirring to coat. Cover or transfer to a zipper-top plastic bag and store in the refrigerator for a few hours to let the flavors mingle. **Diva Do-Ahead:** At this point, you can refrigerate for up to 3 days.

**2.** Preheat the oven to 400°F. Line a baking sheet with aluminum foil or a silicone baking liner. Remove the zest from 1 of the lemons and add it to the olives in the bag. Cut the lemon in half, squeeze the juice into the bag, seal, and squeeze the bag to distribute the zest and juice evenly.

**3.** Pour the olives and juices onto the baking sheet, grate the zest of the remaining lemon over the olives, and arrange them in a single layer. Bake for 10 minutes, until heated through. Remove from the oven, drain, and serve warm.

# Holiday Challah

*Makes 1 large round*

**Challah is on tables for the Sabbath as well as for holiday feasts. Made with lots of eggs, it has a gloriously golden brown crust and rich yellow interior. Traditionally braided into a long loaf, for Rosh Hashanah it is braided into a round to symbolize the circle of life.**

3/4 cup warm water
  (105° to 115°F)
2 packages instant or rapid-
  rise yeast
1/4 cup sugar
4 large eggs
1/3 cup melted and cooled
  unsalted butter
1 teaspoon salt
5 1/2 cups all-purpose flour
1 tablespoon sesame or poppy
  seeds for garnish

**1.** In the bowl of an electric mixer fitted with a dough hook, combine the water, yeast, and sugar.

**2.** Separate one of the eggs and set the white aside. With the mixer running, add the 3 whole eggs and the egg yolk to the yeast mixture, then pour in the butter and salt and begin to add the flour 1 cup at a time, blending until it is incorporated into the liquids. The dough will become a ball and not adhere to the sides of the bowl. (You may have some flour left.)

**3.** Coat the inside of a large bowl with nonstick cooking spray and place the dough into the bowl, turning it to coat. Cover and let rise in a warm place (a turned-off oven is great) for 2 hours, or until doubled in bulk.

**4.** On a floured board, punch down the dough and cut into thirds. Roll each third into a rope about 20 inches long. Bring the ends of the 3 ropes together at the top and braid the dough by laying the right rope over the center rope, then laying the left rope over the center rope, and so on. As you braid, arrange the rope into a circle, and continue to braid until the ends meet and the dough forms a complete circle. **Diva Do-Ahead:** At this point, you can wrap the loaf in plastic and refrigerate it overnight or freeze it for up to 1 month. Defrost in the refrigerator before proceeding.

*continued on next page*

**5.** Line a baking sheet with parchment paper, aluminum foil, or a silicone baking liner and spray with nonstick cooking spray. Arrange the braid on the baking sheet. Cover with a clean kitchen towel and allow to rise for 1 hour.

**6.** Preheat the oven to 375°F. Brush the bread with the reserved egg white and sprinkle with sesame seeds if desired. Bake for 35 to 45 minutes, until the bread is a deep golden brown and sounds hollow when tapped. Remove from the oven and cool on the baking sheet on a wire rack. **Diva Do-Ahead:** At this point, you can store the bread in a 2-gallon zipper-top plastic bag at room temperature overnight or freeze the bread for up to 1 month. Defrost before serving.

# Poached Salmon with Herbed Mayonnaise

*Serves 8 to 10 as a first course*

*Pretty in pink, this do-ahead poached salmon is accompanied by an herbed mayonnaise that can also be used on other occasions as a sandwich spread or dip for veggies. The salmon can be poached, then chilled, the day before; all that's left to do is decorate the platter and bask in the appreciative oohs and aahs of your guests. I suggest serving Chardonnay or Merlot with this first course. If you can find a sparkling Pinot Noir (a rose-colored wine), that's lovely.*

2 cups dry white wine or dry
   vermouth (see page 206)
2 teaspoons Old Bay
   Seasoning
One lemon, quartered
1 medium-size shallot, finely
   chopped
One 2- to 2$\frac{1}{2}$-pound side of
   salmon, filleted and skinned
   (see Diva Note)
Field greens
Herbed Mayonnaise
   (page 206)
Lemon slices for garnish
Chives for garnish
Dill sprigs for garnish

**1.** Preheat the oven to 350°F. Pour the wine into a non-reactive baking dish. Add the Old Bay, squeeze the lemon quarters into the pan, and add the lemon quarters themselves to the pan. Sprinkle with the shallot.

**2.** Arrange the salmon on the top of the ingredients in the pan and spoon some of the wine mixture over the salmon. Cover the baking dish with aluminum foil and bake for 30 to 35 minutes, until the salmon is cooked through. It should be opaque with a pink center. Remove the salmon from the oven, remove the cover, and allow it to cool. **Diva Do-Ahead:** At this point, you can refrigerate for up to 24 hours. Arrange on a bed of field greens, napping some of the herbed mayonnaise over the top and garnishing the platter with lemon slices, chives, and dill sprigs. Serve cold or at room temperature.

## Diva Note

A whole side of salmon generally comes filleted and skinned, but if the skin is left on, there's no need to panic. Once the salmon is poached, it will slip right off the fish. On the underside of the salmon there is a dark layer of fat that I remove as well; it's not strictly necessary but makes the dish prettier.

# Herbed Mayonnaise

*Makes 3 cups*

*This simple mayonnaise is delicious with the salmon, but it's equally good slathered on a sandwich or used as a dip for crudités. Brightly colored and perked up with lemon zest and full of fragrant dill, it's a winner whenever you decide to make it.*

2 cups regular or low-fat
   mayonnaise

$1/2$ cup regular or low-fat sour
   cream

$1/4$ cup chopped fresh dill

$1/4$ cup chopped fresh Italian
   parsley

2 tablespoons chopped fresh
   chives

Zest of 1 lemon

1 teaspoon salt

$1/2$ teaspoon freshly ground
   black pepper

In a large mixing bowl, stir together all the ingredients until blended. Cover with plastic wrap and refrigerate for at least 4 hours. **Diva Do-Ahead:** At this point, you can refrigerate for up to 3 days. Serve cold.

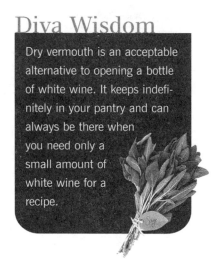

## Diva Wisdom

Dry vermouth is an acceptable alternative to opening a bottle of white wine. It keeps indefinitely in your pantry and can always be there when you need only a small amount of white wine for a recipe.

# Roast Turkey with Pomegranate Glaze

*Serves 8 to 12*

*Turkey is a great entrée to serve when you are having a large gathering because it's economical and it really does all the work by itself, while you get to enjoy the day. This turkey is glazed with pomegranate juice the night before, which will ensure a crispy skin and a deep mahogany-colored bird. The glaze is reapplied during the cooking time to enhance the color and flavor. The stuffing is a delicious mix of rice with dried fruits, and it can either be stuffed into the turkey or served as a side dish. Open some Pinot Noir or Merlot to drink with this entrée.*

One 12-pound turkey
Salt and freshly ground black
   pepper
2 cups pomegranate juice
One recipe Fruited Rice
   Stuffing (optional, page 209)
Kitchen twine
2 cups chicken broth
4 sprigs fresh thyme or
   2 teaspoons dried thyme

**1.** Remove the neck and giblets from the turkey and set aside to make stock if you wish, or discard. Rinse the turkey inside and out under cold running water and pat the inside and outside dry with paper towels. Sprinkle the cavity liberally with salt and pepper.

**2.** Using a basting brush, paint the dry turkey skin with about ¹/₂ cup of the pomegranate juice, allowing time for the skin to absorb the juice. Cover the turkey with paper towels and refrigerate overnight.

**3.** Preheat the oven to 325°F. Remove the paper towels from the turkey and pat the cavity dry. Stuff the cavity with the rice stuffing, if desired. Tie the legs with kitchen twine and transfer the turkey to a rack in a roasting pan. Pour 1 cup of the chicken broth into the roasting pan, add the thyme sprigs, and paint the turkey with a new coat of pomegranate juice.

*continued on next page*

## Roast Turkey with Pomegranate Glaze *continued*

**4.** Bake the turkey for 1½ hours, then baste liberally with the pomegranate juice. If the chicken broth appears to be evaporating, add more. Continue to baste the turkey every 45 minutes or so, until an instant-read thermometer registers 175°F.

**5.** Remove the turkey from the oven to the stovetop, remove the stuffing to a serving bowl, and cover the bowl with aluminum foil to keep warm. Remove the turkey to a warm platter, drape aluminum foil over the turkey, and allow to rest for 30 minutes.

**6.** Strain the turkey drippings through a fat separator and return the drippings to the roasting pan on the stovetop. Bring the juices in the pan to a boil over high heat, adding more chicken broth if needed. Carve the turkey and serve the pan sauce on the side.

### *Diva Safety Note*
When basting liquid comes into contact with raw meats, it becomes contaminated and might be a breeding ground for bacteria. To avoid this hazard, be sure to heat the pan liquid to boiling before serving.

### *Diva Turkey Note*
Follow the turkey cooking instructions on page 248 for timing. It is important to remember that the internal temperature of the turkey, not the length of time it has cooked, is the only way to tell if the turkey is done. The stuffing and the turkey should register 175°F on an instant-read thermometer before removing the turkey from the oven. After resting, the turkey will reach 185°F, which is safe for poultry.

## Diva Tip

Cotton string, kitchen twine, and new silicone "food loops" can all be used for tying poultry.

# Fruited Rice Stuffing

*Serves 8 to 10*

*Filled with dried apricots and cranberries, this stuffing provides a nice balance for the pomegranate-glazed turkey. You can freeze the stuffing a month ahead of time, then defrost it and stuff it into the turkey right before cooking. You can also serve it on the side, if stuffing the turkey isn't your thing.*

2 tablespoons unsalted butter

1/2 cup finely chopped onion

1/2 cup finely chopped celery

1 cup long-grain rice

1/2 cup finely chopped dried apricots

1/2 cup dried cranberries

2 1/2 cups chicken broth

Zest of 1 orange

**1.** Melt the butter in a large saucepan, adding the onion and celery. Sauté the vegetables until they begin to soften. Add the rice, apricots, and cranberries, stirring to coat them with the butter.

**2.** Slowly add the broth and zest, stirring up the bottom of the pan and bringing the mixture to a boil. Cover the pan, reduce the heat, and simmer for 20 to 25 minutes, until the liquid is absorbed and the rice is tender. **Diva Do-Ahead:** At this point, you can store the cooled rice in zipper-top plastic bags and refrigerate for up to 3 days or freeze for up to 1 month. Defrost, then reheat, covered, in the microwave or in a saucepan, with 1/4 cup additional chicken broth.

# Sautéed Spinach

*Serves 8*

*Spinach is a flavorful and colorful addition to any dinner plate, and this typical Italian preparation, which can be served warm or at room temperature, is simple to prepare. It's also delicious as a bruschetta topping: spread goat cheese onto toasted Italian bread, then top with spinach.*

6 quarts water
4 pounds baby spinach
3 teaspoons salt
1/2 cup olive oil
6 cloves garlic, halved
1/2 teaspoon freshly ground
   black pepper

**1.** Bring the water to boil in a large pot. Add the spinach and salt. Remove the pan from the heat and cover for 2 minutes. Drain the spinach and squeeze dry.

**2.** In a large skillet, heat the oil over medium heat and add the garlic, cooking until it begins to turn golden brown, 2 to 3 minutes. Remove the garlic and add the spinach, sautéing for 1 to 2 minutes, until the spinach is coated with the garlic oil. Add the pepper and more salt if desired. **Diva Do-Ahead:** At this point, you can cover and keep at room temperature for up to 4 hours or refrigerate for up to 2 days. Rewarm before serving.

# Roasted Sweet Potatoes, Parsnips, Beets, and Carrots

*Serves 8*

*When roasted in the oven, root vegetables caramelize and become crispy on the outside, with a sweet interior. This combination of sweet roots is in keeping with the sweet hope theme of the dinner. If you would like to substitute Yukon Gold potatoes for the sweet potatoes, feel free. Any leftovers are delicious in soups or tossed with a sherry vinaigrette to serve as a room-temperature side dish.*

1$^1$/2 pounds sweet potatoes, peeled and cut into 1-inch chunks

1 pound carrots, peeled and cut into 1-inch chunks

1/2 pound parsnips, peeled and cut into 1-inch chunks

3 medium-size beets, peeled and quartered

1/4 cup olive oil

1$^1$/2 teaspoons salt

1/2 teaspoon freshly ground black pepper

1/4 cup finely chopped fresh Italian parsley

**1.** Preheat the oven to 400°F. Line a baking sheet with aluminum foil or a silicone baking liner.

**2.** Place all the vegetables on the baking sheet. Drizzle with all but 1 tablespoon of the oil and sprinkle with 1 teaspoon of the salt and all of the pepper. Bake the vegetables for 35 to 45 minutes, until they are tender. Remove from the oven, sprinkle with the remaining 1/2 teaspoon salt, and drizzle with the remaining 1 tablespoon olive oil. **Diva Do-Ahead:** After sprinkling the salt over the roasted vegetables, allow to cool, then cover and refrigerate for up to 2 days. Reheat in a 350°F oven for 10 minutes, until heated through, then drizzle with the reserved oil. Serve warm.

## Diva Quickie

Cut the vegetables into uniform pieces so that they will all cook in the same amount of time.

# Individual Apple Strudels in Phyllo with Caramel Sauce

*Serves 8 to 9*

*I love to make individual desserts: they look like little presents for your guests. These phyllo packets are filled with apples, nuts, and raisins and then served in a puddle of caramel sauce. The best part is that the strudels can be frozen, then baked while you are eating dinner so that you can serve them warm from the oven. Vanilla ice cream or gelato on the side is awesome!*

1/4 cup (1/2 stick) unsalted butter
4 Granny Smith apples, peeled, cored, and diced
1/2 cup granulated sugar
1/4 teaspoon ground cinnamon
Pinch of ground nutmeg
1 tablespoon freshly squeezed lemon juice
1/2 cup golden raisins
1/2 cup chopped walnuts or pecans
1 pound phyllo dough, defrosted
1 1/2 cups (3 sticks) unsalted butter, clarified (see page 59)
1 cup graham cracker or vanilla wafer cookie crumbs
1 recipe Diva Caramel Sauce (page 83)
Confectioners' sugar for garnish

**1.** In a medium-size sauté pan, melt the butter and add the apples, tossing to coat with the butter and cooking for about 3 minutes, until the apples begin to soften.

**2.** Sprinkle in the granulated sugar, cinnamon, nutmeg, lemon juice, raisins, and walnuts, stirring to blend and sautéing for another 5 to 7 minutes, until the apples begin to color and soften. Remove from the heat and allow to cool. **Diva Do-Ahead:** At this point, you can cover and refrigerate for up to 2 days.

**3.** Unwrap the phyllo and lay it flat on the counter, covering with a clean, dry towel.

**4.** Preheat the oven to 400°F. Line a baking sheet with parchment paper, aluminum foil, or a silicone baking liner.

**5.** Uncover 1 sheet of phyllo and lay it on a cutting board or flat surface and cover the remaining sheets with the dishtowel. Using a pastry brush, paint the surface of the phyllo with some clarified butter and sprinkle with some graham cracker crumbs. Repeat with another layer of phyllo. If you are using the larger 18 x 14-inch phyllo sheets, fold the two sheets of phyllo in half, brush with butter, and sprinkle with cracker crumbs. If you are using the smaller 14 x 9-inch phyllo sheets, continue layering phyllo to make a total of

4 sheets; do not fold. Mound a rounded $1/2$-cup measure of the apple filling in the center of the phyllo. Taking opposite ends of the phyllo in each hand, bring them all to the center and twist into a knot. Brush all over with the butter and gently transfer to the prepared baking sheet. Repeat with the remaining phyllo and apple mixture. You should have 8 or 9 packets. **Diva Do-Ahead:** At this point, you can cover the baking sheet with plastic wrap and refrigerate overnight or freeze until firm. When the frozen phyllo is firm, wrap packets individually in plastic, then store in zipper-top plastic bags for up to 1 month. You can bake the packets directly from the freezer.

**6.** Bake for 15 to 20 minutes, until golden brown. Serve warm or at room temperature. (For frozen phyllo packets, bake for 15 to 20 minutes at 400°F, then reduce the oven temperature to 350°F and bake another 10 to 15 minutes, until the pastry is golden brown and you can see some of the apple liquid bubbling around the knot.)

**7.** Pool about 2 tablespoons of caramel sauce on each dessert plate, then place the strudels in the middle of the sauce. Serve dusted with confectioners' sugar.

Treats, Not Tricks

# A Halloween Party for All Ages

Although there's nothing spooky about the menu, this Halloween buffet, which works for anywhere from eight to twelve people, will be a hit in your neighborhood. Because people of all ages might be coming and going at different times, I've devised a couple of appetizers along with a build-your-own-pizza bar and salad bar that will give your guests lots of choices, so that they can graze, go trick-or-treating, and return to eat a little more. And because this is one night when you can't have too much sugar, I've included two sweet treats sure to please all ages.

The pizza bar will prove to be a real conversation starter. With gourmet toppings for the adults and more tried-and-true toppings for the kids, everyone can get into the act. I recommend that you write up note cards with suggested combinations on them to help your friends build a gourmet masterpiece! Because the pita bread crusts and toppings don't spend much time in the oven, you can easily do this dinner with one oven. A salad bar full of healthful choices and two great dressings is also a nice way to let your guests help themselves, or, if you prefer, a

cooling orange and fennel salad complements the pizza nicely. Round out the menu with crispy rice bars studded with candy corn and gourmet caramel apples, and your house will be the one with all the treats!

Decorate your house inside and out with the essence of fall: pumpkins, gourds, leaves, bare branches covered with angel hair to look like cobwebs, dried ears of corn, small winter squashes, and your favorite scary novelty items, like spiders, ghosts, and skeletons. To resemble sheaves of wheat, tie a pound of dry fettuccine in the center with raffia, then weave dried leaves through it, or glue-gun bay leaves or rosemary sprigs to the center of the bow. Indoors, small votive candles to blend with the theme are appropriate—either in a coordinating color or seasonal shape, such as a pumpkin or an apple. Caramel popcorn wrapped in cellophane or crispy rice treats wrapped up to go are wonderful party favors. Creaky music (you can download lots of Halloween songs and sounds to your computer and make a CD) and low lighting are a must (unless you have small, impressionable children in attendance)! Assign someone the task of taking Polaroid or digital photos of your costumed guests as they arrive, and then send them souvenir copies.

A few activities, such as a pumpkin carving contest or a scavenger hunt, are great ideas but require extra space and adult supervision. (Bobbing for apples is messy so do it outside if the temperature allows.) Have a pumpkin carving competition, with teams trying to carve their "greatest" creation, or use a fun theme—alien jack-o'-lanterns or squash gone bad. Young children can get into the act by drawing faces on tiny sugar pumpkins with felt-tip pens. Scavenger hunts are always a great addition to a party. You can have a Polaroid hunt, where the participants have to snap photos of various items while they are trick-or-treating, or you can give them a list of items they must return to the house with. Make it very simple for small children, or more complex, with riddles, for older teens and adults. The last item should be one that's at the party house to encourage everyone to get back within a certain amount of time.

Set up the buffet table with pita bread stacked on aluminum-foil squares that are placed on heavy-duty paper or plastic plates. The aluminum-foil squares will slide directly onto baking sheets and into the preheated oven. The plate will be used for serving the pizza when it comes out of the oven. Follow that with pizza toppings, then plates for the salad bar, then the salad fixings or the orange and fennel salad. You may use your regular flatware, but if you're having a larger crowd, color-coordinated heavy-duty plastic utensils and paper napkins will make your life easier later.

## Do-Ahead Countdown

* **6 weeks ahead**

  Download shopping list and do-ahead calendar and fill them out

  Shop for nonperishables

  Make and freeze Simple Pizza Sauce

* **1 week ahead**

  Make Hot Apple Pie Cocktails

* **4 days ahead**

  Make Sweet Tomato Dressing for salad bar (if serving)

* **3 days ahead**

  Make Warm Spiced Cider

  Assemble Hot Artichoke, Caramelized Onion, and Spinach Dip

  Prepare toppings for pizzas

  Make Diva's Creamy Italian Dressing for salad bar (if serving)

* **2 days ahead**

  Make White Cheddar, Apple, and Bacon Cheesecake

  Prepare and assemble salad bar ingredients (if serving)

* **1 day ahead**

  Set up your buffet table

  Remove Simple Pizza Sauce from freezer and defrost in refrigerator

  Slice oranges and fennel and prepare dressing for Orange and Fennel Salad (if serving)

  Make Crispy Rice and Candy Corn Bars

  Make Pecan and Chocolate Caramel Apples

* **Day of**

  Warm cider and cocktails

  Bake Hot Artichoke, Caramelized Onion, and Spinach Dip

  Bake pizzas

  Assemble Orange and Fennel Salad (if serving)

# Warm Spiced Cider

*Serves 12*

*A favorite with young and old alike, this warm, fragrant cider is just the thing to start a fall or winter party. A splash of rum or brandy is a nice touch for the grownups in the crowd.*

2 quarts apple cider
1 teaspoon whole allspice
  berries
Two 4-inch cinnamon sticks
6 whole cloves
1/4 teaspoon ground ginger

In a large saucepan over low heat, combine the cider and spices and heat for 30 minutes. Strain the cider and discard the spices. **Diva Do-Ahead:** At this point, you can let cool, store in an airtight container, and refrigerate for up to 3 days or freeze for up to 2 months. Serve warm.

## The Diva Says

If you are serving a crowd, double the recipe and store the warm cider in a coffee urn or a few thermal carafes.

## Slow Cooker Savvy

Combine the ingredients in a 5- to 6-quart slow cooker and heat on low for up to 3 to 4 hours.

# Hot Apple Pie Cocktails

*Makes 8 cocktails*

*This is a warm apéritif made with Calvados, a French apple brandy. There are many versions of this, but this one really does taste like a very adult apple pie!*

2 whole cinnamon sticks, broken into pieces

4 whole allspice berries

2 whole cloves

$1/8$ teaspoon finely grated nutmeg, plus more for garnish

Pinch of ground ginger

3 cups apple cider

$1/3$ cup Calvados

$1/3$ cup light rum

Place the cinnamon, allspice, cloves, $1/8$ teaspoon nutmeg, and ginger in a medium-size saucepan. Stir in the apple cider, Calvados, and rum, and warm over low heat for 30 minutes, until the mixture reaches a hot serving temperature. Strain out the spices. **Diva Do-Ahead:** At this point, you can store in an airtight container and refrigerate for up to 1 week. Serve warm, garnished with freshly grated nutmeg.

# White Cheddar, Apple, and Bacon Cheesecake

*Serves 12 to 16*

*I don't recommend freezing this cheesecake because the bacon loses a little bit in the translation. But it's still a do-ahead dish, and it's definitely worth a try for a fall party, with its sweet apple, tart cheddar, and smoky bacon filling. I also like to serve this cheesecake as a starter for a casual soup-and-salad dinner for friends, as its unusual presentation gets the conversation going.*

1/4 cup (1/2 stick) butter

1/2 cup firmly packed light brown sugar

4 medium-size Granny Smith apples, peeled, cored, and cut into 1/4-inch-thick slices

1 teaspoon freshly squeezed lemon juice

1/4 teaspoon ground cinnamon

Pinch of ground nutmeg

6 strips bacon, cooked and crumbled

Two 8-ounce packages cream cheese, softened

2 large eggs

2 cups finely shredded sharp white cheddar cheese

1 teaspoon hot sauce

Crackers, cocktail rye, or pumpernickel rounds for serving

**1.** Line the bottom and sides of a 9-inch springform pan or a cake pan with 3-inch-tall sides with parchment paper or aluminum foil and coat with nonstick cooking spray.

**2.** In a medium-size skillet over medium heat, melt the butter, then add the brown sugar and stir until dissolved. Add the apples and stir to coat them with the sugar mixture. Add the lemon juice, cinnamon, and nutmeg, and continue to cook, stirring a few times, for 4 to 5 minutes. The apples will retain their crispness but should have absorbed some of the sauce. Pour the apples and sauce into the prepared pan and arrange in a decorative pattern if you like. Sprinkle the bacon evenly over the apples. Set aside.

**3.** Preheat the oven to 350°F.

**4.** In the bowl of an electric mixer, beat the cream cheese until smooth. Add the eggs, one at a time, beating until light and fluffy. Stir in the cheddar and hot sauce. Gently pour the mixture over the apples and bacon in the prepared pan, smoothing the top with a rubber spatula.

*continued on next page*

# White Cheddar, Apple, and Bacon Cheesecake *continued*

**5.** Bake until a skewer inserted into the middle of the cheesecake comes out clean, about 45 minutes. Leave the cheesecake in the oven with the door ajar for another 30 minutes (to help prevent cracks from developing).

**6.** Remove the cheesecake from the oven and let cool on a rack for another 30 to 45 minutes.

**7.** Place a large serving plate over the pan, invert, and remove the pan from the cheesecake. Peel away the parchment. **Diva Do-Ahead:** At this point, you can let the cheesecake cool completely, cover with plastic wrap, and refrigerate for up to 2 days. Bring to room temperature before serving. Serve at room temperature with crackers or bread.

# Hot Artichoke, Caramelized Onion, and Spinach Dip

*Serves 8 to 10*

*This dip combines three different dips to make a winner when it's set out with crackers, bread sticks, baguette slices, or crudités. The bright green spinach, sweet caramelized onions, and chunks of artichoke swirled in the rich cheesy sauce are perfect on a cold, crisp evening. (For a terrific Christmas appetizer, serve this dip with red bell pepper slices to evoke the colors of the season.)*

2 tablespoons unsalted butter

1 teaspoon olive oil

2 cloves garlic, minced

1 cup chopped sweet onion, such as Vidalia, Walla Walla, or Texas sweet

One 10-ounce package baby spinach

1 teaspoon salt

1/2 teaspoon hot sauce

One 15-ounce can artichoke hearts, drained and chopped

1 cup regular or low-fat mayonnaise

2/3 cup grated Swiss cheese

2/3 cup grated Parmesan cheese

**1.** In a medium-size sauté pan over high heat, melt the butter with the oil and sauté the garlic for 1 minute, until fragrant. Reduce the heat and add the onion, cooking for 5 to 7 minutes, until it begins to turn golden. Add the spinach and stir until the spinach is wilted, then cook until the moisture from the spinach is evaporated, about 5 minutes. Stir in the salt and hot sauce and transfer to a large mixing bowl to cool. **Diva Do-Ahead:** At this point, you can cover and refrigerate for up to 3 days. Drain off any liquid that has accumulated before proceeding.

**2.** Preheat the oven to 350°F. Coat the inside of a 1-quart baking dish with nonstick cooking spray. Add the artichokes, mayonnaise, Swiss cheese, and Parmesan cheese to the spinach mixture, stirring until blended. Transfer to the baking dish. **Diva Do-Ahead:** At this point, you can cover and refrigerate for up to 3 days. Remove from the refrigerator 30 minutes before proceeding. Bake the dip for 20 minutes, until bubbling and golden brown. Serve hot.

## Diva Variations

- Add 1 cup lump crabmeat along with the artichokes.
- Add one 4-ounce can diced green chiles, rinsed and drained, along with the artichokes.
- Add 6 strips crumbled crisp bacon along with the artichokes.
- Bake the dip in a scooped-out large round loaf of bread.

# Build-Your-Own-Pizza Bar

*Serves 10*

*This pizza bar is really more of a concept than an actual recipe, although I provide the template here and give you recipes for specialty pizzas on pages 226–227. You can set up the pizza bar area before your guests arrive, and they can make their own pizzas at their leisure throughout the evening. You can make your own pizza dough if you'd like, but pita bread is a simpler, quicker alternative. The 6-inch size stays sturdy with toppings. Beer or Chianti is a classic pizza accompaniment.*

Twelve 6-inch pita breads

3 cups Simple Pizza Sauce (recipe follows) or your favorite store-bought sauce

Assorted toppings of your choice (see opposite)

3 to 4 cups shredded cheeses of your choice

**1.** Preheat the oven to 425°F. Spread about $1/4$ cup of the sauce over each pita and top with your favorite toppings and cheeses.

**2.** Slide the pita onto baking sheets (you can get 3 to 4 on one sheet) and bake for 7 to 10 minutes, until the cheese is melted and golden brown.

**3.** Transfer the pizzas to a cutting board and slice with a pizza cutter. Lift onto plates and serve hot.

## Diva Wisdom

Pita versus Boboli—Boboli makes an individual pizza shell that is precooked and works well for this presentation, but I prefer the pita bread because it doesn't have the additional cheese and other flavorings, giving you a blank canvas to work on. Plus, pita bread is less expensive for a crowd.

# Traditional Toppings for a Build-Your-Own-Pizza Bar

Traditional pizza begins by spreading the dough with a layer of pizza sauce, adding your favorite toppings, then topping with cheeses and baking until the cheese is golden brown. These toppings are a few of my favorites. You can assemble them 2 to 3 days ahead of time and keep them covered in the refrigerator until it is time for your Halloween party.

* Tomato sauce
* Roasted red pepper strips
* Sautéed sliced mushrooms
* Drained canned pineapple chunks
* Thinly sliced sweet onions, either sautéed or raw
* Canned artichoke hearts, drained and chopped
* Pitted and sliced Kalamata olives
* Anchovies, drained and chopped
* Chopped or thinly sliced meatballs
* Chopped cooked Italian sausages
* Thinly sliced pepperoni
* Chopped or sliced ham (hot capicola for the spicy-food freaks in the crowd)
* Shredded mozzarella cheese
* Shredded Monterey Jack cheese
* Shredded Muenster cheese
* Shredded aged provolone cheese
* Grated Parmesan cheese
* Grated Romano cheese
* Red pepper flakes
* Dried Italian oregano
* Extra-virgin olive oil

# Gourmet or Tried and True?

The kinds of pizzas you make are up to you and your guests. Here are some great combinations for individual 6-inch pizzas. Simply multiply upward for however many you wish to make.

## Peking Pizza

*This Asian-inspired pizza is a delicious change of pace, and it uses up leftovers to boot.*

**2 to 3 tablespoons hoisin sauce**
**1/4 cup finely sliced or chopped smoked turkey or chopped cooked duck or chicken**
**1/4 cup finely shredded smoked Gouda cheese**
**1 scallion (white and some tender green parts), chopped**
**2 tablespoons bean sprouts**

Spread the hoisin sauce evenly over the pita. Sprinkle with the turkey and cheese. Bake for 7 to 10 minutes. Garnish with scallion and bean sprouts.

## Ryan's BBQ Chicken Pizza

*This pizza is my son's favorite, and it couldn't be easier to make at home.*

**2 to 3 tablespoons store-bought barbecue sauce (Ryan likes KC Masterpiece)**
**1/4 cup finely chopped cooked chicken**
**1/4 cup finely shredded smoked Gouda or smoked mozzarella cheese**
**1 thin slice red onion, separated into rings**

Spread the barbecue sauce over the pita. Top with the remaining ingredients, and bake for 7 to 10 minutes, until the cheese is bubbly and golden.

## Goat Cheese and Artichoke Pizza

*Smooth goat cheese, marinated artichokes, and sun-dried tomatoes make this pizza a sophisticated addition to a build-your-own bar.*

**2 to 3 tablespoons goat cheese**
**1/4 cup coarsely chopped marinated artichokes**
**1 tablespoon sun-dried tomatoes, finely chopped**
**2 teaspoons toasted pine nuts**
**1/4 cup grated Parmesan cheese**
**2 tablespoons extra-virgin olive oil**
**1 clove garlic, minced**

Spread the goat cheese evenly over the pita. Spread the artichokes, sun-dried tomatoes, pine nuts, and then Parmesan evenly over the cheese. Stir the oil and garlic together in a small bowl and drizzle over the pizza. Bake for 7 to 10 minutes, until the pizza is bubbly and the cheese begins to turn golden.

## Garlic Clam Pizza

*Spicy clams and molten cheese make this pizza a winner in my book.*

**2 tablespoons olive oil**
**2 cloves garlic, minced**
**2 tablespoons chopped clams**
**2 tablespoons oil-packed sun-dried tomatoes, drained and finely chopped**
**$^1/_4$ cup grated Parmesan cheese**

In a small bowl, combine the oil, garlic, clams, and sun-dried tomatoes. Spread over the pita and sprinkle with the cheese. Bake for 7 to 10 minutes, until the cheese begins to turn golden brown.

## Four-Cheese Pizza

*I've never met a cheese I didn't like, and this four-cheese pizza is a delicious mélange of cheese, crust, and garlic.*

**2 tablespoons olive oil**
**1 clove garlic, minced**
**1 teaspoon dried oregano**
**2 tablespoons crumbled Gorgonzola cheese**
**2 tablespoons shredded fontina cheese**
**2 tablespoons shredded mozzarella cheese**
**2 tablespoons grated Parmesan cheese**

In a small bowl, combine the oil, garlic, and oregano. Spread half of the garlic oil over the pita, top with the cheeses, and drizzle with the remaining oil. Bake for 7 to 10 minutes, until the cheese is bubbling and golden brown.

## Buffalo Chicken Pizza

*Blue cheese, chicken, and hot sauce all on one crust—I think I'm in heaven!*

**3 tablespoons melted butter**
**2 teaspoons hot sauce (or more to your taste)**
**$^1/_4$ cup finely chopped cooked chicken**
**$^1/_4$ cup crumbled Maytag blue cheese**

In a small bowl, combine the butter and hot sauce. Spread half of the mixture on the pita bread, top with the chicken and blue cheese, and drizzle the remaining butter mixture over the top of the pizza. Bake for 7 to 10 minutes, until the cheese is melted.

## Pesto Shrimp Pizza

*Pink shrimp resting on spicy basil pesto and sprinkled with cheese is a nice addition to any party menu.*

**2 tablespoons mascarpone cheese blended with $^1/_4$ cup pesto (basil or sun-dried tomato)**
**$^1/_4$ cup chopped cooked shrimp**
**$^1/_4$ cup shredded mozzarella cheese**
**2 tablespoons grated Parmesan cheese**

Spread the pesto mixture evenly over the pita. Spread the shrimp, mozzarella, and Parmesan over the pesto mixture. Bake for 7 to 10 minutes, until the cheese is bubbly and golden brown.

# Simple Pizza Sauce

*Makes about 4 cups*

*Pizza sauce is simple to put together and have on hand in the refrigerator or freezer, but if time is of the essence, there are lots of commercial brands to choose from at your supermarket. Garlic doesn't freeze well, so if you will be freezing this sauce, I recommend that you remove the garlic.*

2 tablespoons extra-virgin
olive oil

2 cloves garlic, minced

1 large onion, chopped

2 teaspoons dried oregano

1/2 teaspoon dried basil

One 32-ounce can tomato
puree

2 teaspoons sugar

1 1/2 teaspoons salt

1/2 teaspoon freshly ground
black pepper

1/4 cup finely chopped fresh
Italian parsley

**1.** Heat the oil in a large saucepan over medium heat and add the garlic, sautéing for about 1 minute, until the garlic is fragrant but not browned. If you are freezing the sauce, remove the garlic; otherwise, leave it in and add the onion, oregano, and basil to the pan. Sauté until the onion is softened, 4 to 5 minutes.

**2.** Add the tomato puree, sugar, salt, and pepper, and simmer the sauce, uncovered, for 30 to 40 minutes. Taste the sauce, adjust the seasonings if desired, and add the parsley. **Diva Do-Ahead:** At this point, you can cover and refrigerate for up to 5 days or freeze for 6 weeks. Present the sauce cold at your pizza bar.

# Orange and Fennel Salad

*Serves 8 to 10*

*This refreshing salad of fresh fennel and oranges is delicious along with the pizza. Blood oranges are beautiful (and appropriate for Halloween!) to add to this presentation, if they are available and economical. Otherwise, standard navel oranges work well.*

6 large navel or blood oranges

2 heads of fennel, wispy ends trimmed and reserved for garnish, bulb ends trimmed, and thinly sliced on an angle

1/3 cup extra-virgin olive oil

2 tablespoons red wine vinegar

1 teaspoon dried oregano

**1.** Slice the bottom and top from the oranges. Stand each orange on a flat end and, using a boning knife or thin flexible knife, cut down the sides to remove all the peel and white pith. Cut the oranges into 1/2-inch-thick slices and arrange on a serving platter with the thinly sliced fennel. **Diva Do-Ahead:** At this point, you can cover and refrigerate overnight.

**2.** In a small bowl, whisk together the oil, vinegar, and oregano until thickened. Pour over the salad. Garnish with some of the wispy ends of the fennel. Allow to marinate for at least 2 hours at room temperature. **Diva Do-Ahead:** At this point, you can marinate for up to 6 hours at room temperature.

# Build-Your-Own-Salad Bar

*Serves 10*

*Salad bars are a wonderful way to allow your guests to choose their favorite veggies, and they can either practice restraint or throw caution to the wind and load up. Some of the salad bar components will also be used for the pizza bar, so make sure to cross-reference your shopping list and have enough for each area. A food processor will make quick work of the slicing and shredding chores, giving you more time to focus on other areas of the meal. The sliced and shredded components for the salad bar will keep, covered, in the refrigerator for up to two days. Two simple dressings will round out your bar, and, of course, if you don't have time to make the dressings, you can use bottled dressings—Marie's and Newman's Own are two of my favorite brands.*

Four 10-ounce bags mixed greens (such as 1 bag spinach, 1 iceberg blend, 1 romaine, and 1 field greens, or all of 1 type)

1 cup finely sliced red onion

1 cup finely sliced red or yellow bell pepper

1 cup shredded carrots

Two 6-ounce jars marinated artichoke hearts, drained and quartered

2 cups cherry tomatoes

One 15-ounce can baby beets, drained and quartered

2 cups frozen petite green peas, defrosted and drained

2 cups frozen white corn, defrosted and drained

4 cups flavored croutons

4 individual cups various cheeses (such as shredded cheddar, crumbled blue, crumbled feta, and/or shredded Parmesan)

1 cup pitted and sliced Kalamata olives

One 6-ounce jar roasted red peppers, drained and chopped

1 European cucumber, washed and thinly sliced

1 pound bacon, cooked crisp and crumbled

1 cup mandarin orange segments

1 cup chopped nuts (walnuts, pecans, or almonds)

1 cup dried cranberries

Salad dressings of your choice (recipes follow)

Arrange the salad greens in a large salad bowl with tongs. If using different kinds of greens, you may either put them all together in one bowl or set them out separately in smaller bowls. Arrange the other items in bowls with spoons, forks, and tongs for serving as needed. Make sure to label each ingredient with a small sign to let people know what they are choosing.

## Diva Tip

When you are using a store-bought dressing, freshen the taste by adding fresh herbs, fresh lemon zest, fresh minced garlic, and/or finely chopped onion or shallot.

# Diva's Creamy Italian Dressing

*Makes 3 cups*

*This dressing is my idea of an Italian ranch-style dressing, and it's terrific on pasta and potato salads, as well as greens and tomatoes.*

2 cups regular or low-fat
   mayonnaise
1/4 cup whole milk
1/4 cup finely chopped red
   onion
1/4 cup finely chopped red bell
   pepper
1/4 cup red wine vinegar
1 teaspoon dried oregano
1/2 teaspoon dried basil
1/2 cup grated Parmesan
   cheese

1/2 teaspoon freshly ground
   black pepper
Pinch of red pepper flakes

In a large mixing bowl, whisk together all the ingredients until blended. Cover and store the dressing in the refrigerator for at least 4 hours. **Diva Do-Ahead:** At this point, you can refrigerate for up to 3 days. Rewhisk to blend and serve. If the dressing is a bit thick, thin it with additional milk a few drops at a time.

# Sweet Tomato Dressing

*Makes about 2 cups*

*This dressing reminds me of the old-fashioned Kraft Catalina dressing, and it's a real hit with the kids in the crowd. The dressing keeps in the refrigerator for four days, but it will solidify when it's cold, so remember to remove it from the refrigerator about one hour before serving.*

1 1/2 cups vegetable oil
2/3 cup sugar
1/2 cup ketchup
1/2 cup red wine vinegar
1/2 cup finely chopped red
   onion
1 teaspoon Worcestershire
   sauce

1 teaspoon freshly ground
   black pepper
1/2 teaspoon dry mustard

In a mixing bowl, whisk together all the ingredients until blended. Cover and refrigerate for at least 1 hour. **Diva Do-Ahead:** At this point, you can refrigerate for up to 4 days. Remove from the refrigerator an hour before serving and rewhisk to blend.

# Crispy Rice and Candy Corn Bars

*Makes twenty-four 2-inch bars*

*You don't have to be a kid to enjoy these crispy treats; I find that adults are the first to devour them when they are placed on the dessert table. I've added some candy corn to make them coordinate with the Halloween theme. (For Christmas, substitute reindeer corn in red, white, and green.)*

5 tablespoons unsalted butter

Two 10.5-ounce bags miniature marshmallows

One 7-ounce jar marshmallow crème, such as Marshmallow Fluff

7 1/2 cups crispy rice cereal

1 1/2 cups candy corn

**1.** Coat the inside of a 13 x 9-inch baking dish with nonstick cooking spray.

**2.** In a 5-quart saucepan, melt the butter and add the marshmallows and marshmallow crème, cooking until the mixture is smooth and the marshmallows are melted. Remove from the heat and stir in the cereal and the candy corn.

**3.** Spoon into the prepared baking dish and smooth the top with an offset spatula dipped in warm water. Allow to cool completely and then cut into 2-inch squares with a sharp knife. **Diva Do-Ahead:** At this point, you can cover the bars and keep them at room temperature for up to 24 hours.

# Pecan and Chocolate Caramel Apples

*Makes 12 caramel apples*

*Crisp Granny Smith apple wedges dipped into caramel, milk chocolate, and chopped pecans are a perfect pick-up dessert for your Halloween party. They are so much easier to handle than whole caramel apples and so simple to prepare ahead and have waiting on the buffet table that you may want to make this dessert for other holidays. I prefer the flavor of milk chocolate in this recipe, but fans of semisweet can make the substitution. Those who can't decide can melt six ounces of each!*

8 large Granny Smith apples, wax scrubbed from the skin, cored, and sliced into 8 wedges

Sixty-four 6-inch wooden skewers

One 14-ounce bag Kraft caramels

2 tablespoons water

12 ounces milk chocolate, chopped

1 1/2 cups toasted chopped pecans (see page 114)

**1.** Line a baking sheet with parchment paper, aluminum foil, or a silicone baking liner. Skewer each apple wedge with a 6-inch wooden skewer.

**2.** In a small saucepan, melt the caramels over low heat and add the water. Dip each apple wedge into the warm caramel, allowing any excess to drip back into the pan. Arrange the wedges on the baking sheet and refrigerate until firm.

**3.** Melt the chocolate in the microwave or on the stovetop over simmering water. Place the pecans in a wide shallow bowl. Line another baking sheet with parchment paper, aluminum foil, or a silicone baking liner.

**4.** Dip the cold caramel-dipped apples into the chocolate, allowing any excess to drip off into the warm chocolate. Dip each end of the apple in the pecans and arrange on the prepared baking sheet. Refrigerate until firm. **Diva Do-Ahead:** At this point, you can cover and refrigerate for up to 24 hours. Remove from the refrigerator about 30 minutes before serving.

## Diva Note

I like to leave the skewers in the apples so that my guests have a "handle." Otherwise, the heat from their fingers will melt the chocolate and a sticky mess will result.

# The Diva's Famous Do-Ahead Thanksgiving Dinner

I've lost count of how many times I've taught this do-ahead Thanksgiving dinner, but I do remember one year when I cooked 52 turkeys in cooking classes before my own Thanksgiving dinner! In all the years that I've taught home cooks how to prepare this meal, I've never gotten tired of the dishes that we serve, and I've given you a choice of starters, stuffings, vegetables, and desserts. All are simple, delicious, and can be done ahead of time—what could be better? I tell my students when we begin the class, "I know why you are here," and they all laugh. Then I tell them my tale of woe, when I worked 10 hours to put Thanksgiving on the table only to have my family inhale it in 10 minutes. I knew there had to be a better way, so I embarked on a quest for the easiest and best do-ahead Thanksgiving possible. And 15 years later, I am still teaching this class to sellout audiences.

What you need to know is that each dish can be broken down into manageable steps, then refrigerated or frozen. Several days before Thanksgiving, defrost the frozen items, and on Thanksgiving Day all you need to do is roast the turkey. When the turkey comes out of the oven, you reheat your side dishes while the turkey rests for 30 minutes. By the time the turkey is carved, all the side dishes are ready to be served. It *is* that simple.

Thanksgiving is one of my favorite holidays. I love the food, and I love that we have a day in which we take time to give thanks with our family and friends. I've prepared this dinner in many places all over the world: in my tiny kitchen in Okinawa, Japan, for more than 20 people; with my cousin Dave in his small kitchen north of London; in a retreat center near Washington, D.C.; and for the past few years on Maui, where my family has rented a condo. You can do the cooking anywhere, in a gourmet kitchen, a small apartment with a basic oven, or a rented condo with unknown equipment. It's possible to do it all and keep your sanity!

This dinner demands your best: the food, the table settings, the wines, flowers, and decorations all should say that you care about your guests and have put out your very best—whatever that is for you. If you are serving more than eight guests, set up a buffet service and then direct your guests to the dinner table to sit down and eat, or if you have set up numerous tables, have place cards so each guest knows where to sit. Make sure to have extras on the table: butter, rolls, water, and wine. When the guests have finished their first plate, they can get up and go back for more when they are ready. Keep gravy warm in a slow cooker or fondue pot or on the stovetop, and then pour it into a gravy boat as needed.

A beautiful low (no more than eight to nine inches high) arrangement of seasonal flowers makes a nice statement on your table, as does a cornucopia filled with fresh fruits and nuts sitting on autumn leaves. For a rustic feel, use a long shallow wooden bowl and fill it with autumn leaves, fruits, nuts, small gourds, sheaves of wheat, dried corn, and small pumpkins. Or hollow out small pumpkins and other gourd-like vegetables and fill them with flowers or votive candles for your centerpieces. For flower arrangements in spots other than the dining table, cut a piece from the bottom of the vegetable so that it will stand flat on the table, hollow it out, fill it with an oasis

(a dry floral foam that you can find in floral supply and craft stores), and then arrange your flowers, greenery, and taper candles in the foam. This will give you that professional-centerpiece look for a lot less money. Make pomanders for your guest bathroom or living room by studding citrus fruits with cloves and nesting them in a basket. I sometimes make cookie-cutter place cards for my guests, using seasonal cookie cutters and filling them with melted chocolate, then wrapping them in cellophane bags tied with a colorful seasonal ribbon. This makes a nice party favor as well.

Votive candles give your dinner table a beautiful glow, especially if you are eating in the evening. If you serve the meal earlier, when the room is still bright with sunlight, candles are nice, though not necessary. You can light them later, with dessert, if you'd like.

Cloth linens are a must, as well as your best china, flatware, and glassware. If you don't have enough for all your guests, you can always borrow from friends, and renting them is another option. If you are just starting out, buy large white or cream-colored dinner plates—they go with

everything. You can generally find them on sale at discount stores, and then you can accent them with seasonal colors. If your plates aren't as posh as you'd like, elaborately decorate around them—the food will decorate the plates, and your table setting will add to the ambiance. There are lots of Diva tricks for making the most of what's at hand, and you don't have to spend a fortune to do it. If you have mismatched plates, or are borrowing some from friends, use that to your advantage: find a common color in the plates to inspire your selection of linens, flowers, and candles. Alternate the plates at the table so that the mixing and matching looks deliberate. Use a different shade for your napkins. Your glassware can be eclectic as well, but do hide the jelly glasses for this special holiday! This style actually makes the table much more interesting, and your guests will think you are a very talented decorator.

Last, if you have invited any newcomers to join your group, it's always a thoughtful idea to ask if there's a certain family dish that will make their Thanksgiving complete—and then try to make it. You will have very grateful guests.

# Do-Ahead Countdown

Because so much of this meal can be made ahead and frozen, I provide three countdowns here: one for the freezer, one for the refrigerator, and one for the big day itself. Feel free to pick and choose recipes you make ahead and refrigerate versus recipes you make ahead and freeze.

## Freezer Countdown

### ✳ 3 months ahead

Download shopping list and do-ahead calendar and fill them out

Shop for nonperishables

Make and freeze Cranberry-Peach Chutney

### ✳ 6 weeks ahead

Make and freeze Make-Ahead Gravy

### ✳ 2 months ahead

Make and freeze streusel for Hot Apple Pie Sundaes

### ✳ 1 month ahead

Make and freeze Curried Cream of Pumpkin Soup *or* base for Triple Mushroom Soup

Make (but don't bake) Old-Fashioned Do-Ahead Bread Stuffing *or* Old-Fashioned Do-Ahead Cornbread Stuffing

Make Make-Ahead Mashed Potatoes *or* make (but don't bake) Sweet Potato and Apple Gratin *or* Creamy Butternut Squash

Make (but don't bake) Parmesan-Crusted Creamed Corn

Make and freeze Orange-Ginger Custard Sauce

## Refrigerator Countdown

### ✳ 1 month ahead

Make Cranberry-Peach Chutney

### ✳ 1 week ahead

Make streusel for Hot Apple Pie Sundaes

### ✳ 5 days ahead

Make Hot Cranberry Punch

Make Chocolate Cookie-Cutter Place Cards

### ✳ 4 days ahead

Make Curried Cream of Pumpkin Soup

Make gravy

Make (but don't bake) Sweet Potato and Apple Gratin

Make Orange-Ginger Custard Sauce

Make filling for Hot Apple Pie Sundaes

### ✳ 3 days ahead

Make (reserving cheese and chives) Triple Mushroom Soup with Brie

Clean and season turkey

Make (but don't bake) Old Fashioned Do-Ahead Bread Stuffing

Make Creamy Butternut Squash

Make (but don't bake) Parmesan-Crusted Creamed Corn

Make (but don't bake) Pumpkin Bread Pudding

### ✳ 2 days ahead

Make (but don't bake) Old Fashioned Do-Ahead Cornbread Stuffing

Make Make-Ahead Mashed Potatoes

*continued on next page*

## Do-Ahead Countdown *continued*

* **1 day ahead**

   Make Green Beans with
   Caramelized Shallots and
   Roasted Mushrooms

   *Thanksgiving Day
   Countdown*

   Make sure that all your
   dishes are defrosted in the
   refrigerator

   Roast the turkey

   Set the table (if not done
   already)

* **30 minutes before the
   turkey is ready**

   Remove all your side dishes
   and the bread pudding (if
   serving) from the refrigerator
   to come to room temperature.

Pour the gravy into a
saucepan and bring to a
simmer; keep warm.

When the turkey comes out of
the oven, remove from the
rack and cover loosely with
aluminum foil.

Set oven to 350°F.

Remove the stuffing from the
turkey, cover with foil, and
keep warm.

Place corn, potatoes, squash,
and sweet potatoes in the
oven.

Pour drippings into fat
separator, and pour drippings
into the gravy, whisking to
blend. Keep warm over low
heat.

Reheat Green Beans with
Caramelized Shallots and
Roasted Mushrooms.

After turkey has rested for
30 minutes, carve and cover
with aluminum foil. By the
time the turkey has been
carved, your side dishes
should be baked, and you
will be able to serve the
dinner.

When you remove the side
dishes from the oven, place
the Pumpkin Bread Pudding
into the oven (if serving) and
allow it to bake while you are
eating dinner.

# Hot Cranberry Punch

*Serves 12*

*This ruby-red spiced drink is terrific for serving at holiday time. The inviting aroma of cranberries, cloves, and allspice will permeate your house. I also like to serve this punch over ice with a splash of sparkling water for a refreshing and different drink during warmer weather.*

One 48-ounce bottle cranberry juice cocktail

1 cup water

1/2 cup firmly packed dark brown sugar

Three 4-inch cinnamon sticks

1 teaspoon whole allspice berries

3/4 teaspoon whole cloves

1/4 teaspoon ground nutmeg

4 cups fresh orange juice

2 oranges, halved and thinly sliced into half-moons

**1.** Combine all the ingredients except the orange juice and orange slices in a large saucepan, stirring to blend. Bring to a boil, add the orange juice, and return to a boil. Reduce the heat to medium and simmer for 5 minutes. **Diva Do-Ahead:** At this point, you can cool, strain the spices from the punch, and refrigerate for up to 5 days.

**2.** Serve warm, garnished with the orange slices.

## Diva Variation

To serve this drink cold, fill a 12-ounce tumbler with ice, add 4 ounces cranberry punch, and fill the rest of the way with either sparkling water or 7UP. Garnish with the orange slices.

## Slow Cooker Savvy

Combine all the ingredients, except the orange slices, in a 5- to 6-quart slow cooker and warm them on low for 3 to 4 hours until heated through. Strain out the spices and serve the punch garnished with the orange slices.

## Diva Wisdom

I tell my students that if they will be serving children (or adults who act like children) not to serve this drink—it will stain everything that you own. If that is a concern for you, substitute the Warm Spiced Cider (page 219) from the Halloween menu.

# Chocolate Cookie-Cutter Place Cards

Makes 8 place cards

*Years ago I bought some darling turkey-shaped cookie cutters that were filled with chocolate and had candy corn imbedded into the tail section. Wrapped in cellophane, they made the perfect party favor to arrange with a place card at the table. I decided that they would be fun to replicate. You can get very creative, using white, milk, or semisweet chocolate and using different types of decorations. Because these "place cards" will be thick, if you wish to imbed candy decorations you'll need to wait until the chocolate has set a bit; otherwise, they will sink to the bottom.*

**1¹/₂ pounds semisweet, milk, or white chocolate, chopped**
**2 tablespoons vegetable oil**
**Eight 2- or 3-inch turkey-shaped cookie cutters, preferably metal**
**Candy corn or other candy for decorations**
**8 cellophane bags and ribbon ties**

**1.** Line a sheet pan with parchment paper, aluminum foil, or a silicone baking liner. Coat with nonstick cooking spray.

**2.** In a large glass bowl, combine the chocolate with the oil, and microwave on high power for 4 minutes, watching carefully so the chocolate doesn't burn. Stir the chocolate, and microwave at 15-second intervals until it is melted. (The timing will depend upon your microwave.) Or place the bowl over barely simmering water and melt the chocolate, stirring with a heatproof spatula until melted.

**3.** Place the cookie cutters on the prepared sheet very carefully and slowly pour the chocolate into each mold about three-quarters of the way up to the top. Allow the chocolate to set for about 30 minutes and then add candy decorations: candy corn for the tail, the white tip of the candy corn cut to make an eye, and so forth. Transfer the cookie sheet to the refrigerator and refrigerate until firm. **Diva Do-Ahead:** At this point, you can wrap each cutter in plastic wrap and refrigerate for up to 5 days. Remove from the refrigerator at least 3 hours before using. The chocolate may sweat when brought to room temperature, so blot with paper towels if necessary. Using a thin, flexible spatula, transfer each cookie cutter to a cellophane bag and close with a decorative ribbon.

## Diva Variation

Use different cookie cutters for other holidays. At Easter, use bunny-shaped cutters with white chocolate and jelly beans; for Christmas, make semisweet chocolate trees decorated with red and green sprinkles; at Hanukkah, use dreidel-shaped cutters and decorate with gold leaf; and at Halloween, use pumpkin-shaped cutters and tint white chocolate with orange food-coloring paste.

# Curried Cream of Pumpkin Soup

*Serves 8 to 10*

*Smooth and creamy with a hint of curry, this soup is the perfect prelude to your Thanksgiving dinner, especially if you won't be serving a pumpkin dessert. It lends itself well to serving in small pumpkins that you've hollowed out. I have never found that cooking a fresh pumpkin and using it for this soup is worth the trouble, when canned pumpkin is so good. Just make sure to use pumpkin puree and not pumpkin pie filling. Serve along with glasses of Pinot Grigio.*

1/4 cup (1/2 stick) unsalted butter

1/2 cup chopped onion

1 bay leaf

1/3 teaspoon curry powder (or more to taste)

2 cups pumpkin puree

4 cups chicken broth

Salt to taste

2 cups half-and-half

1/4 cup finely chopped fresh Italian parsley, for garnish

1/2 cup toasted pumpkin seeds, for garnish (see page 114)

**1.** Melt the butter in a large saucepan and add the onion, bay leaf, and 1/3 teaspoon curry powder. Cook until the onion is softened but not browned, about 3 minutes.

**2.** Add the pumpkin puree and broth, stirring well, and bring to a boil. Reduce the heat to a simmer and cook, uncovered, for 20 minutes. Taste for seasoning after about 15 minutes, and add more curry powder and salt, if desired. Remove from the heat and remove the bay leaf. **Diva Do-Ahead:** At this point, you can cool, cover, and refrigerate for 4 days or freeze for up to 1 month. Bring to a simmer before proceeding. Add the half-and-half. Bring the soup to a hot serving temperature, but do not boil. **Diva Do-Ahead:** At this point, you can cool and refrigerate for up to 4 days. Serve garnished with parsley and toasted pumpkin seeds.

# Triple Mushroom Soup with Brie

*Serves 8*

*This delicious soup is a terrific warm-up before dinner, with its earthy mushrooms and melted Brie in every bite. A great beginning to any meal, it gives your Thanksgiving guests a little fuel before the main event. You can serve it as a first course or keep it in a soup tureen or slow cooker for your guests to help themselves. Any leftover soup is great with bits of leftover turkey added the next day. As with the pumpkin soup, Pinot Grigio is a good wine choice.*

1/4 cup (1/2 stick) tablespoons
  unsalted butter

1/2 cup chopped shallots

1/2 pound shiitake mushrooms,
  stems removed and sliced

1/2 pound button mushrooms,
  sliced

1/2 pound cremini mushrooms,
  sliced

2 tablespoons flour

3 cups chicken broth

1 cup heavy cream

2 tablespoons sherry

1/3 pound Brie cheese, cut into
  thin slices (rind left on)

1/2 cup chopped chives, for
  garnish

**1.** In a large saucepan over high heat, melt the butter and add the shallots, stirring for 2 to 3 minutes. Add all the mushrooms and sauté for 5 minutes, until the mushroom liquid has begun to evaporate.

**2.** Sprinkle the flour over the mushrooms and stir until the flour begins to cook.

**3.** Gradually add the chicken broth, whisking until the soup is smooth and comes to a boil. **Diva Do-Ahead:** At this point, you can freeze the soup for up to 1 month. Defrost before proceeding. Add the heavy cream and sherry and bring the soup to a simmer. **Diva Do-Ahead:** At this point, you can refrigerate for up to 3 days. Ladle soup into bowls and top each with 2 thin slices of Brie. Garnish with chives.

## Diva Notes

Although I usually don't freeze this soup, you can do it. Just keep in mind that the mushrooms will be a little softer after they have been frozen.

Also, if you object to the heavy cream (even though 1 cup for 8 people isn't really a lot), I recommend that you substitute more chicken broth instead of a lower-fat dairy product.

## Diva Variation

If you would like to puree the soup with an immersion blender or in a conventional blender, you can. Just make sure that you cool the soup before putting it into the blender, to avoid a soup explosion.

# Perfect Roast Turkey

*Serves 12 to 14*

*Every year all the national food magazines tout new ways to roast turkeys to make them more flavorful and juicy. I have taught this method to my students for more than 15 years and have never had one complaint about dry or tough turkey. The most recent fad is "brining," or soaking the turkey in a salt-water solution overnight. The turkey absorbs the brine, becoming juicier, but it also gets saltier and the texture of the meat changes. And you can't use the drippings from a brined turkey, as they are too salty to add to the gravy. If you want to try a brined bird, roast a kosher chicken and see if you like the texture of the meat. If you do, then buy a Butterball or kosher turkey for Thanksgiving because both have already been brined, saving you the mess of a huge container of salted water and a floating turkey.*

*Also, buy a fresh turkey if at all possible. Your local grocery stores will be practically giving away frozen turkeys, and there's a reason for that. I usually pick up a frozen bird and donate it to a shelter or keep it in the freezer and cook it later in the year for a regular dinner. A fresh turkey has better flavor and texture, and I think it's juicier. If you do buy a frozen bird, however, you should defrost it in the refrigerator for three days.*

*When figuring amounts of turkey to serve a crowd, I usually go with $1/2$ to $3/4$ pound per person if I want a few leftovers; $3/4$ to 1 pound per person for a substantial amount of leftovers, and 1 to $1^1/4$ pounds per person if I want to send people home with doggy bags. I also recommend that you don't cook a bird over 18 pounds, because when turkeys get that large the ratio of meat to bone throws off your timing and the bird will be dry. If you need 24 pounds of turkey, roast two 12-pounders; they are more tender and cook in less time, and you'll be happier. Make sure to buy an instant-read thermometer to gauge whether the turkey is cooked—the little plastic thermometers that come imbedded in turkeys sold commercially work on a moisture principle, so when that thing pops up, your turkey has turned to jerky!*

*I think sparkling Pinot Noir is delicious with this turkey. You can also serve regular Pinot Noir, Merlot, or Syrah.*

One 12- to 14-pound fresh
  turkey
Salt and freshly ground black
  pepper to taste
3 ribs celery, cut into 1-inch
  lengths

2 carrots, cut into 1-inch
  lengths
1 onion, quartered
Kitchen twine
6 strips bacon

*continued on next page*

## Perfect Roast Turkey *continued*

**1.** Remove the neck and giblets from the turkey and set aside for other use if you wish, or discard them. Rinse the turkey inside and out under cold running water and pat the inside and outside dry with paper towels. Sprinkle the cavity liberally with salt and pepper. **Diva Do-Ahead:** At this point, you can cover and refrigerate for up to 3 days. Dry the inside of the turkey again if you store it for any length of time.

**2.** Preheat the oven to 325°F. Put the celery, carrots, and onion inside the cavity and tie the legs together with kitchen twine. (If you would like to stuff the turkey, put the stuffing into both cavities, and then tie the legs together with twine and fold the skin flap over the other cavity so that it rests underneath the bird.) Transfer the turkey to a rack in a heavy-duty roasting pan. Drape the bacon over the turkey and roast for 1$^1$/$_2$ hours, then remove and discard the bacon. Continue roasting until an instant-read thermometer inserted into the thickest part of the thigh (behind the drumstick) without touching the bone registers 170° to 175°F, another 1$^1$/$_2$ to 2 hours. If you would like to baste the turkey with pan drippings, start doing so after 2 hours. If the turkey is browned to your liking before it reaches 170°F, loosely tent it with aluminum foil for the duration of the cooking time.

**3.** Remove the turkey from the oven, transfer to a cutting board, and cover with foil. Allow the turkey to rest for at least 30 minutes, then carve as directed on page 249.

### Diva Tip

I've roasted turkeys in conventional ovens and convection ovens, and I find that convection ovens don't provide as many caramelized drippings as roasting low and slow in a conventional oven.

## Diva Variations

**Maple-Glazed Turkey:** Follow the basic recipe, but baste the turkey with 1/4 cup of pure maple syrup during the last hour of cooking.

**Cider-Glazed Roast Turkey:** Omit the onion, carrots, celery, and bacon. Stuff the turkey with 6 cored and quartered Gala or Golden Delicious apples. In a 2-quart saucepan over medium heat, combine 2 cups apple cider and 1/2 cup firmly packed light brown sugar and stir until the cider is hot and the sugar dissolves. **Diva Do-Ahead:** At this point, you can cool and refrigerate until ready to use, up to 2 weeks. Brush the turkey liberally with the cider syrup before it goes into the oven. Roast the turkey as directed, basting with more of the syrup every half hour. Discard remaining syrup.

**Hoisin-Glazed Roasted Turkey:** In a large bowl, combine 2 cups hoisin sauce, 1/2 cup soy sauce, and 1/2 cup rice wine or seasoned rice vinegar until smooth. Divide the sauce in half, refrigerating one half and painting the turkey liberally with the rest. **Diva Do-Ahead:** At this point, cover and refrigerate the sauce and turkey for at least 24 hours and up to 3 days. Bring to room temperature before continuing. Substitute 6 scallions, chopped, for the onion and omit the celery and bacon. Stuff the turkey with the scallions and carrots and roast as directed, basting with the reserved hoisin glaze every half hour. Transfer the roasted turkey to a cutting board, drizzle with 1/4 cup toasted sesame oil, cover with aluminum foil, and let rest at least 30 minutes. Carve and serve with warm flour tortillas, more hoisin sauce, and chopped scallions, as you would Peking duck.

**Thyme-and-Sage-Rubbed Turkey:** Omit the bacon. Combine 1 cup (2 sticks) of unsalted butter, melted, and 2 tablespoons each of chopped fresh thyme and sage and brush it liberally over the turkey; keep the butter warm over very low heat. Roast the turkey as directed, basting every half hour with the herbed butter baste. Discard remaining baste.

# Turkey Roasting Times

The following estimates are for roasting a turkey in a conventional oven preheated to 325°F. Remember the internal temperature, not the cooking time, is the only accurate way to know if the turkey is done.

| WEIGHT OF TURKEY | ROASTING TIMES | |
| --- | --- | --- |
| | UNSTUFFED | STUFFED |
| 4 to 8 pounds | 1$^1$/$_2$ to 2 hours | 2$^1$/$_2$ to 3$^1$/$_2$ hours |
| 8 to 12 pounds | 2$^3$/$_4$ to 3 hours | 3 to 3$^1$/$_2$ hours |
| 12 to 14 pounds | 3 to 3$^3$/$_4$ hours | 3$^1$/$_2$ to 4 hours |
| 14 to 18 pounds | 3$^3$/$_4$ to 4$^1$/$_4$ hours | 4 to 4$^1$/$_4$ hours |
| 18 to 20 pounds | 4$^1$/$_4$ to 4$^1$/$_2$ hours | 4$^1$/$_4$ to 4$^3$/$_4$ hours |
| 20 to 24 pounds | 4$^1$/$_2$ to 5 hours | 4$^3$/$_4$ to 5$^1$/$_4$ hours |
| 24 to 30 pounds | 5 to 5$^1$/$_4$ hours | 5$^1$/$_4$ to 6$^1$/$_4$ hours |

The stuffing should register 165°F on an instant-read thermometer, and the turkey should register 170° to 175°F at the thickest part of the thigh or breast.

## Do-Ahead Turkey?

Everyone asks me if you can roast turkey ahead of time. The answer to this question is yes and no. It's not my first choice, but you can do it, and it comes in handy if you need to roast more than one turkey.

Roast one turkey the day before according to the directions on pages 245–246, allow it to cool, and slice the meat. Arrange the meat in a baking dish and pour $^1$/$_2$ to 1 cup chicken or turkey broth over the turkey. Cover with aluminum foil and refrigerate overnight. On Thanksgiving Day, roast another turkey as directed. When the turkey is roasted, remove from the oven and let it rest. Have the baking dish with your do-ahead turkey at room temperature and bake at 350°F, covered with aluminum foil, for 20 to 30 minutes until heated through. Carve the freshly roasted turkey and serve that first, then for second helpings, serve the other.

# Carving the Bird

Every year, thousands of turkey lovers watch as a dear loved one carves the golden turkey directly out of the oven for the eagerly expectant diners—resulting in a shredded mess rather than beautifully sliced meat. Because someone isn't patient enough to wait for the turkey to rest, many people end up with little bits of meat, rather than nice thick slabs of white meat or rich nuggets of dark meat.

The Diva recommends that you don't carve at the table. First of all, it will be loaded with food, crystal, and chinaware, giving you a very small area to work in. Second, bringing in a cutting board robs the dinner of its ambiance, and if the turkey is particularly juicy, the juices may run off the carving board and onto the table. So it's not a good idea, period! Finally, I've seen more carving-at-the-table disasters than I care to remember, with turkeys flying off the serving platter and dads having a few too many martinis before dinner and hacking away at the bird as if it's a redwood. So take my advice, learn from my mistakes, and carve in the kitchen. People will be congregated there anyway, so you can dramatically pull the turkey out of the oven and show it off before allowing it to rest and reheating your side dishes.

Whenever you cook a good-sized piece of protein like a turkey, roast beef, or fish, you need to let it rest a bit, so that the meat reaches its proper internal cooking temperature without overcooking in the oven and the juices reabsorb into the meat, making it much easier to carve. You will need a sharp carving knife, so a few weeks before the main event have your knives sharpened (mark your do-ahead calendar). I recommend a meat carving knife that is hollow-ground, meaning that it has what look like scallops along the edge, but it's not serrated. The scallops help the knife slide through the cooked meat, rather than drag through it.

If you have stuffed the turkey, immediately upon taking the turkey from the oven remove all the stuffing to a serving dish, cover with aluminum foil, and keep warm in the oven. Allow your turkey to rest, loosely covered with aluminum foil, for at least 30 minutes, and *do not* listen to those in the kitchen who are whispering, "It's going to get cold." I've taught this dinner many times, sometimes waiting more than an hour before carving—and the turkey can still burn my hands because it has retained its heat.

*continued on next page*

Remove the drumsticks by cutting through the joint that connects the drumstick to the thigh. Cut some of the meat off one drumstick and then leave the other whole on the platter. Slice down through the joint that attaches the thigh to the turkey and then slice off the meat from the thighbone. Starting at the top of the breastbone, cut down along the breast-bone, following the contour of the meat along the bone, until you reach the bottom of the breast, and remove the entire piece of breast meat. Slice this piece across the grain into $1/2$-inch-thick slices and arrange on your serving platter. Repeat this process on the other side of the turkey. Garnish the platter with some fresh parsley, thyme, and sage sprigs, and if you want to gild the lily, fill hollowed-out orange halves with whole fresh cranberries or cranberry chutney. Enjoy!

# Make-Ahead Gravy

*Makes 4 cups*

*Last-minute whisking and stirring can make even the most seasoned kitchen veteran a little frazzled, but this Diva trick will make you the gravy champ in your family. The gravy base is made weeks ahead and frozen. On Thanksgiving, while the turkey is resting after it comes out of the oven, separate the fat from the drippings. Then pour the drippings into the gravy base, and you'll have a deep, rich gravy for all to enjoy. If you have a family of gravy lovers, double or triple the recipe. Leftovers freeze beautifully.*

6 tablespoons unsalted butter
  or margarine
6 tablespoons all-purpose flour
4 cups chicken broth or turkey
  broth
Salt and freshly ground black
  pepper to taste
Drippings from the turkey pan

**1.** In a medium-size saucepan, melt the butter and whisk in the flour. Cook over medium-high heat until the flour is incorporated and white bubbles begin to form on the top of the roux. Cook the roux for 2 to 3 minutes, after the white bubbles have formed, whisking constantly.

**2.** Gradually add the broth, whisking constantly and stirring until the gravy is thickened and comes to a boil. Remove from the heat and season with salt and pepper. **Diva Do-Ahead:**

At this point, you can cool, cover, and refrigerate for up to 4 days or freeze for up to 6 weeks. Defrost before proceeding.

**3.** On Thanksgiving Day, heat the gravy in a medium-size saucepan. When the turkey is done, pour off all the drippings into a jar or fat separator. Skim or spoon off all the fat and discard. Add the drippings to the gravy and bring it to serving temperature.

## Diva Variations

Inside the turkey is a bag containing the heart, liver, and gizzard. If your family enjoys these in the gravy, poach them in a saucepan with 2 cups of chicken broth for about 45 minutes, until they are cooked through. Cool and finely chop. Add them to the finished gravy.

If you like the gravy thicker, make a paste of 1 part flour to 1 part softened or melted butter, kneading the flour into the butter with a tablespoon. This is called a *beurre manié*, and it is used to help thicken sauces. Whisk some *beurre manié* into the gravy after adding the drippings. Bring back to a boil after each addition, and add more *beurre manié* until the gravy is thickened to your preference.

## Diva Tip

Keeping the gravy hot is always a dilemma, so here are a few suggestions:

* Buy a thermal gravy carafe or other thermal container.
* Keep the gravy warm on low in a slow cooker.
* Pour boiling water into your gravy boat about 15 minutes before serving and let it sit. Pour the water out, pour in the gravy, and the boat should remain warm for about half an hour.

## What? No Drippings?

Some people swear by grilling, smoking, or deep-frying their turkeys, but they end up without drippings to stir into the gravy. If this is you, never fear! Two weeks before Thanksgiving, roast a chicken or chicken parts, which will give you some nice caramelized drippings that can be frozen, then stirred into your gravy. You can actually have the gravy completely ready to go on Thanksgiving if you choose to do it this way.

# Old-Fashioned Do-Ahead Bread Stuffing

*Makes enough to stuff a 14- to 18-pound bird or to serve 12*

*I've never met a stuffing I didn't like, and this simple stuffing flavored with sage, thyme, onion, and celery can be jazzed up with your favorite additions. Although you can buy herb-seasoned dry bread cubes in the grocery store, I urge you to use stale bread and dry it out in the oven, then add your own herbs. The difference in effort is small, but the difference in flavor is huge! If you are using leftover baguettes with a hard crust, remove the tough parts of the crust, because they will absorb most of the liquid. I like to use a high-quality white sandwich bread like Pepperidge Farm and include the crusts.*

1 cup (2 sticks) unsalted butter

2 cups chopped celery

2 cups chopped onion

1 tablespoon finely chopped fresh sage or 1 teaspoon dried sage

1 tablespoon finely chopped fresh thyme leaves or 1 teaspoon dried thyme

12 cups stale dry bread cubes

1 tablespoon salt

1/2 teaspoon freshly ground black pepper

1 1/2 to 2 cups chicken broth, as needed

1 large egg, beaten

**1.** Melt the butter over low heat in a large sauté pan and cook the celery, onion, sage, and thyme until the onion is golden.

**2.** Place the bread cubes, salt, and pepper in a large mixing bowl and add the celery mixture, tossing to blend.

**3.** Pour the broth over the stuffing ingredients, add the egg, and stir to blend. **Diva Do-Ahead:** At this point, you can cool, cover, and refrigerate for up to 3 days or freeze for up to 1 month.

**4.** Preheat the oven to 350°F. Coat the inside of a 3-quart baking dish with nonstick cooking spray. Transfer the stuffing to the baking dish and bake for 30 minutes, basting with turkey drippings or butter halfway through the cooking time. If you put the stuffing into the turkey, it will roast according to the timing chart on page 248.

## Diva Note

If you like crispy stuffing, don't drown your bread cubes in liquid, and bake the stuffing outside the turkey. For those who like a moist stuffing, stuff it inside the turkey, or add more liquid to the stuffing and bake it covered with aluminum foil in the oven.

## Diva Variations

While sautéing the onion and celery, add any of the following:

- 1 pound sliced mushrooms
- $1/2$ pound crawfish tails
- $1/2$ cup dried chopped apricots
- $1/2$ cup dried cranberries
- 1 dozen chopped oysters
- 1 cup pecan halves
- 1 cup giblets, poached in broth or water for about 30 minutes and finely chopped

## Diva Tip

If you are serving a crowd, pack the stuffing into greased loaf pans and bake as directed. Turn the stuffing out of the loaf pans and let rest for 5 minutes. Cut the stuffing with a serrated knife that has been coated with nonstick cooking spray and arrange the slices on a platter. Or, fill 18 wells in greased muffin tins with the stuffing and bake for 15 to 17 minutes, until golden.

# Old-Fashioned Do-Ahead Cornbread Stuffing

*Makes enough to stuff a 14- to 18-pound turkey or to serve 12*

**Southerners love their cornbread stuffing, and many Southern cooks add seafood to their versions, either crawfish or oysters, but my favorite is made with crawfish and nuggets of spicy andouille sausage, giving the stuffing a terrific flavor and balancing the relative blandness of the turkey. If you use Jiffy mix to make your cornbread, you'll need two boxes for this recipe.**

1/2 pound andouille sausage, finely chopped

1/4 cup (1/2 stick) unsalted butter

1 cup finely chopped onion

1 cup finely chopped celery

1/2 cup finely chopped green bell pepper

Pinch of cayenne pepper (optional)

2 tablespoons finely chopped fresh sage or 2 teaspoons dried sage

1/2 pound cooked shelled crawfish tails (if not available, substitute lump crabmeat or chopped cooked shrimp)

1 to 1 1/2 cups chicken broth, as needed

Salt and freshly ground black pepper to taste

8 cups crumbled cornbread (contents of one 13 x 9-inch baking dish)

1 large egg

1/2 cup chopped fresh Italian parsley

**1.** In a large skillet over medium heat, cook the sausage until the fat is rendered. Drain the fat from the pan, add the butter, then add the onion, celery, bell pepper, cayenne if using, and sage. Cook for about 5 minutes, until the onion is translucent and the other vegetables are softened. Add the crawfish and 1 cup broth. Season with salt and pepper to taste. The mixture should be highly seasoned.

**2.** Preheat the oven to 350°F. Coat a 13 x 9-inch baking dish with nonstick cooking spray.

**3.** Crumble the cornbread into a large bowl and pour the broth mixture over it. Add the egg, stirring to blend. The stuffing should be slightly moist but not wet; add more broth if it seems too dry. Stir in the parsley, then transfer to the prepared dish. **Diva Do-Ahead:** At this point, you can cover and refrigerate for up to 2 days or freeze for 1 month. Bring to room temperature before continuing. Bake the stuffing until the top is golden brown, 30 to 40 minutes. Let rest for 5 to 10 minutes before serving.

# Make-Ahead Mashed Potatoes

*Serves 10 to 12*

*Remember Mom and Grandma struggling to get the potatoes mashed just before the big Thanksgiving dinner and how they often seemed lumpy, or watery, or not quite right? Well, this recipe will ensure that you never have to stand over the stove as everyone is waiting for dinner, sweating over all those potatoes, and no one has to know that they have been ready for days! The additions of cream cheese and sour cream make these potatoes puff up in the oven like a soufflé, which makes them even more delicious.*

8 to 10 medium-size russet baking potatoes, peeled and cut into 1-inch chunks (see Diva Quickie)

6 tablespoons (3/4 stick) unsalted butter, softened

3/4 cup freshly grated Parmesan cheese

1 cup sour cream

One 8-ounce package cream cheese, softened

1/3 cup chopped fresh chives (optional)

Salt and freshly ground black pepper to taste

**1.** Boil the potatoes in salted water to cover, until tender, and drain.

**2.** Preheat the oven to 350°F. Rub a 13 x 9-inch baking dish with 2 tablespoons of the butter. Sprinkle 1/4 cup of the Parmesan into the dish and tip the dish so the cheese is evenly distributed and adheres to the butter.

*continued on next page*

## Diva Quickie

The smaller the potato cubes, the faster they will cook, so if you have lots of time for your potatoes to boil, leave them larger; otherwise, cut them into a smaller dice to cook them in a flash. When boiling potatoes, I use a pasta pot with a colander insert; that way I can remove the potatoes from the water and drain them over the stove before I put them in a bowl.

## Skins On or Off?

For Thanksgiving I love pure white potatoes, but if you like to leave the skins on (and they are unblemished), you can. If there is a greenish tinge on the potato skin, however, remove it with a peeler.

**3.** Place the hot cooked potatoes in a large bowl and add the sour cream, cream cheese, 2 tablespoons of the remaining butter, 1/4 cup of the Parmesan, and the chives, if using. Using an electric mixer, beat the potatoes until smooth. Taste for seasoning and add with salt and pepper as desired.

**4.** Transfer to the prepared dish, dot with the remaining 2 tablespoons butter, and sprinkle with the remaining 1/4 cup Parmesan. **Diva Do-Ahead:** At this point, you can cover and refrigerate for 2 to 3 days or freeze for up to 1 month. Bring to room temperature before continuing. Bake the potatoes until golden, about 25 minutes. Serve hot.

## What Kind of Potato?

The best potatoes for mashing are Idaho baking potatoes, or russet-type potatoes. They are drier and will give you a fluffy potato dish. But I also like to make mashed red-skinned potatoes and Yukon Golds. They are just a bit waxier and moister, though, and won't have the ethereal fluffy quality of the russet.

# The Diva on Low-Fat and Nonfat Products

I look at nonfat foods as if they were a blind date: the expectations are enormous, but they are almost never met. Low-fat products are acceptable in most cases, although they do leave a bit to be desired in the flavor department. When they reduce the fat, manufacturers add sugar and/or water to the product to make up the difference, so your cooking times will vary when using a low-fat dairy product such as sour cream or cream cheese. A new product on the market is fat-free half-and-half, but it has too much sugar to be used in savory dishes, so I don't recommend it. Nonfat sour cream, cream cheese, and cheeses have a distinct waxy quality. If you use them in the Make-Ahead Mashed Potatoes (page 255), your potatoes will become gluey and waxy, so please, don't do it. That recipe also will not work if you substitute chicken broth for any of the sour cream or cream cheese, so I don't recommend that either.

Those of us who are health-conscious try to watch fat intake. But on holidays, I do pull out all the stops and use full-fat dairy products for all these dishes. But I did also test them with low-fat products, which are an acceptable alternative.

## Slow Cooker Savvy

These potatoes can be prepared in a 4-quart slow cooker if you have a removable ceramic insert. Butter the insert and dust it with the cheese as directed in step 2. Follow the recipe through step 3, then fill the insert with the mashed potatoes. Cover and cook on low for 4 to 6 hours, until heated through. An extra dusting of Parmesan and butter before serving makes them look divine.

# Sweet Potato and Apple Gratin

*Serves 8*

*Tart Granny Smiths and sherry-spiked sweet potatoes are a perfect combination for this delicious side dish, which is terrific with poultry or pork and a welcome change from the usual marshmallow-and-yam casserole served at Thanksgiving. I have taught this dish in my do-ahead Thanksgiving classes for more than 20 years, and it is even a hit with people who don't like sweet potatoes!*

Two 32-ounce cans sweet potatoes, drained (see The Diva Says)

$2/3$ cup firmly packed light brown sugar

$2/3$ cup dark corn syrup

$1/2$ cup (1 stick) unsalted butter, melted

3 tablespoons cream sherry

$1^1/2$ teaspoons ground cinnamon

$1/8$ teaspoon ground nutmeg

4 medium-size Granny Smith or other tart apples, peeled, cored, and sliced $1/4$-inch thick

**1.** Preheat the oven to 350°F.

**2.** Put the sweet potatoes in a large bowl. With an electric mixer, beat until smooth. Add the brown sugar, corn syrup, $1/4$ cup ($1/2$ stick) of the butter, the sherry, cinnamon, and nutmeg, and blend until creamy.

**2.** Spread half of the sweet potato mixture into a 10- to 12-inch pie plate 2 inches deep or a 13 x 9-inch baking dish. Arrange half the apple slices over the potato layer and brush with some of the remaining butter. The butter will seal the apples and prevent discoloration. Spread the remaining sweet potato mixture over the apples and arrange the remaining apple slices on top in an attractive pattern. Brush with the remaining butter, covering the apples completely.

**Diva Do-Ahead:** At this point, you can cover and refrigerate for up to 4 days or freeze for up to 1 month. Defrost and bring to room temperature before continuing. Bake the dish, uncovered, until the apples are golden brown, 30 to 40 minutes. Serve warm.

**The Diva Says**

If you would prefer to use fresh sweet potatoes, bake 8 medium-size sweet potatoes (remember to poke holes in them) at 425°F until tender when squeezed with an oven mitt, 50 to 60 minutes. When cool enough to handle, cut in half and scoop out the flesh. Proceed as directed.

# Creamy Butternut Squash

*Serves 8 to 10*

*For some families, if there isn't butternut squash on the table, it isn't Thanksgiving. This creamy dish adds color and flavor to your Thanksgiving table, and, of course, it can be made a few days ahead of time.*

1/2 cup (1 stick) unsalted butter

1 cup finely chopped sweet yellow onion

1 butternut squash, peeled, seeded, and cut into 1-inch chunks

2 tablespoons fresh thyme leaves, chopped, or 2 teaspoons dried thyme

1 teaspoon salt (or more to taste)

1/2 teaspoon freshly ground black pepper (or more to taste)

1/4 to 1/2 cup chicken broth

1/4 cup heavy cream (optional)

**1.** In a large stockpot, melt 4 tablespoons (1/2 stick) of the butter over medium-high heat and add the onion, sautéing until the onion is softened, about 4 minutes.

**2.** Add the squash, thyme, 1 teaspoon salt, and 1/2 teaspoon pepper, stirring to blend. Cover the pan and allow the vegetables to sweat for about 4 minutes. Some liquid should form in the pan; then stir in enough chicken broth to cover half the squash chunks. Cover the pan and simmer until the squash is soft, about 10 minutes. Remove from the heat, drain the squash, return to the pan, add 2 tablespoons butter, and puree the mixture with an immersion blender, or cool and puree in a blender or food processor. **Diva Do-Ahead:** At this point, you can cover and refrigerate for up to 3 days or freeze for up to 1 month. Defrost before proceeding.

**3.** Reheat the squash in a saucepan, adding the remaining 2 tablespoons butter and the cream, if using. (The cream is optional but really adds to the flavor.) Taste the dish for seasoning and add additional salt and pepper if needed. Keep the squash warm on the stovetop until ready to serve.

# Cranberry-Peach Chutney

*Makes about 4 1/2 cups*

**Peaches, onions, and cranberries combine in this stunning relish to make a sweet and pungent side dish. You can also serve it with other poultry and pork, and it's terrific on a turkey sandwich the next day!**

One 16-ounce can peach
  halves packed in syrup,
  drained and syrup reserved
One 12-ounce package fresh
  or frozen cranberries
1 1/2 cups sugar
1 medium-size onion, chopped
1 cup pecan halves
1/2 teaspoon ground cinnamon
1/4 teaspoon ground ginger

**1.** Coarsely chop the peaches and set aside.

**2.** Combine the cranberries, reserved peach syrup, sugar, and onion in a large saucepan over medium-high heat and cook until the cranberries begin to pop, about 10 minutes. Stir in the pecans, cinnamon, ginger, and peaches and cook 10 minutes longer.

**3.** Remove from the heat and let cool. **Diva Do-Ahead:** At this point, you can cover and refrigerate for up to 1 month or freeze for up to 3 months. Serve the chutney cold, warm, or at room temperature.

# Green Beans with Caramelized Shallots and Roasted Mushrooms

*Serves 10*

**Serving something other than the ubiquitous green bean bake (there are more than 15 million made each Thanksgiving) on the holiday is unheard-of in some parts, but this simple, elegant dish has gained a lot of converts.**

2 pounds green beans, ends trimmed and halved

1 tablespoon salt

2 teaspoons freshly ground black pepper

10 medium-size shallots, halved

1 1/2 pounds mushrcoms, such as cremini (my favorite), shiitake, white, or a mixture, quartered

1/2 cup olive oil

2 teaspoons chopped fresh thyme leaves

**The Diva Says**

This dish also makes a great room-temperature salad, with the addition of 2 to 3 tablespoons red wine vinegar tossed with the finished beans and mushrooms.

**1.** Fill a steamer pan with water to about 1/2 inch below the steamer insert. Place the insert in the pot, cover, and bring the water to a boil. Spread out the beans evenly in the steamer with a long-handled spoon, cover, and cook until the beans are crisp-tender, about 5 minutes. Remove the steamer with oven mitts, and shake the beans dry in the basket. (If you are steaming the beans ahead of time, plunge them into cold water and drain immediately so they will retain their color.) Sprinkle with 1 1/2 teaspoons of the salt and 1 teaspoon of the pepper. **Diva Do-Ahead**: At this point, you can place in a zipper-top plastic bag and refrigerate overnight.

**2.** Preheat the oven to 375°F. Line a baking sheet with aluminum foil or a silicone baking liner.

**3.** In a large bowl, toss together the shallots, mushrooms, olive oil, remaining 1 1/2 teaspoons salt and 1 teaspoon pepper, and the thyme. Spread the mushroom mixture over the baking sheet and roast for 20 minutes, turning once. **Diva Do-Ahead:** At this point, you can cool, transfer to a zipper-top plastic bag, and refrigerate overnight.

**4.** If beans have been refrigerated, poke 3 holes into the plastic bag with the beans and microwave on high power for 2 minutes. Remove beans from the bag and arrange in a serving bowl. While beans are warming, reheat the mushrooms if necessary in a medium-size skillet over high heat, tossing them until heated through. Pour the mushrooms over the beans and serve warm or at room temperature.

# Parmesan-Crusted Creamed Corn

*Serves 8 to 10*

*This luxuriously creamy and comforting corn dish is the most requested recipe from my Thanksgiving classes. I think the reason is that the simplicity of the ingredients belies the sophistication and scrumptious flavor. You may substitute whole milk for the cream, but the finished dish will not be as luxurious.*

6 tablespoons (³/4 stick)
    unsalted butter, melted
²/3 cup freshly grated
    Parmesan cheese
1¹/2 cups heavy cream
Two 16-ounce packages frozen
    white corn, defrosted
2 teaspoons salt
1 teaspoon sugar
3 tablespoons all-purpose flour

**1.** Preheat the oven to 350°F. Brush a 13 x 9-inch baking dish with some of the butter.

**2.** Sprinkle ¹/3 cup of the cheese over the bottom of the dish and tilt so the cheese is evenly distributed and adheres to the butter. (Or you can use ten 4-ounce ramekins for individual servings.)

**3.** In a large saucepan, heat the cream until it begins to boil. Add the corn, salt, and sugar and heat, stirring occasionally, until the mixture is almost at a boil.

**4.** In the meantime, make a paste out of the remaining melted butter and the flour. Stir it into the mixture in the saucepan and cook until thickened and the liquid comes to a boil. Remove the pan from the heat, transfer the mixture to the prepared dish (or ramekins), and sprinkle with the remaining ¹/3 cup cheese. **Diva Do-Ahead:** At this point, you can let cool, cover, and refrigerate for up to 3 days or freeze for up to 1 month. Bring to room temperature before continuing.

**5.** Bake the corn until bubbling and golden brown, about 30 minutes. (Individual ramekins will take 15 to 20 minutes.) Serve immediately.

## Diva Tip

I usually don't recommend skim milk in cream sauces, because it will sometimes give the sauce a bluish tinge—not attractive at all!

# Pumpkin Bread Pudding with Orange-Ginger Custard Sauce

*Serves 12*

*Flavored with pumpkin, cinnamon, cloves, and ginger, this bread pudding will make a stellar ending to your Thanksgiving celebration. Serve it in a pool of orange custard sauce or top it with whipped cream for an amazing dessert. I like to make the pudding with an egg bread, such as challah. It has to be made at least a day ahead of time to soak in the pumpkin mixture, but that gives you more time to relax. It bakes in the oven while you and your guests are enjoying the main course.*

9 cups challah or other egg
   bread, torn into chunks
   (about 1 pound)
1 1/2 cups heavy cream
One 16-ounce can pumpkin
   puree
4 large eggs
1 cup firmly packed light
   brown sugar
2 teaspoons ground cinnamon
1/4 teaspoon ground cloves
1/4 teaspoon ground nutmeg
1/8 teaspoon ground ginger
Orange-Ginger Custard Sauce
   (page 264)

**1.** Preheat the oven to 350°F. Coat a 13 x 9-inch baking dish with nonstick cooking spray.

**2.** Put the bread in a large bowl. In another large bowl, whisk together the cream, pumpkin, eggs, brown sugar, and all the spices. Pour over the bread and stir to blend, pushing the bread down into the mixture. Transfer to the prepared dish. Cover and refrigerate for at least 12 hours. **Diva Do-Ahead:** At this point, you can refrigerate for up to 72 hours. Bring to room temperature before continuing.

**3.** Bake the pudding until puffed and golden brown, 35 to 40 minutes. Remove from the oven and let rest for 10 minutes. Serve individual portions in a pool of custard sauce, or drizzle sauce over the top.

## Diva Variation

Sprinkle the pudding with about 1 cup chopped pecans or walnuts before baking to send it over the top!

# Orange-Ginger Custard Sauce

*Makes about 3 cups*

*This gingery smooth custard sauce is just the right thing to serve with an apple cake, gingerbread, spice cake, or this bread pudding.*

3 cups whole milk

Zest of 1 orange

2 teaspoons chopped
   crystallized ginger

$1/3$ cup sugar

$1/4$ cup cornstarch

6 large egg yolks

1 cup heavy cream

1 to 2 teaspoons orange
   liqueur or orange extract

**1.** In a medium-size saucepan, heat the milk, orange zest, and ginger over medium high heat until the milk beings to form bubbles around the sides of the pan. Remove from the heat and allow to steep for 5 minutes. Strain the zest and ginger out of the milk, returning the milk to the saucepan.

**2.** Whisk in the sugar, cornstarch, and egg yolks, and, over medium heat, whisk until the mixture thickens and comes to a boil, 4 to 5 minutes. Remove from the heat and stir in the cream and liqueur. Transfer to a glass bowl, let cool slightly, and press plastic wrap directly against the surface to keep a skin from forming. Refrigerate for at least 4 hours. **Diva Do-Ahead:** At this point, you may refrigerate for up to 4 days or freeze for up to 1 month.

**3.** When ready to serve, rewhisk the sauce and serve cold or warm.

# Hot Apple Pie Sundaes

*Serves 8 to 10*

*This simple hot and crunchy dessert is a wonderful ending to your Thanksgiving meal. The hot apple pie filling can be prepared three to four days in advance, then heated up before layering in sundae or parfait glasses with a crunchy streusel topping. Store scoops of ice cream separated by waxed paper in plastic containers in the freezer for quick serving.*

### Streusel Topping
1/2 cup (1 stick) unsalted butter
1/2 cup all-purpose flour
1/2 cup firmly packed light brown sugar
1/2 cup chopped pecans

### Apple Filling
1/2 cup (1 stick) unsalted butter, cut into pieces
2/3 cup firmly packed light brown sugar
3 Granny Smith apples, peeled, cored, and chopped
1 teaspoon ground cinnamon
1/8 teaspoon ground nutmeg

### Assembly
1 recipe streusel topping
1 recipe apple filling
1 quart good-quality vanilla ice cream
2 cups heavy cream, whipped to stiff peaks, for garnish (optional)

**1.** To make the streusel, preheat the oven to 400°F. Line a baking sheet with parchment paper, aluminum foil, or a silicone baking liner.

**2.** In a medium-size mixing bowl, cut the butter into the flour and sugar, until the mixture begins to look like peas. Add the pecans and stir to blend.

**3.** Transfer the mixture to the baking sheet, breaking up any bits that are large. Bake the streusel for 10 to 15 minutes, or until golden brown. **Diva Do-Ahead:** At this point, you can cool, transfer to a zipper-top plastic bag, and refrigerate for up to 1 week or freeze for up to 2 months. Defrost and bring to room temperature before proceeding.

**4.** To make the apple filling, melt the butter in a large skillet and add the brown sugar, cooking until the sugar is melted. Add the apples, cinnamon, and nutmeg and cook until the sauce is thickened and the apples are golden and soft, 10 to 15 minutes. Remove from the heat and use immediately. **Diva Do-Ahead:** At this point you can cool and refrigerate in an airtight container for up to 4 days. Reheat before serving.

**5.** To assemble the sundaes, sprinkle a bit of the streusel in the bottom of 8 to 10 sundae glasses and ladle some of the hot apple filling into each glass. Top with a scoop of ice cream, more apple filling, and another scoop of ice cream. Top with more apple topping and sprinkle with some of the streusel topping. Garnish with whipped cream if desired, and serve immediately.

We Spring from
Our Beds
# A Christmas
# Breakfast and
# Dinner

# A Simple but Festive Christmas Breakfast

Holiday breakfasts can be either a little frantic or a little forlorn. Whether it's Christmas or Easter or Thanksgiving, you want to give your family and guests something to satisfy them so that they are not gnawing on the dining room table by the time dinner is ready later in the day, but you don't want to spend too much time in the kitchen. At Christmas, there is the added excitement of opening presents, and then everyone saying "What's for breakfast?" My family has been eating Dutch Baby Pancakes every Christmas morning since my daughter, Carrie, can remember, and it isn't Christmas at our house without this traditional and simple puffed pancake. If you need more inspiration, I've got a few other selections here to round out the menu. You can serve all or part of it for your family, depending upon their appetites, the number of guests you have, and what you'll be serving later in the day. I've designed it to serve about 12 people, but you can easily cut recipes in half to serve a more intimate group.

Decorations for this breakfast should be simple. You've already decorated the house for Christmas, and you have probably set the dining room table for dinner, so serve this meal buffet-style in the kitchen. Or if your family has the main Christmas dinner on Christmas Eve, serve this breakfast at the dinner table with all the beautiful arrangements from the night before. Traditional, family-friendly Christmas carols are the obvious and best choice for music!

# Do-Ahead Countdown

## ✳ 1 month ahead

Download shopping list and do-ahead calendar and fill them out

Shop for nonperishables

Make and freeze Sweet Corn, Spinach, and Bacon Breakfast Tortes

## ✳ 3 days ahead

Prepare fruit for Breakfast Ambrosia

## ✳ 2 days ahead

Make Ultimate Hot Chocolate

Prepare Traditional Dutch Baby Pancake batter

Prepare Volcanic Apple-Cinnamon Pancake components

Make Denver Omelet Casserole

## ✳ 1 day ahead

Remove Sweet Corn, Spinach, and Bacon Breakfast Tortes from freezer and defrost in refrigerator

Whip cream for hot chocolate

## ✳ Day of

Make Traditional Dutch Baby Pancakes

Bake Volcanic Apple-Cinnamon Pancake

Rewarm hot chocolate, tortes, and casserole

Assemble Breakfast Ambrosia

# Ultimate Hot Chocolate

*Serves 12*

*My favorite hot chocolates are those that are thick, creamy, chocolatey, and topped with a crown of freshly whipped cream and a few chocolate curls or shavings. (Unfortunately, too many hot chocolates are made from a packaged, powdered mix that's been reconstituted with water—how sad.) This ultimate hot chocolate can be put together the day before, then heated up just before serving. Whip the cream the day before and then rewhisk before topping off each mug, or buy a $CO_2$-charged whipped cream dispenser (available at gourmet and specialty shops) and keep that cold in the fridge. My friend Lora Brody, the author of many wonderful cookbooks, my favorite of which is* Chocolate American Style *(Clarkson Potter, 2004), inspired this recipe.*

6 cups whole milk

3³/₄ cups heavy cream

³/₄ pound semisweet
  chocolate, chopped

Chocolate shavings or curls for
  garnish (optional)

Candy canes for swizzle sticks
  (optional)

Mini marshmallows
  (if you must)

**1.** In a medium-size saucepan, heat the milk and 2¹/₄ cups of the cream until small bubbles form around the outside edges of the pan. Remove the pan from the heat and stir in the chocolate a bit at a time, until it is melted. **Diva Do-Ahead:** At this point, you can cool and refrigerate the chocolate mixture overnight. Rewarm over low heat until serving temperature.

**2.** Using an electric mixer, whip the remaining 1¹/₂ cups cream until very stiff. **Diva Do-Ahead:** At this point, you can cover and refrigerate for up to 1 day. Rewhisk before serving.

**3.** To serve, pour the hot chocolate into mugs to within about ¹/₂ inch of the top. Dollop with the whipped cream. If desired, dust with chocolate shavings, add a candy cane as a stirrer, and/or sprinkle with marshmallows.

# Traditional Dutch Baby Pancake

*Serves 6*

*Dutch Babies are much like popovers in that they are made with eggs, milk, and flour, but after that the similarity ends. These magic pancakes rise to great heights in a hot oven and are then served with maple syrup, berries, and whipped cream, or traditionally with powdered sugar and fresh lemon juice squeezed over them. Whichever way you choose to serve them, your family will love them. You can have all the ingredients ready in the fridge the day before. Make sure that the ingredients for the batter are ice-cold—when they hit the hot butter they will rise dramatically, winning you "wow"s when you remove them from the oven.*

6 tablespoons unsalted butter

6 large eggs

1 cup all-purpose flour

1 cup cold whole milk

1 teaspoon pure vanilla extract or vanilla bean paste (see page 171)

2 tablespoons cinnamon sugar (combine 4½ teaspoons sugar with 1½ teaspoons cinnamon)

½ cup confectioners' sugar

One lemon, cut into 6 wedges

Warm maple syrup (optional)

**1.** Preheat the oven to 425°F. Melt the butter in a 10-inch round ovenproof pie plate or skillet in the oven.

**2.** While the butter is melting, combine the eggs, flour, milk, vanilla extract, and cinnamon sugar in a blender and blend for 45 seconds to 1 minute, until frothy, scraping down the sides if necessary. **Diva Do-Ahead:** At this point, you can refrigerate the entire blender container for up to 2 days. Reblend the batter before proceeding.

**3.** Make sure the butter is hot and bubbling, then pour the batter into the pan. Bake for 17 to 22 minutes, or until puffed and golden brown. Remove from the oven and cut into wedges. Serve immediately with a dusting of sifted confectioners' sugar and a squeeze of fresh lemon, or maple syrup if desired.

## Diva Tip

If you have a large group, you can make several pancakes at the same time. Just stagger them, from front to back, on your oven racks so that they aren't on top of one another.

# Volcanic Apple-Cinnamon Pancake

*Serves 6*

*This dramatic pancake rises high in your oven, with a molten base of caramelized cinnamon sugar, butter, and apples. When it comes to the table, the smell of the apples and cinnamon permeates the room, making it a real showstopper! Although it must be cooked and then eaten immediately, you can prepare the components ahead and keep them in the refrigerator for up to two days. Just preheat your oven, and you are on your way to breakfast nirvana.*

6 tablespoons unsalted butter

1/3 cup firmly packed light brown sugar

1/4 cup granulated sugar

1 teaspoon ground cinnamon

3 Granny Smith apples, peeled, cored, and sliced 1/2 inch thick

3 eggs

1/2 cup whole milk

1/2 cup all-purpose flour

1/4 teaspoon salt

Cinnamon sugar for garnish (combine 1 cup sugar with 1 to 2 teaspoons ground cinnamon, reserving any left over for another use)

**1.** Preheat the oven to 450°F. In a 10-inch ovenproof skillet over medium heat, melt the butter, and add the light brown sugar, granulated sugar, and cinnamon, stirring until the sugars melt and the mixture begins to bubble. Add the apples and cook for 7 to 8 minutes, until they caramelize. **Diva Do-Ahead:** At this point, you can cool the apples and refrigerate for up to 4 days. Reheat the skillet and the apples until they are bubbling hot before proceeding.

**2.** In a blender, combine the eggs, milk, flour, and salt, blending until the mixture is frothy. **Diva Do-Ahead:** At this point, you can refrigerate the blender container for up to 2 days. Remove from the refrigerator and reblend for 45 seconds before proceeding.

**3.** Pour the cold batter over the apples, and bake for 20 to 25 minutes, until the pancake is puffed and golden. Remove from the oven, invert onto a serving plate, and cut into wedges. Serve immediately, garnished with cinnamon sugar.

# Sweet Corn, Spinach, and Bacon Breakfast Tortes

*Makes 12 tortes*

*Each savory little torte is cooked in a ring of bacon, forming the base for an individual breakfast cake. Corn, spinach, and egg make a delicious contrast to the crisp bacon, and, best of all, you can bake this entrée ahead of time and then reheat it before serving.*

12 strips thick-cut bacon (applewood-smoked bacon is my favorite)

1 tablespoon unsalted butter

4 scallions (white and some tender green parts), chopped

One 16-ounce package frozen white corn, defrosted

One 16-ounce package frozen spinach, defrosted and squeezed dry

1 1/2 teaspoons salt

1 teaspoon freshly ground black pepper

1/8 teaspoon ground nutmeg

4 large eggs

1 cup whole or 2 percent milk

3 cups frozen shredded hash brown potatoes, defrosted

2 cups shredded sharp white cheddar cheese

**1.** Preheat the oven to 400°F. Arrange bacon on a baking sheet lined with parchment paper, aluminum foil, or a silicone baking liner. Cook the bacon for about 10 minutes, until it has rendered its fat and is beginning to turn golden, but is still not crisp. Remove from the oven and drain on paper towels. **Diva Do-Ahead:** At this point, you can refrigerate for up to 2 days.

**2.** In a medium-size sauté pan, melt the butter and sauté the scallions for 1 minute. Add the corn, spinach, salt, pepper, and nutmeg, sautéing until the mixture is dry. Set the mixture aside to cool. **Diva Do-Ahead:** At this point, you can cover and refrigerate for up to 2 days. Drain off any excess liquid before proceeding.

**3.** Reduce the oven temperature to 350°F. Coat the inside of 12 muffin cups with nonstick cooking spray and line the sides of each cup with a strip of the bacon.

**4.** In a large mixing bowl, whisk together the eggs and milk. Add the hash browns, cheese, and the corn mixture, stirring to blend. Scoop 1/2 cup of the mixture into each muffin cup and bake for 20 to 25 minutes, until the mixture is puffed, golden, and set. Remove from the oven and allow to rest for 10 minutes before serving. Serve warm or at room temperature. **Diva Do-Ahead:** At this point, you can cool and refrigerate for up to 2 days or freeze for 1 month. Defrost before proceeding and then reheat on a cookie sheet in a 350°F oven, covered loosely with aluminum foil, for 10 minutes.

# Denver Omelet Casserole

*Serves 6 to 8*

*Traditional Denver omelets have a filling of sautéed onions, peppers, and ham. Some cooks gild the lily and add cheese or other ingredients, but I think the original combination is best. On a morning like Christmas you don't want to be flipping omelets on the stove while everyone else is busy opening presents, so this combination is just the ticket for a lazy morning breakfast or brunch. The entire casserole can be baked and then refrigerated or frozen, and reheated before serving either hot or at room temperature.*

4 tablespoons unsalted butter

1 cup sweet yellow onion, finely chopped

1 medium-size green bell pepper, cored, seeded, and finely chopped

1 medium-size red bell pepper, cored, seeded, and finely chopped

1/4 pound boiled imported ham, finely chopped

4 cups sturdy white bread (any tough crusts removed), torn into 1/2-inch pieces

6 large eggs

1 cup heavy cream

2 tablespoons all-purpose flour

1 1/2 teaspoons salt

6 shakes hot sauce

**1.** Preheat the oven to 350°F. Coat the inside of a 13 x 9-inch baking dish with nonstick cooking spray.

**2.** In a large skillet, melt the butter and sauté the onion and bell peppers until they are softened, about 5 minutes. Add the ham and continue to sauté until the onion is translucent. Transfer the mixture to a large mixing bowl to cool, adding the bread cubes and stirring until blended.

**3.** In a medium-size mixing bowl, whisk together the eggs, cream, flour, salt, and hot sauce until blended. Pour over the ham mixture, stirring to blend. Transfer the entire contents of the bowl to the prepared pan. Cover and refrigerate for at least 6 hours. **Diva Do-Ahead:** At this point, you can cover and refrigerate for up to 2 days. Bring to room temperature before proceeding.

**4.** Bake for 35 to 45 minutes, until the casserole is puffed and golden brown and set in the center. Remove from the oven and allow to rest for 15 minutes before cutting into squares.

**Diva Do-Ahead:** If you would like to make this casserole ahead of time, bake until the middle registers 140°F on an instant-read thermometer (about 25 minutes); it will not be set, but the eggs will be cooked. Remove from the oven and allow to cool. Cover and refrigerate for up to 3 days or freeze for up to 6 weeks. Allow to come to room temperature before reheating, loosely tented with foil, in a 350°F oven for 15 minutes, or until the center is heated through.

## Diva Variation

To make cheesy Denver quiche, add 1 cup shredded cheese to the final mixture. Good choices are mild cheddar, sharp white cheddar, Monterey Jack, pepper Jack, fontina, or provolone.

# Breakfast Ambrosia

*Serves 6 to 8*

*In most parts of the country, December is not a good time to find many fresh fruits, but citrus is the exception, so this salad includes grapefruit and oranges, as well as bananas, which are all reliable during the winter. Feel free to include some of your favorites if the selection looks good—say, kiwi or melon, or splurge on a few fresh berries for some color if you can find them. (I don't recommend using frozen berries or peaches; they tend to drool a lot when exposed to the citrus, making a soupy mess.)*

4 navel oranges (see Diva Tip)

2 pink grapefruits (see Diva Tip)

4 bananas

1 cup sweetened flaked coconut

1/4 cup sifted confectioners' sugar

Mint leaves for garnish

**1.** Slice the bottom and top from the oranges and grapefruits. Stand each fruit on a flat end and, using a boning knife or thin flexible knife, cut down the sides to remove all the peel and white pith. Place your knife at the side of a segment and then run it down to the middle. Repeat on the other side of the segment and place it in a large serving bowl. Repeat until all the oranges and grapefruit are sectioned. **Diva Do-Ahead:** At this point, you can cover and refrigerate for up to 3 days.

**2.** Just before serving, drain off the juice that has accumulated in the bottom of the bowl. Peel and slice the banana into 1/2-inch-thick rounds and add to the bowl.

**3.** Sprinkle the coconut and confectioners' sugar over the fruit and toss to combine. Serve the ambrosia garnished with mint leaves.

## Diva Tip

More and more in your grocer's produce section, you can find sectioned grapefruit and other citrus. Buy these fruits and forgo your own slicing and peeling if time is of the essence.

# Christmas Dinner

The celebration of Christ's birth brings family and friends together to share in this joyous holiday. The Christmas season, however, is fraught with anxiety between the parties, the presents, and the stress of thinking that you can't get it all done without the help of medication and therapy.

This dinner for 10 is going to be the most relaxing part of your Christmas, whether you serve it on Christmas Eve or Christmas Day. You can make most dishes ahead of time, including the main-course roast. Many of my students tell me that this dinner is a lifesaver because it is so easy. I know that a whole beef tenderloin is expensive, but there is hardly any fat or waste on it, so it's really a better buy than a prime rib. I usually buy the tenderloin at a warehouse store like Costco and trim it myself, but I've noticed that at the holidays, many stores sell it trimmed for you, for a slightly higher cost. Your butcher can trim the meat too, but this service may increase the price.

Your holiday table should be a festive affair, in the colors of the season. You can make it as elaborate as you want. For a less formal, more country-ish Christmas, I recommend that you lay pine boughs down the center of the table, then decorate with natural or spray-painted pinecones, winter fruits, nuts in their shells, and holly branches. Arrange these items in a long shallow bowl centered on the table or scatter them down the length of the table. Wheatgrass is becoming more and more popular as a centerpiece. Cut it to fit your vessel, then decorate by glue-gunning some seasonal colored ribbon to the vessel itself or securing it with double-stick tape. Intersperse some votive candles into your table scheme, for pretty twinkling lights, or arrange a string of battery-powered Christmas lights or candles on the table.

For a more elegant table setting, get out the glitz! Decorate in the colors of the season, but think deep burgundies and forest greens, with velvet, gold, or silver accents. A fabric runner in velvet with gold or silver wired ribbon for accent is a beautiful contrast. An all-white table with white and silver accents, or an all-cream table with red accents, has a look of elegance and luxury. Tie thin velvet ribbons in your choice of colors, or gold and silver ribbons, to the stems of wineglasses to give the table an even more festive feel. For flowers, try low arrangements in silver or gold tones, perhaps that silver soup tureen or Revere bowl you haven't used in ages. I have a set of silver punch cups that are a family heirloom, and I fill each with an oasis to within half an inch of the top. Then I arrange flowers in each oasis, top it off with some sphagnum moss, and tack in some small shiny ornaments for extra color. You can do the same with low glasses. Filling glass bowls with shiny ornaments or sugared fruits also makes a nice statement. Achieve the look of a professional floral arrangement by placing flowers, ornaments, and other items in an oasis in a long, low display, and then decorating it with ribbons and candy canes. Low pillars (three inches), votives, or floating candles provide a beautiful glow for this elegant table. Fill shallow glass bowls with cranberries or red marbles, then float candles or arrange low pillars in the bowls for interesting lighting. Other colorful table accents: gold or silver charger plates at each place.

You can decorate gingerbread men or holiday sugar cookies with your guests' names written in frosting to make place cards, or wrap the cookies in cellophane bags with guests' names printed on them as combination party favors and place cards. Another idea: give each guest a small (four-inch)

Christmas tree or pink, cream, or variegated poinsettia. Decorate the base with ribbon or glitter. Candy canes also make delightful party favors, especially for the kids in the crowd.

Small bud vases can serve as anchors for place cards, as can commemorative ornaments, which can also double as party favors. I like to include the Christmas story from Luke's Gospel at each place. I print out the story and ask several guests at the table read it. You can also find children's versions, and you may want to include Nativity scenes for them to color. Other ideas for place-card holders are labeled gift boxes with small mementos inside, or photos of your guests from days gone by, reproduced on your computer and inserted into small frames. Baby photos are a fun choice, and you can document when and where each photo was taken. Most importantly, make your guests feel welcome and give them a sense of belonging.

Again, for music, Christmas carols are the way to go. There are loads of options: Bing Crosby, *The Nutcracker*, or something a little more contemporary, such as the Trans-Siberian Orchestra or the Boston Pops.

## 3...2...1...

## Do-Ahead Countdown

* **2 months ahead**

  Download shopping list and do-ahead calendar and fill them out

  Shop for nonperishables

  Make and freeze base for Butternut Squash Soup with Crab

* **6 weeks ahead**

  Make and freeze Roasted Tomato and Pesto Cheesecake with Polenta Crust

  Make and freeze Port Wine Reduction Sauce

* **1 month ahead**

  Make and freeze Garlic-Herb Make-Ahead Mashed Potatoes

* **2 weeks ahead**

  Make dressing for Mango-Cranberry Salad

* **1 week ahead**

  Make sauce for Garlic Prawns

* **5 days ahead**

  Make Garlic-Herb Marinade for beef tenderloin

* **3 days ahead**

  Make custard for Holiday Eggnog

* **2 days ahead**

  Chill champagne for Kir Royales

  Marinate beef tenderloin (up to 36 hours before roasting)

  Make Creamy Spinach Gratin

Prepare Chocolate Crème Brûlée

* **1 day ahead**

  Set the table

  Chop ingredients for Mango-Cranberry Salad

  Remove soup, cheesecake, sauce for tenderloin, and potatoes from freezer and defrost in refrigerator

  Roast beef tenderloin and cook prawns

* **Day of**

  Finish eggnog, squash soup, and crème brûlée

  Assemble Mango-Cranberry Salad

## Keeping Eggnog Cold

It's hard to keep milk-based drinks cold, but you can make an ice mold in a bundt pan from the cooked custard for your eggnog. Make two batches of custard, one for your block and one for the nog. If you like, after you've poured the custard into the mold, drop in a few berries and then freeze for up to a month. When ready to serve, run hot water over the bottom of the pan to loosen the ice mold and place in the punch bowl. Pour the eggnog over the mold and serve. For smaller decorative ice molds, place a few raspberries or a strawberry into the bottom of clean muffin tins. Fill with eggnog custard and freeze. When frozen, transfer to zipper-top plastic bags and freeze for up to a month.

# Holiday Eggnog

*Serves 10*

*You can serve this beverage when guests arrive or for dessert (or both!). Because there has been so much talk about the bacteria in raw eggs, I cook my eggnog on the stovetop long enough to eliminate any risk. You will need to make the base the day before so that it is cooled and ready to go. Freshly grated nutmeg is essential for great eggnog, and so is good Kentucky bourbon. There are lots of people who prefer their eggnog with rum or brandy, but I'm betting that once you try mine, you won't go back! Leftover eggnog is terrific in pancake batter in place of milk and is delicious frozen as a dessert. It doesn't freeze rock-solid, making it like a semifreddo. I garnish each frozen dessert with chocolate curls or chopped pistachios.*

1½ quarts whole milk

1½ cups superfine sugar

8 large egg yolks

2 teaspoons pure vanilla extract or vanilla bean paste (see page 171)

2 cups heavy cream

2 cups Kentucky bourbon

Freshly grated nutmeg for garnish

**1.** In a large saucepan over medium heat, warm the milk and sugar together, stirring until the sugar is dissolved and fine bubbles form along the side of the pan.

**2.** In a large bowl, beat the egg yolks, then gradually add a cup of the warm milk, whisking until the milk is absorbed. Stir the egg-milk mixture into the saucepan, reduce the heat to low, and simmer until the mixture is thickened and coats the back of a spoon, 10 to 15 minutes. Remove from the heat and stir in the vanilla bean paste.

**3.** Strain the custard through a fine-mesh strainer into a bowl and place a piece of plastic wrap directly onto the surface of the custard to keep a skin from forming. Cover and refrigerate for at least 8 hours. **Diva Do-Ahead:** At this point, you can refrigerate for up to 3 days.

**4.** With an electric mixer, whip the heavy cream in a large bowl until stiff peaks form.

**5.** Remove the custard from the refrigerator and whisk in the bourbon and whipped cream. Pour into a chilled punch bowl, garnish liberally with nutmeg, and serve immediately.

## Diva Variation

Omit the bourbon to make Virgin Eggnog—but that would be a shame!

# Kir Royales

*Serves 10*

This combination of crème de cassis and champagne is a ruby-colored bubbly apéritif from days gone by. Its red color is particularly appealing during the holiday season. Of course, your guests can elect to have their champagne without the cassis if they wish. You can't make this drink ahead of time (the champagne will go flat), but you can certainly have the champagne chilled and be ready to go when your guests arrive.

Two 750-milliliter bottles
    chilled champagne
1/4 cup crème de cassis

Pour 1/2 cup champagne into each champagne flute. Slowly pour 1 teaspoon of crème de cassis down the inside of each glass. Serve immediately.

# Roasted Tomato and Pesto Cheesecake with Polenta Crust

*Makes one 9-inch cheesecake to serve 12 to 16*

*Swirled with garlicky basil pesto, topped with roasted tomatoes, and nestled in a cornmeal crust, this cheesecake is not only visually appealing, it's also a terrific starter for any party. Serve it with baguette slices, crackers, or European cucumber rounds.*

1/4 cup (1/2 stick) unsalted butter

1 cup cornmeal

1 teaspoon salt

1/2 teaspoon freshly ground black pepper

1/4 cup boiling chicken broth

1 cup freshly grated Parmesan cheese

Two 8-ounce packages cream cheese, softened

8 ounces mascarpone cheese, softened

2 large eggs

1 cup finely shredded mozzarella cheese

1 cup basil pesto, homemade (page 36) or store-bought

2 cups Herb-Roasted Tomatoes (page 285)

Sprigs of fresh basil for garnish

Pine nuts for garnish

**1.** Combine the butter, cornmeal, salt, and pepper in a large bowl. Pour in the broth, stirring to blend. Add 1/2 cup of the Parmesan and mix to combine.

**2.** Line the inside of a 9-inch springform pan or a cake pan with aluminum foil and spray the inside with nonstick cooking spray. Press the cornmeal mixture onto the bottom, but not up the sides.

**3.** Preheat the oven to 325°F.

**4.** Using an electric mixer, cream the cream cheese and mascarpone together in a large bowl until smooth. Beat in the eggs 1 at a time, then the mozzarella, beating until light. Pour into the prepared pan. Drop the pesto by tablespoonfuls onto the batter and, with the tip of a knife, swirl it through the cheesecake for a marbled effect. Sprinkle the top evenly with the remaining 1/2 cup Parmesan.

**5.** Bake until a skewer inserted into the middle comes out with some cheesecake on it but is not liquid, 45 to 50 minutes. Turn off the oven and leave the door ajar for 30 minutes (to prevent cracks from forming).

*continued on next page*

# Roasted Tomato and Pesto Cheesecake with Polenta Crust *continued*

**6.** Allow the cheesecake to cool completely, then remove it from the pan and peel away the foil. **Diva Do-Ahead:** At this point, you can let cool completely, cover with plastic wrap, and refrigerate for up to 3 days or freeze for up to 6 weeks. Defrost overnight in the refrigerator and bring to room temperature before serving.

**7.** Decorate the top of the cheesecake with a layer of Herb-Roasted Tomatoes and sprinkle with basil leaves and pine nuts.

## *Diva Variation*

Chop up the roasted tomatoes or process them until chunky and swirl them into the cheesecake before baking, then smooth the basil pesto over the cooled cheesecake just before serving.

# Herb-Roasted Tomatoes

*Makes about 4 cups*

*These savory roasted tomatoes are a way to get intense flavor from otherwise boring canned tomatoes. The tomatoes caramelize and sweeten up in the oven. This recipe makes a lot more than you will need for the cheesecake, but it freezes beautifully, providing you with a great topping down the road for bruschetta, grilled chicken, fish, or meats, or a sauce to toss with fresh pasta.*

Two 28-ounce cans peeled whole tomatoes, drained and juice reserved
1/2 cup extra-virgin olive oil
1/2 cup chopped red onion
2 teaspoons dried basil
1 teaspoon fresh rosemary leaves, crushed
6 cloves garlic, coarsely chopped
1 1/2 teaspoons salt
1/2 teaspoon freshly ground black pepper

**1.** Preheat the oven to 350°F. Line a jelly-roll pan with aluminum foil or a silicone baking liner.

**2.** Cut the tomatoes in half and place in a large glass bowl. Stir in the olive oil, onion, basil, rosemary, garlic, salt, and pepper, being careful not to tear the tomatoes. Pour onto the prepared pan, spreading the mixture out in a single layer. Bake until the tomato liquid is absorbed and the tomatoes have firmed up and turned a deep red color, 1 to 1 1/2 hours, checking to make sure that the tomatoes and garlic don't brown.

**3.** Transfer the tomato mixture to a clean glass bowl and let it mellow at room temperature for about 6 hours. **Diva Do-Ahead:** At this point, you can cover and refrigerate for up to 4 days or freeze for up to 3 months. Defrost in the refrigerator overnight and bring to room temperature before using.

## Diva Wisdom

Sometimes fresh tomatoes aren't the most flavorful, so take a tip from my Italian cousin Nella, who will slice the tomatoes into 1/2-inch-thick slices, place them on a baking sheet, drizzle with salt, pepper, chopped fresh garlic, and extra-virgin olive oil, and bake at 300°F for 40 to 50 minutes. Roasting intensifies the flavor of the tomatoes.

# Butternut Squash Soup with Crab

*Serves 10*

*Creamy, with a hint of sweetness, this soup will become a favorite for entertaining. You can freeze the soup base, then defrost it the night before you plan to serve it, which gives you lots of flexibility. You can also serve this soup as a light lunch with crusty bread.*

2 tablespoons unsalted butter

1 cup finely chopped onion

1 cup finely chopped, peeled Granny Smith apple (1 large apple)

2 teaspoons dried thyme

1/4 teaspoon ground ginger

3 pounds butternut squash, peeled, seeded, and cut into 1-inch chunks

4 cups chicken broth

1 1/2 teaspoons salt

1/2 teaspoon freshly ground black pepper

1 cup heavy cream

1 pound lump crabmeat

1 tablespoon Old Bay Seasoning

1/2 cup melted butter

Fresh Italian parsley or chopped chives for garnish

**1.** In a large stockpot, melt the 2 tablespoons butter and sauté the onion, apple, thyme, and ginger for 5 minutes, until the onion and apple are softened.

**2.** Add the squash and sauté for another 10 minutes, until the squash begins to soften.

**3.** Stir in the broth, salt, and pepper, and simmer for 15 to 20 minutes, until the squash begins to fall apart. Using an immersion blender, puree the soup, or cool the soup and puree in a blender or food processor. **Diva Do-Ahead:** At this point, you can cover and refrigerate for up to 3 days or freeze for up to 2 months. Defrost before proceeding.

**4.** Add the cream and heat to serving temperature.

**5.** In a small bowl, toss the crabmeat with the Old Bay Seasoning and 1/2 cup melted butter. Ladle the soup into bowls and top each with 2 to 3 tablespoons of the crab. Serve garnished with parsley or chopped chives, if desired.

# Roast Beef Tenderloin with Port Wine Reduction Sauce

*Serves 10*

*This piece of meat, while costly, is a showstopper, and there is hardly any waste. Because it has little fat, you need to marinate it to add flavor. Then roast it the day before Christmas and serve warm or at room temperature with your choice of sauce. Many wholesale clubs like Costco sell a whole beef tenderloin for $50 to $70, and because it will serve a lot of people as a main course it's really not as big a splurge as you might think.*

*To trim the roast, remove the silver skin, a tendon sheath that surrounds the center portion of the meat. You can do so easily with a sharp knife; cut close to the skin and peel it off the meat. Also remove any fat extending down the roast and connecting a thin strip of meat to the center portion. I prefer to cut off this thin strip of meat and freeze it for kebobs and stir-fries because it cooks much faster than the rest of the tenderloin. If you decide to roast this piece, remove it from the pan and cover it with aluminum foil after it reaches 130°F on an instant-read meat thermometer.*

*The trimmed meat should weigh four to five pounds (seven to eight pounds before trimming). Because the tapered end portion of the roast would otherwise cook more quickly than the center, fold the tapered piece under itself in the pan; it will cook to medium, not medium-rare. I like to include this portion for those who don't like their meat too pink.*

*Roast your beef in a heavy-duty roasting pan, which will leave some caramelized pan juices for you to serve as is or to incorporate into a wine sauce (see page 289). Tying the roast with cooking twine will ensure that it cooks evenly and that the meat stays compact for easy carving. You can ask your butcher to do the tying for you.*

*Serve a rich Cabernet Sauvignon or Pinot Noir with this sumptuous tenderloin.*

One 4- to 5-pound trimmed beef tenderloin, tapered end tucked under and roast tied with kitchen twine every 1½ inches

Garlic-Herb Marinade (page 288)

**1.** Put the trimmed and tied tenderloin in a 2-gallon zipper-top plastic bag. Pour in the marinade and seal. Refrigerate for at least 24 hours. **Diva Do-Ahead:** At this point, you can refrigerate for up to 36 hours. Bring to room temperature for about 45 minutes before continuing.

*continued on next page*

**2.** Preheat the oven to 400°F.

**3.** Drain the meat and pat it dry with paper towels. Place in a heavy-duty roasting pan and roast, uncovered, until an instant-read meat thermometer inserted in the thickest part registers 135°F, 45 to 55 minutes. (When taken out at this temperature, your roast will be medium-rare to medium when it finishes resting.)

**4.** Remove the meat from the oven, cover with aluminum foil, and let rest at least 15 minutes. **Diva Do-Ahead:** At this point, you can let cool completely, cover, and refrigerate overnight. Bring to room temperature before continuing. Clip the strings from the meat and slice thinly, arranging the slices on a platter according to their degree of doneness. Serve with the garlic prawns (page 290) arranged around the edges of the platter.

# Garlic-Herb Marinade

*Makes about 1 1/2 cups (enough for 5 pounds of meat)*
*This soy-based marinade is great for roasts as well as steaks and kabobs. After a long soak in the marinade, the roasted meat will be tender and juicy, no matter which cut of beef you try.*

1/2 cup olive oil
1/2 cup soy sauce
2 tablespoons red wine vinegar
4 cloves garlic, minced
2 teaspoons dried thyme
1 bay leaf
1 teaspoon freshly ground
 black pepper

In a small glass bowl, whisk together all the ingredients.
**Diva Do-Ahead:** At this point, you can cover and refrigerate for up to 5 days.

# Port Wine Reduction Sauce

*Makes about 3 cups*

*This luxurious sauce is perfect to serve with tenderloin, and it's equally good with pork. The reduction can be made ahead and frozen for two months. Simply defrost, reheat, and thicken with the beurre manié (butter and flour paste) just before serving.*

1/2 cup (1 stick) unsalted
    butter, softened
2/3 cup chopped shallots
8 sprigs fresh thyme or
    1 1/2 tablespoons dried
    thyme
Two 10.75-ounce cans
    condensed beef broth
1 cup ruby port
1/2 cup Cabernet Sauvignon
1/4 cup all-purpose flour

**1.** In a large saucepan, melt 1/4 cup (1/2 stick) of the butter over medium heat. Add the shallots and thyme and cook, stirring, until the shallots soften, 3 to 4 minutes.

**2.** Pour in the broth, port, and Cabernet and bring to a boil over high heat. Reduce the heat to medium and simmer until it begins to thicken, about 30 minutes. Strain through a fine-mesh strainer. **Diva Do-Ahead:** At this point, you can let cool, cover, and refrigerate for up to 5 days or freeze for up to 2 months. Defrost and reheat gently before continuing.

**3.** In a small bowl, blend together the flour and remaining 1/4 cup (1/2 stick) of butter until it forms a smooth paste. This is the *beurre manié*.

**4.** Bring the sauce to a boil, then add the flour mixture a tablespoon at a time, bringing the sauce to a boil after each addition. Add just enough of the *beurre manié* to achieve the thickness you prefer. Remove from the heat and serve warm. **Diva Do-Ahead:** At this point, you can let cool, cover, and refrigerate for up to 5 days. Reheat gently.

## The Diva Says

Sometimes this sauce has a pronounced wine flavor even after boiling it down, which has to do with the wine and not the recipe. To counteract this, I recommend that you deglaze the roasting pan with the sauce—the drippings from your roast will round out all the flavors. Add the sauce to the pan after you have removed the tenderloin. Place the pan over medium heat and cook, stirring and scraping up the browned bits from the bottom of the pan to incorporate into the sauce.

# Garlic Prawns

*Serves 10*

*This half of your surf-and-turf entrée is simple to put together, with just a last-minute sauté to heat it through. This recipe also makes a simple dinner on its own when tossed with linguine or your favorite pasta. To serve with the tenderloin, arrange the shrimp around the edges of the platter that holds the tenderloin slices and top the shrimp with their pan sauce. Or you may arrange the shrimp separately on a platter or in a serving bowl. If you wish to serve a white wine with the shrimp, choose something that can stand up to the tenderloin as well, such as a white Bordeaux or a French Chenin Blanc.*

1 cup (2 sticks) unsalted
 butter
1/4 cup olive oil
8 cloves garlic, minced
1 tablespoon Old Bay
 Seasoning
1/4 cup cream sherry
2 tablespoons freshly squeezed
 lemon juice
2 pounds jumbo shrimp,
 peeled and deveined
1/4 cup chopped fresh Italian
 parsley

**1.** Melt the butter and oil in a medium-size skillet over low heat. Add the garlic and cook until softened, about 10 minutes, but don't let the garlic brown.

**2.** Add the Old Bay and cook for another 2 minutes, stirring constantly so the garlic doesn't burn. Add the sherry and lemon juice and bring to a boil. Reduce the heat to low, simmer for 1 minute, and remove from the heat. **Diva Do-Ahead:** At this point, you can let cool, cover, and refrigerate for up to 1 week. Reheat gently before proceeding.

**3.** Add the shrimp and parsley to the garlic butter and toss together. Cook over medium heat until the shrimp turn completely pink. **Diva Do-Ahead:** At this point, you can cool and refrigerate for up to 24 hours. Gently reheat before serving.

# Garlic-Herb Make-Ahead Mashed Potatoes

*Serves 10*

*The technique in this recipe is similar to that of the Thanksgiving mashed potatoes (see page 255), but here the additions are garlic and Boursin cheese. Like the others, these fluffy potatoes will rise like a soufflé, and the best part is that they can be ready several days before your big dinner.*

8 medium-size russet potatoes, peeled and cut into chunks

4 cloves garlic

6 tablespoons (3/4 stick) unsalted butter, softened

1/4 cup freshly grated Parmesan cheese

1 cup sour cream

Two 3.5-ounce packages Boursin or other garlic-herb cream cheese

1/3 cup chopped fresh chives (optional)

Salt and freshly ground black pepper to taste

**1.** Boil the potatoes and garlic in salted water to cover until tender. Drain.

**2.** Preheat the oven to 350°F. Rub a 13 x 9-inch baking dish with 2 tablespoons of the butter. Sprinkle the Parmesan into the dish and tip the dish so the cheese is evenly distributed and adheres to the butter.

**3.** Put the potatoes and garlic into a large bowl, add the sour cream, Boursin, 2 tablespoons of the remaining butter, and the chives, if using. Using an electric mixer, beat the potatoes until smooth. Taste for seasoning and add salt and pepper to taste.

**4.** Transfer to the prepared dish and dot with the remaining 2 tablespoons butter. **Diva Do-Ahead:** At this point, you can cover and refrigerate for 2 to 3 days or freeze for up to 1 month. Bring to room temperature before continuing.

Bake the potatoes until golden, about 25 minutes. Serve hot.

## Slow Cooker Savvy

These potatoes can be heated in a 4-quart slow cooker if you have a removable ceramic insert. Butter the insert and dust it with the cheese as directed in step 2. Follow the recipe through step 3 and fill the insert with the mashed potatoes. Cover and cook on low for 4 to 6 hours, until heated through. Dust the top with more Parmesan and butter before serving.

# Creamy Spinach Gratin

*Serves 10*

*Creamed spinach is one of my favorite dishes, but I often order it in restaurants only to be disappointed by gluey sauce or tasteless spinach. This dish is a combination of some of the best versions that I've had, and the good news is not only that it doesn't take long to make, but also that you can make it up ahead of time and refrigerate it until you are ready to bake it. This recipe also lends itself to being made in individual gratin dishes or soufflé ramekins. The truffle oil is optional, but I have to tell you it is awesome, and it is well worth buying a small bottle to make this dish.*

4 quarts water

Four 10-ounce packages baby spinach

6 tablespoons unsalted butter, softened

1/2 cup freshly grated Parmesan cheese

1 clove garlic, minced

1 shallot, finely chopped

1 teaspoon salt

1/2 teaspoon freshly ground black pepper

1/4 teaspoon ground nutmeg

1 cup heavy cream

2 tablespoons black truffle oil (optional)

**1.** In a large pot, bring the water to a boil. Place the spinach in the water, cover the pot, turn off the heat, and allow to sit for 3 minutes. Drain the spinach, removing all the liquid by pressing down on the spinach in a colander. Coarsely chop the spinach and set aside. **Diva Do-Ahead:** At this point, you can refrigerate for up to 2 days.

**2.** Preheat the oven to 350°F. Rub the inside of a 10-inch round or square baking dish with 2 tablespoons of the butter. Sprinkle 1/4 cup of the cheese over the butter and tip the dish so the cheese is evenly distributed and adheres to the butter. Set aside.

**3.** In a medium-size saucepan, heat the remaining butter and sauté the garlic and shallot for 3 minutes, until softened. Add the spinach to the pan and season with the salt, pepper, and nutmeg, stirring to combine. Slowly add the cream and bring back to a simmer, cooking for about 5 minutes, until the mixture is thickened.

**4.** Stir in the truffle oil, if desired, and turn the mixture into the prepared dish. Sprinkle the spinach with the remaining ¹/₄ cup cheese. **Diva Do-Ahead:** At this point, you can cool, cover, and refrigerate for up to 2 days. Bring to room temperature before proceeding. Bake for 20 to 25 minutes, or until bubbling and the cheese begins to turn golden brown. For individual ramekins, bake about 15 minutes. Serve hot or warm.

### Diva Variation

The spinach mixture is also delicious when used to fill large mushroom caps or artichoke bottoms. Bake for 10 to 15 minutes at 350°F and serve hot or at room temperature.

# Diva Tip

I've found that white truffle oil works well, too, although it has a more subtle flavor. It's generally more widely available and less expensive than black truffle oil.

# Mango-Cranberry Salad

*Serves 10 to 12*

*This colorful salad is both sweet and tart because of the finely chopped mango and the dried cranberries. If mangoes aren't available, use chopped cantaloupe instead; either way, you'll love the salad's unique flavor.*

### Dressing

1½ cups vegetable oil

⅔ cup rice vinegar

2 tablespoons sugar

1½ teaspoons salt

1 teaspoon freshly ground
   black pepper

### Salad

Four 10-ounce packages
   mixed greens

1 large ripe mango, peeled,
   flesh cut away from pit, and
   finely chopped

½ cup finely chopped red
   onion

1 cup unsweetened dried
   cranberries

**1.** In a medium-size bowl, whisk together the dressing ingredients until thickened. **Diva Do-Ahead:** At this point, you can cover and refrigerate for up to 2 weeks.

**2.** To assemble the salad, place the greens, mango, onion, and cranberries in a large salad bowl. Pour the vinaigrette over and toss to coat everything. Serve immediately.

# Chocolate Crème Brûlée

*Serves 8*

*Smooth and creamy, with an intense chocolate flavor and crackly sugar topping, this dessert is sure to please all your guests. I recommend that you use a high-quality chocolate with a high percentage of cacao. For testing, I used Scharffen Berger, which produced an ethereal dessert. For a little variation and a surprise for your guests, place a few fresh raspberries in the bottom of each ramekin.*

4 cups heavy cream, chilled

2/3 cup granulated sugar

Pinch of salt

2 teaspoons vanilla bean paste

8 ounces semisweet chocolate, chopped

12 large egg yolks

8 to 12 teaspoons Demerara or turbinado sugar

1 cup heavy cream, whipped to stiff peaks, for garnish (optional)

**1.** Preheat the oven to 300°F. Place a kitchen towel in a large baking dish or on a rimmed baking sheet and arrange eight 4-ounce ramekins on the towel. Bring a kettle of water to a boil on high heat.

**2.** Pour 2 cups of the cream, the granulated sugar, salt, and vanilla bean paste into a 2-quart saucepan and bring to a boil. Remove from the heat and add the chocolate, stirring until the chocolate is melted. Add the remaining 2 cups chilled cream and stir. Set aside.

**3.** In the bowl of an electric mixer, beat the egg yolks until they break up and combine. Slowly pour in the cooled chocolate-cream mixture, beating until it is all combined. Pour the chocolate cream through a sieve to strain it, discarding the solids left in the strainer.

**4.** Slowly pour the chocolate cream into the ramekins, dividing it equally. Place the baking dish with the ramekins on an oven rack, and pour boiling water into the baking dish until it is halfway up the sides of the ramekins. Bake the custards until they are just barely set and no longer loose, 30 to 35 minutes. (If the ramekins are shallow, as with heart-shaped

*continued on next page*

# Chocolate Crème Brûlée *continued*

ones, bake 25 to 30 minutes.) An instant-read thermometer will register 170°F when inserted in the center. Remove from the oven and transfer to a rack to cool at room temperature, about 2 hours. **Diva Do-Ahead:** At this point, you can cover with plastic wrap and refrigerate for up to 2 days. Gently remove any condensation that forms on the custard with a paper towel.

**5.** Sprinkle each custard evenly with the Demerara sugar. Ignite a kitchen torch and caramelize the sugar. Serve immediately. **Diva Do-Ahead:** At this point, you can refrigerate, uncovered, for up to 4 hours, and serve chilled. Garnish with whipped cream if desired.

## Diva Note

If you don't have a small kitchen torch or crème brûlée torch, you can run the ramekins under the broiler until the sugar is melted, but watch them carefully so that the sugar doesn't burn. The torch is a great tool to have because it gives you more control.

# Measurement Equivalents

## LIQUID CONVERSIONS

| U.S. | Metric |
|---|---|
| 1 tsp | 5 ml |
| 1 tbs | 15 ml |
| 2 tbs | 30 ml |
| 3 tbs | 45 ml |
| 1/4 cup | 60 ml |
| 1/3 cup | 75 ml |
| 1/3 cup + 1 tbs | 90 ml |
| 1/3 cup + 2 tbs | 100 ml |
| 1/2 cup | 120 ml |
| 2/3 cup | 150 ml |
| 3/4 cup | 180 ml |
| 3/4 cup + 2 tbs | 200 ml |
| 1 cup | 240 ml |
| 1 cup + 2 tbs | 275 ml |
| 1 1/4 cups | 300 ml |
| 1 1/3 cups | 325 ml |
| 1 1/2 cups | 350 ml |
| 1 2/3 cups | 375 ml |
| 1 3/4 cups | 400 ml |
| 1 3/4 cups + 2 tbs | 450 ml |
| 2 cups (1 pint) | 475 ml |
| 2 1/2 cups | 600 ml |
| 3 cups | 720 ml |
| 4 cups (1 quart) | 945 ml (1,000 ml is 1 liter) |

## WEIGHT CONVERSIONS

| U.S./U.K. | Metric |
|---|---|
| 1/2 oz | 14 g |
| 1 oz | 28 g |
| 1 1/2 oz | 43 g |
| 2 oz | 57 g |
| 2$^c$ oz | 71 g |
| 3 oz | 85 g |
| 3 1/2 oz | 100 g |
| 4 oz | 113 g |
| 5 oz | 142 g |
| 6 oz | 170 g |
| 7 oz | 200 g |
| 8 oz | 227 g |
| 9 oz | 255 g |
| 10 oz | 284 g |
| 11 oz | 312 g |
| 12 oz | 340 g |
| 13 oz | 368 g |
| 14 oz | 400 g |
| 15 oz | 425 g |
| 1 lb | 454 g |

## OVEN TEMPERATURES

| °F | Gas Mark | °C |
|---|---|---|
| 250 | 1/2 | 120 |
| 275 | 1 | 140 |
| 300 | 2 | 150 |
| 325 | 3 | 165 |
| 350 | 4 | 180 |
| 375 | 5 | 190 |
| 400 | 6 | 200 |
| 425 | 7 | 220 |
| 450 | 8 | 230 |
| 475 | 9 | 240 |
| 500 | 10 | 260 |
| 550 | Broil | 290 |

# Index

Strawberry(ies)
-Apricot Crostata, Rustic, 129
Fresh Fruit Parfaits with
Orange Mascarpone Crème,
138–39
Lemonade, 146
Lime Pound Cake with Fresh
Lime Glaze and, 154–55
Old Glory Cake, 193–94
Smoothies, 134
Virgin Pineapple Coolers, 103
Strudels
Individual Apple, in Phyllo with
Caramel Sauce, 212–13
Sausage and Egg, 57–59
Stuffings
Bread, Old-Fashioned
Do-Ahead, 252–53
Cornbread, Old-Fashioned
Do-Ahead, 254
Fruited Rice, 209
Pineapple, 112
serving, tip for, 253
Sweet Potato(es)
and Apple Gratin, 258
Roasted Parsnips, Beets,
Carrots, and, 211

•T•
Tablecloths, 12, 13
Tarragon-Mustard Dip, Crudités
with, 22
Teriyaki-Sesame Butter, 184
Thanksgiving Dinner, Diva's
Famous Do-Ahead
do-ahead countdown, 239–40
menu, 235
planning, 236–38
recipes, 241–65
Thermal carafes, 8
Thermometer, instant-read,
6–7
Thermometer, oven, 4
Thyme-and-Sage-Rubbed Turkey,
248

Toffee Bars, Almond, 47
Tomato(es)
adding to strata recipe, 107
Dressing, Sweet, 231
Eggplant Napoleons, 124
Greens and Veggies with
Sun-Dried Tomato
Vinaigrette, 189
Herb-Roasted, 285
preparing, for crudité platter,
25
Roasted, and Pesto
Cheesecake with Polenta
Crust, 283–84
roasting, 285
Simple Pizza Sauce, 228
Sun-Dried, Butter, 182
Sun-Dried, Vinaigrette, 189
Tongs, for serving salad, 5
Tortes
Mediterranean Artichoke
Pesto, 29–30
Sweet Corn, Spinach, and
Bacon Breakfast, 273
Tortillas
for fajitas, numbers per
serving, 167
warming, 166
Trays, lap, 9
Tuna Niçoise Sandwich, 148
Turkey
carving, 249–50
in egg strudel recipe, 59
Peking Pizza, 226
Roast, Cider-Glazed, 247
Roast, Hoisin-Glazed, 247
Roast, Maple-Glazed, 247
Roast, Perfect, 245–47
Roast, Thyme-and-Sage-
Rubbed, 247
Roast, with Pomegranate
Glaze, 207–8
roasting ahead of time, 248
roasting times, 248
testing for doneness, 208

•V•
Valentine's Day Sweetheart
Dinner
do-ahead countdown, 68
menu, 65
planning, 66–67
recipes, 69–83
Vanilla bean paste, about, 171
Vanilla extract, about, 171
Vanilla Frosting, Creamy, 117
Vegetable(s). See also specific
vegetables
Build-Your-Own-Salad Bar, 230
crudités, arranging, 23–25
Crudités with Tarragon-
Mustard Dip, 22
estimating quantity, 3–4
Greens and Veggies with
Sun-Dried Tomato
Vinaigrette, 189
Roasted, and Chicken Soup, 91
Roasted, Soup, 91
Velouté Sauce, Lemon-Dill, 80
Vermouth, as wine substitute,
206
Vinaigrettes
Apple, 61
Poppy Seed, 81
Red Wine–Citrus, 128
Sun-Dried Tomato, 189

•W•
Walnut(s)
adding to bread pudding, 263
-Gorgonzola Crostini Topping,
45
Individual Apple Strudels in
Phyllo with Caramel Sauce,
212–13
Red Cabbage and Apple Sauté,
95
Spicy Nuts, 62
Sweet and Nutty Nibbles, 201
Watermelon Lemonade, 146
Whisks, 6